FINDING & FUNDING
GREAT
DEALS

FINDING & FUNDING
GREAT
DEALS

*The hands-on guide to acquiring
real estate in any market.*

By Anson Young

BiggerPockets
PUBLISHING

Finding and Funding Great Deals
Anson Young

Published by BiggerPockets Publishing LLC, Denver, CO
Copyright © 2017 by Anson Publishing, LLC
All Rights Reserved.

Publisher's Cataloging-in-Publication
(Provided by Quality Books, Inc.)

    Young, Anson, author.
      Finding and funding great deals : the hands-on guide
    to acquiring real estate in any market / Anson Young. --
    First edition.
      pages cm
      ISBN 978-0-9907117-7-3
      ISBN 978-0-9907117-8-0

      1. Real estate investment--United States. 2. Real.
    property--purchasing--United States. 3. Real property--
    Valuation--United States. 4. Real estate management--
    United States. I. Title.

    HD255.Y675 2017   333.63'240973
                    QBI17-900011

Printed in the United State of America
10 9 8 7 6 5 4 3 2 1

Dedication

This book is for real estate investors and agents who like to push the envelope and more importantly, take massive action towards their goals. Whether you want to buy a house to live in, rent out, or flip, this book is the first step.

And, of course, for Stacy and Wesley—my family, my core, my drive, my inspiration and my adventure partners. I love you both more than words could ever express.

Contents

Introductions Are in Order   **1**

CHAPTER 1:
What I Do   **5**
    Why I Wrote This Book   7
    Who This Book Is For   9

CHAPTER 2:
Market Analysis   **13**
    Time to Get Your Hands Dirty   16
    What Is This Magical MLS System Anyway?   25
    Market Analysis for Reverse Wholesaling   27
    Case Study—Virtual Wholesaling Is Real!   29

CHAPTER 3:
Reaching Your Market   **31**
    Distressed Properties   33
    Foreclosures   35
    Other Property Types and Their Owners   48
    Case Study—REO Auction   59

CHAPTER 4:
Networking, Agents, and MLS   **61**
    Networking   61
    Agents   65
    Multiple Listing Service (MLS)   67
    Case Study—Four-Way Deal   77

CHAPTER 5:
Marketing Methods   **79**
    Broad Direct Marketing   80
    Targeted Direct Marketing   93
    Direct Mail: The Method   118
    Case Study—Mail Out Land Deal   129

CHAPTER 6:
Evaluating the Deal   **131**
    Evaluating Property   132
    Case Study—Vindication   154

CHAPTER 7:
Financing the Deal   **157**
    Types of Financing and Who Uses Them   159
    Bank Financing   161
    Other Funding Methods   167
    Transactional Funding   173
    Summing It Up   176
    Case Study—Partnering as a funding method   180

CHAPTER 8:
Negotiation   **181**
    Getting Over Fear of Rejection   182
    Case Study—Rapport Wins the Day   208

CHAPTER 9:
Locking it Up   **209**
    What Contracts Should I Use?   212
    Case Study—Nine-Offer REO   217

CHAPTER 10:
Closing the Deal   **219**
    How to Find an Investor-friendly Title Company or Attorney   223
    Case Study—Short Sale Time Machine   224

CHAPTER 11:
How to Build a Business Around Finding Deals   **227**

    Big Picture   228

    Systems   230

    Case Study—Ten Cats Live(d) Here, Two Are Missing   235

Introductions Are in Order

"Seek thee out, the diamond in the rough."

–*Aladdin*, 1992

Knee-deep in twenty years of someone else's trash, I reflected on how I came to be here. My year-long journey to this mountain of filth began like most real estate deals. I'd mailed a letter to someone in foreclosure. The work of finding the homeowner, learning her story, and convincing her I could help spanned the better part of a year. When most investors would have stopped, I pushed on, tracking down a new address to contact the absentee owner. I'd driven by the property before and knew its stench drifted all the way to the street. Now, hunched over five and a half feet of accumulated garbage, my back against the ceiling, I steeled my resolve and reminded myself why I was there—to fix the property and alleviate the homeowner of a desperate situation. Nine dumpsters and countless untold horrors later, as we stripped a history of neglect from the three-bedroom, two-bath ranch-style home, the property finally emerged as what I'd seen it all along—one heck of a deal.

Believe it or not, this is the beauty of investing in real estate. In the stock market, you wait for something to happen that will affect your end price. Even so much as a rumor about the CEO can tank your stock price. Instead, I like seeing and feeling my investment in brick and mortar, wood frame and nails, 70s shag carpeting with wood paneling, hoarded piles of junk, and cat-pee soaked carpets. Well, maybe not so much the latter, but know this: You will see some crazy stuff on your real estate journey. You will be

1

looking for the worst house in the neighborhood, seeking out the proverbial diamond in the rough. The worse the property condition, the more excited you should be at the potential that lies within. Instead of waiting for factors outside your control to affect your profit, you can be hands-on every step of the way to ensure you maximize your profits.

Who Am I—And Why Should You Care?

It all started with a copy of Robert Kiyosaki's *Rich Dad Poor Dad*. I was about to move from Denver to Phoenix when my friend handed me this book. I read it all the way there, leaving my wife to drive the entire route *(Sorry honey!)*. When we arrived in Arizona, I declared I was going to start investing in real estate.

To that end, I attended every investor meeting and association group I could, talking to every expert I could find. My method was somewhat aimless, taking menial jobs doing whatever I could for agents or investors, bugging anybody I could to get more experience in real estate. In all my wisdom, I also paid a mentor ten states away to help me. The information, while good, was too general, spanning a dozen sections of real estate. Needless to say, I didn't close any deals. What I needed to do was pick a niche in real estate, laser-focus on it, and run after it 100 percent. That's really the key to real estate: running after it 100 percent. You can have all the talent in the world, but it will only get you so far. The rest is hard work. I didn't find that total focus until a few years later.

I landed my first deal in 2005, a year after declaring myself a real estate investor. By 2017, I've now done over a hundred wholesale deals, as well as dozens of fix-and-flips with a few partners. I don't say all of this to boast, but to offer that I'm an actual person with gritty, real world experience who knows that if you don't have deals, you don't have anything.

I've made more money than I thought possible during some months and less money than I needed during others. I started off wholesaling as a necessity. I didn't have much money and wanted to dive into real estate investing. I lacked the down payment or credit to buy a rental property, and I didn't have the capital or knowledge to buy a property to fix and sell for profit. If you'd mentioned the term "note," I would've assumed you left "sticky" off the front. I had no experience, but I made up for it with enthusiasm to learn as much as possible and to take action on it. The road during my journey hasn't always been smooth, but I want to make your journey *much* smoother. I want you to enjoy the hunt for deals.

Here's a quick story: When I first started out in real estate, I was in Phoenix, Arizona. Finding what I thought was a good deal, I called on an ad for a fourplex, a single building that housed four separate apartment units. I ended up talking to the listing agent, who sounded like he was in his late forties and a bit steeled, experience-wise. I asked about the condition and he paused for a second, probably deciding whether to sugar coat it. He proceeded to tell me all about the poor conditions, the massive amount of work needed, and, of course, the filth and cockroaches. I must have sounded a bit put off, so he probably knew I couldn't handle the real thing. He then gave me the first—and what I think is some of the best—real estate advice I've heard: "I understand you're just starting out, so let's get this out of the way. If you want to be an investor, you will likely see some serious filth and conditions you couldn't imagine living in. You have to get past that. You can't judge people for the way they live, and many times, you can help someone out of a poor situation. If you approach it from the perspective that you want to help first, the rest falls into place."

He was right. I wasn't ready to see the cockroach-infested fourplex that was baking in the fires of Hades they call the Valley of the Sun. But that advice has always stuck with me: Don't judge others on the way they live, and if you are truly there to help, the rest will fall in place.

So, with that in mind, imagine standing in a house with holes in the roof, trash piled on the floor, the overwhelming smell of twenty cats, maybe a Schrodinger's Cat situation in the attic where you don't know if a critter is alive or dead, and a damp basement that's something out of your worst nightmares. Did you smile just now? Did you feel a twang of excitement and twinge of hope? Where the general public would run away screaming, I specifically seek these types of properties out because I know the following:

- I have the chance to help someone deal with problematic real estate.

- I have the chance to get creative.

- I have the chance to make as much money as I can negotiate.

If you didn't get excited, don't worry. It's a long book. I have plenty of time to convince you that these are signs of great potential deals. Of course, there are also nice houses you can invest in that are sold at a discount or using creative financing. That's the best thing about real estate! From undeveloped raw land to mansions, $1 houses (yes, they exist) to multimillion-dollar apartment complexes—if the numbers are right, you can invest in it.

What do you need to know to invest in these deals? *How to find them.* That's right—before we get to step two or three or a hundred, we need to start at step one.

CHAPTER 1:
What I Do

> Phil: What would you do if you were stuck in one
> place and every day was exactly the same, and
> nothing that you did mattered?
> Ralph: That about sums it up for me.
>
> —*Groundhog Day*, 1993

I'm a treasure hunter, a situation solver, and a master at spying potential. It could boil down to "deal-getter guy." Or if you wanted to get fancy, you could say I'm in acquisitions. I can see your eyes sparkle, imagining mansions, private jets, fur coats, and a gold chain that reads "deal-getter guy." Glamorous, isn't it?

If you ask a room of third graders what they want to be when they grow up, though, nobody says "acquisitions." Most people don't truly understand what this role entails. That could be because the methods used to find deals vary from investor to investor and market to market. When people pry for more detail as to what I do, I break it down a little further.

> Wholesaler: I find properties, put them under contract, then assign that contract to another investor for a fee. Essentially, I'm the middleman. If the mansions and champagne got you excited about being the deal-getter guy, imagine being a professional middleman. That's essentially what wholesaling is. I find properties and then pass them on to another investor. The spread could be

between $1,000 and $100,000. It's all in how good you are at finding deals.

Fix-and-Flipper: I find properties, buy them, then fix them up and sell them to someone else to make money. Instead of selling the property to another investor, I close on the property and send in swarms of contractors to fix it up. While I'm working on finding the next deal, my tool-equipped crews take the house from nasty to nice. When it's all done, I put it on the market and sell it to a nice family who will love it forever. I'm less of a middleman in this capacity and more of a caped neighborhood-improving, value-giving, home-saving crusader.

Real Estate Agent: I help retail or investor clients find properties to live in, house hack, rent out, or fix and sell. I combine my special agent powers with my investor powers to find properties many agents can't or won't seek out. I personally like being licensed. I feel like my access to direct data via the Multiple Listing Service (MLS) helps immensely in what I do day-to-day. I also feel like I have a bit more credibility than my unlicensed competition when building trust with homeowners. I have an entire government body regulating what I can and can't do, and I use state-approved, standard contracts. This can go a long way with the average homeowner when compared to the guy with a business card and no license. But to each his own. Most investors I know aren't licensed, and they do just fine. If you are an agent, the techniques in this book can make you the go-to resource for homeowners and investors in your market. Most agents wouldn't dream of thinking outside the box (or the MLS) to get deals for their clients.

These are just three facets of real estate investing. Soon I will transition my business into rentals and development (building brand new houses), but there's one constant I will continue to focus on. It's something any good investor will need to know how to do consistently, and it's the one thing you need to build a business: find deals.

After that, we can get into all the fun that comes after finding deals—things like how you can negotiate, analyze, determine the repair cost and after-repair value, and, of course, how—if you are consistent—you can build a business around those deals.

Why I Wrote This Book

One of my favorite movies of all time is *Groundhog Day*. Even though it came out twenty-four years ago, I still watch it once a month or so. It must run in the family. When it came out, my brother saw it eight times in the theater, and years later, my son was born on Groundhog Day. In it, Bill Murray plays Phil, a TV weatherman who relives the same day, February 2nd, over and over again. The trial and error process is hilarious, daunting, and sometimes depressing. He is stuck in this cycle of purgatory until he can somehow break his way out. This is a great reflection of how I feel when I meet with new investors. Time and time again, I'll connect with someone in my local area through the BiggerPockets Forums, and we will message back and forth. Eventually, I'll meet them at Starbucks. We'll talk for about an hour, then part ways. Most of the time, I'll hear the exact same statement: "I'm going to start with wholesaling to build up capital to fund fix-and-flips/rentals." I ask them what steps they're taking to get there, and I inevitably get this list:

1. Build my team.

2. Form an LLC.

3. Get business cards.

4. Create my website.

5. Build a buyer list.

Then they disappear, never to be heard from again. I'd start putting "missing newbies" on milk cartons, but I'm pretty sure they just gave up and quit. Wholesalers likely have the worst reputation of all investors in part because of this high dropout rate. It is also because many new investors call themselves wholesalers and then make mistakes that mess up deals for other investors, sometimes mishandling transactions, and hurting distressed sellers. Let's agree, here and now, not to be *that* guy.

Those steps listed above are all well and good—you *will* eventually need a team, an LLC (or some sort of entity), some business cards, and a website. You will need many things, but as a real estate investor, the one thing you will need more than anything else is property. Deals. You want to find deals, source deals, fund deals, and dive into a large pool full of deals Scrooge McDuck style.

Brandon Turner, the author of *The Book on Investing in Real Estate with No (and Low) Money Down*, hit on some great points about how new investors get sucked into the "easy button" philosophy that many gurus teach. They try it for a while, then eventually quit because:

- "Experts" make it sound easier than it is.

- It takes more time to get started than new investors anticipate.

- Many are inconsistent with their efforts and quit when they don't get results as quickly as they hoped.

The guru trap breeds misguided individuals who are sold on the "easy" idea—and they ultimately fail. Wholesaling is not easy, folks. In fact, it's likely one of the hardest things you can do in real estate investing. You have to find properties that others can't and buy them for less than others might manage. When a wholesaler sells a deal to another investor, the property *still* has to be a good deal to that investor, even after the wholesaler makes her profit. An amazing but difficult skill to master, wholesaling can be boiled down into one concept: Who can find the better deals?

So, just like Bill Murray breaks out of his cycle, I'm hoping to help break new investors out of quitting before they even start. I've spent hours with new investors who have been sold by a guy in a suit that this business is easy. Some are fresh out of a seminar or training program taught by a late-night TV guru. "Guru" isn't always a bad word. While they have their place in this world, when a guru sells motivation more than they sell real world tips and tools, then there's a problem.

Of course, some courses are great. Some might be totally worth it, but most don't care at all if you succeed or fail. After all, they already have your money. These systems prey on a newbie's hopes and dreams. While everyone in the room is bouncing up and down to rock music, all hyped up after the presentation, the "coaches" and "experts" selling the systems see dollar signs. Then you have the free, two-hour presentation that funnels into the $49-per-day seminar, which gets you into their $499 weekend or three-day getaway, during which they sell you into a $20,000 mentorship program. I know people who've spent $40,000+ on their education, and not all of them are actually doing deals.

The knowhow in this book—just like the advice presented in those courses or seminars—won't break new ground. This information is free for you to go find through the magic of the Internet. Sites like BiggerPockets. com are great resources where you can find most of this expertise via forums, blogs, articles, and free resources. This is a master compilation coming from someone who buys from wholesalers, fixes up properties, sells deals to landlords and builders, and has been licensed for a decade. Real estate is not rocket science. It's not difficult to grasp the concepts outlined in this book and run away with massive action to make it work, but there's the keyword: work. While there are many facets and segments of real estate investing, you're still going to have to pay your dues and work to make it succeed.

Here goes, the big mission statement for this book:

I want this book to be the ultimate guide to finding real estate deals.

Who This Book Is For

There are no secrets in real estate. This book is meant to be the ultimate guide to finding deals, not a secret formula to make you a ba-jillionaire. It's all about learning to be awesome at finding houses at a significant discount. I'll give you the ingredients and a few recipes, but you still have to do the work to make your real estate business thrive.

- Real Estate Investors: This book is for you if you fix-and-flip, wholesale, wholetail, or buy and hold single family, multifamily, land deals, development, etc.

- New Real Estate Investors: This book is for those of you getting through the research phase of beginning something new, big, and daunting. New investors should focus on one thing: finding deals. I want you to blast through analysis paralysis, where investors become so caught up crunching numbers that they never do their first deal. Too many new investors sit on the fence—and admittedly, it's scary up there. I want to make that drop easier so you aren't afraid to jump—and hit the ground running.

- Veteran Real Estate Investors: Just because you have a bunch of deals under your belt doesn't mean you're done growing. This book isn't just for the new kids on the block. I also want to talk to the guys who, like me, have been doing this for years. My philosophy when listening to a podcast, watching a video, attending an event or class, or traveling to a conference is that if I get one actionable, usable piece of information out of it, then it was 100 percent worth it. If you've been in the game for more than a few years, you know the target is constantly moving. The more tools you have, the faster you can react when the market shifts from bank owned foreclosures to short sales to private sellers to who knows what else.

- Real Estate Agents: I get it—I'm licensed, too. When the market is super tight, it can feel like you are guiding your client through a stretch of shark-frenzied waters in a rickety canoe. The frustration of bidding wars, escalation clauses, and overpaying for a house in a super-hot market will make your job difficult. Knowing how to find deals for your clients, whether on or off market, is invaluable. How about expanding into taking on investor clients? A normal client will buy one property every eight years, while an investor client might buy eight properties in one year. If you're an agent willing to knock on doors of pre-foreclosures and mail out to vacant properties or absentee owners, you will close more houses than the agent surfing the MLS and putting clients on the auto-email list.

- House Hackers: These brilliant folks decide to leverage their first home purchase into one of the smartest deals they have at their disposal. A house hacker uses an FHA first-time home loan to buy a house or a multi-unit building, living in one room or unit and renting out the rest. I've witnessed young families and single people pull off house hacks where their housing expense went to zero thanks to renters covering their mortgage. If I had a time machine, I would likely house hack a fourplex as my first purchase.

- Homeowners: What could this book have to offer someone looking for his or her next home? Well, especially in a hot market, the skills in this book will help find owners who want to sell but haven't put their house on the market yet. Some homeowners like fixer-uppers, and this is a great way to find those with instant equity. Some homeowners want to find something so special and specific that there might be only a handful of them on the market. Case in point: My dad was looking for a single-acreage property with two single-family houses on it. How many did we find on the market? Two. How many were in the county? At least a hundred. I see that as a hundred opportunities to go out and find what I'm looking for.

I want to help you learn all the nuts and bolts that go into this process of finding real estate deals. I want this book to demystify the strategies for new investors. I want to push people who are on that fence into action. I want veteran investors to keep it on their shelf as a complete resource to reference. I want flippers and landlords to give it to the people they will inevitably meet for coffee who tell them, "I'm going to start with wholesaling to build up capital to fund fix-and-flips/rentals." I want agents to creatively use the information to better service their buyers and get more listings. I want house hackers and homeowners to read this and go out and find exactly what they're seeking. You may have some knowledge or zero knowledge; maybe you've never closed a deal, or perhaps you've done fifty deals in your career. My hope is there is something here for everyone.

What I've learned in my career is this: When it comes to surviving as an investor, you will hit walls, you will fall into analysis paralysis, and you will not know what to do next. You will want to quit. I don't want you to burn out before you get a chance to hit your stride. As in most businesses, the momentum when you first start is slow. Once you create a small snowball and start pushing it, you may not think you are working with much, but the more you push, the bigger it gets.

What does this look like in the real world? You might start marketing and networking, and it may seem like you're not getting anywhere at first. Will you get frustrated and quit? *No!* You'll work the system, market and network consistently, keep it up, and all the sudden, you'll do your first deal.

There's nothing sweeter than holding your first check, total confirmation that your effort, hard work, blood, sweat, and tears paid off. The possibilities of this business suddenly become a reality. One deal turns into two, which turn into a handful. Do you stop marketing and networking now that you have a little success? *No!* You reinvest profits into the business and ramp up your efforts. After a period of calling, marketing, and networking, your success will become known. Suddenly, you'll have people bringing deals to you—and your snowball will turn into an avalanche of deal flow. Success begets success, and it all starts with consistency and hard work.

This book is not a system. It's not a roadmap that tells you to do X and Y that will get you to Z. This is a how-to-find-a-great-deal guide, covered front to back and sideways, with actionable steps along the way. It *can* be a step-by-step guide if you follow along, but it's not a business-in-a-box system that's done for you. It's merely a tool box; *you* must invest time into learning the process, figuring out which methods work for you and your market, and then act upon that information. There is a lot of information in these pages, but there's also real world examples of deals I have personally completed. I describe how I built my business, how I look at deals, and how you can learn from my mistakes. Sure, I've been broke. I've worked side jobs for agents and investors when I was getting started. What you might not guess is that wholesaling was my method of choice to get into real estate investing way back when I had no money. I've screwed up, made rookie mistakes, and wasted plenty of time. I've been right where you are today, hoping for more information in a field that excites me. I've learned from my mistakes, picked myself up plenty of times, made a bunch of money in this business, and now I'm here to share it all with you.

CHAPTER 2:
Market Analysis

"To find something, anything, a great truth or a lost pair of glasses, you must first believe there will be some advantage in finding it."

–All the King's Men, 2006

When I was younger, my brothers and I had one rule before we went to bed. Every night, our mom would make us read an hour before bedtime. This is probably where I first caught the bug to read. Still, there was one book I couldn't stand: *Where's Waldo?* I couldn't understand why he was hiding or what he was hiding from. Why was I trying to find him? Why did he wear the same clothes day in and day out, in all different climates and locations? Was the reader a secret CIA operative hunting down a stocking-capped double agent? Did Waldo owe someone money?

Similar to the task of finding our striped friend in a crowd, we're aiming to look for deals in the real estate market. There are a dozen or more methods to find Waldo in the crowd—we can strain our eyes, scan everyone in the crowd, or meticulously hunt him down. Or we could work smarter. What if we could get Waldo to call us and tell us where he is? What if Waldo was searching the Internet for a solution to his predicament, came across our website, and filled in his info voluntarily? What if we could enlist help, so we had two or three sets of eyes trying to find this Waldo character, grabbing him off the street into the back of a van and bringing him straight to us?

Those are the kinds of strategies we'll be exploring in this chapters.

Deals are what drive this business. Remember, our job as deal-getter guys is to *consistently find great deals*. These four words stand out.

- Consistently. We have to repeat this process over and over again. When you are building a business, you need to have a consistent flow of deals to keep your business running.

- Find. Our strengths lie in being able to dig up deals where no one else is. The ability to market or go find these deals and then negotiate and lock them up legally (with contracts) is what we are all about.

- Great. We are looking for deals that will actually make money—not mediocre deals where your margins are so slim, the deal isn't worth the time you spent on it.

- Deals. There should always be legitimate deals in the pipeline, which will require you to put in hard work and run the numbers forwards and backwards.

Where to Find Waldo

Consistently finding great deals is possibly the hardest part of this business. Acquisitions easily take up 50 percent of my effort and time, especially in a difficult or competitive market. You need to know what areas investors are avoiding and what areas they are flocking to, and then you need to make decisions. Are these deals on the market or off the market? Well, why limit ourselves? We will cover both on and off market deals. We need to strategically look at our target market to pinpoint the best areas to find properties. This is known as market analysis and is a key skill to have.

What is a market anyway? A market is a geographical area, usually encompassed within city limits or a city/metro area. In each market are several neighborhoods and countless houses. The conditions of the market are much more ambiguous than geographic area; this could include inventory, economic factors, social considerations, and a dozen more items. We will explore some of these factors, but only as they pertain to what we are trying to do here.

Can I say that my market conditions here in Denver, Colorado are the exact same as those in Phoenix, Arizona? No way—it's not even the same as an hour south or north, and things change quickly block by block. A ton of factors can drive inventory, sales, and desirability in each market and each neighborhood in that market. Many factors are out of your control, but it's now your job to figure out what is going on so we can invest intelligently rather than being too quick on that buy button. We want to make sure we're confident in a certain target area before we start spending marketing dollars.

When a flipper or a landlord is doing market research, they should consider the following:

- Crime rate
- Who's buying
- Whether the area houses starter homes or move-up homes
- Proximity to schools/shopping/highways/transportation
- Proximity to business centers
- Desirability
- Employment trends
- Days on market
- The city's general plan for expansion

A **fix-and-flip** investor cares about all these factors because when he buys a house in a neighborhood, they will come into play after he fixes it and tries to sell it. A landlord investor will care about most of these since they will dictate what kind of tenant she will eventually attract. A **builder or developer** will want to monitor the growth in the area—whether there are any other new-build comparables and whether the land value is worth more than if the property was just fixed up. **Wholesalers** mostly care about one thing: Are investors buying in this area? Wholesalers are scoping the demand, feeling it out, and then offering the supply.

Investor's want to know the track record of recent sales for properties in a given market. Notice how I said "recent" sales? That is an important factor here. We're looking for the last three-to-six months' worth of activity, usually not longer than six months. The more recent, the better. I start with three months and expand out from there. Data never lies, and getting a recent snapshot of activity in the area can tell you nearly everything you need to know.

Your target areas will likely be no more than a zip code or a few neighborhoods in the beginning. They might include a few thousand houses or a few thousand names on a target list. You can always start from there and expand once you outgrow that smaller list. Looking at an overhead map of your area and picking a needle out of that haystack is daunting. That's why you want to break it down even further and isolate the areas where the types of properties you want to invest in are located.

Time to Get Your Hands Dirty

Let's get to work. We can talk about theory all day long, but I'd rather get right to it. We are going to analyze *your* market now. There are three main ways to determine your target market:

1. Use online tools to determine where high numbers of recent investor sales are.

2. Network with agents and have them send you reports of recent cash/investor sales.

3. Use the reverse wholesale approach by networking with other investors to find out where they're buying and target those same areas.

Don't use just one of these, use them all. The more you use, the better you will know your area and your target markets.

Online Tools

The Internet is a wonderful place. It's not just buzzword lists and cat pictures. The tools we can use as real estate investors are getting better every year. It used to be that if you didn't have access to the listing service that agents use, the Multiple Listing Service (MLS), you were sunk. But now, the free tools are getting better and better. These are the tools that I use to determine where there are high concentrations of investor sales.

• Multiple Listing Service (MLS). This is the most direct access to the data we are trying to filter and the platform real estate agents use to publish new listings. This is also where agents report when properties go under contract and are sold, how much they sold for, and the type of financing or cash used to purchase them. Since most houses sold are sold through the MLS, we can assume this is likely the best source of information.

- Redfin.com. If you can't get MLS access (it's not easy and in some cases not possible at all when you don't have your real estate license), Redfin is the next best thing. These types of sites pull data from the MLS, so it's well sourced. It might be a secondhand source and heavily-filtered based on your state or area's rules for sharing this information, but it's better than nothing and it's free. You can take an overhead view of the map of your area, select a few different criteria, and suddenly the info you are looking for appears on the map. Amazingly simple. Unfortunately, it's not available in every market.

- Zillow.com. If the MLS and Redfin aren't available, this is my last-ditch effort. This site also pulls from the MLS, but I don't like the search or layout as much. Like with all these sites, we drill down to individual houses and what's going on with the comparables, leaving the "Zestimates" and other approximate value estimates alone. They are nearly always too far off to use reliably.

- ListSource.com. We will talk about this resource a few times in this book. What is ListSource? It's basically a huge collection of data on properties across the United States, searchable by building your own custom lists. I buy lists from ListSource and then use those lists to market to my target areas. CoreLogic owns ListSource and it runs the backend data for many title companies and owns an MLS platform that areas can license to use. The MLS in my market here in Colorado is a CoreLogic system, so when it comes to the "source" of the data, ListSource is among the best, although that may not be the case for your market.

- County Tax Records. This is a good place to start looking up information on properties, but it's not a great way to search for recent cash or investor sales. Unless you like blindly looking up every property, most county search websites are not very user-friendly. Note: If your state is a non-disclosure state, this will be a very difficult process. In most states, sold property information is public information. You can look up what a property sold for, the date it sold, and even the name of the lender used to fund the transaction. In non-disclosure states however, this information is not public. Check your state to find out if it is a non-disclosure state. If it is, the more access you have to the MLS, the better.

Now it's time to take these concepts and apply them to the three methods above—MLS, Redfin, and Zillow. The objective is to find the highest concentrations of properties recently sold to investors. This will tell you the types of investment activities going on in the area. In each system, the goal is to limit the filters to search the most recent "solds." With Zillow and Redfin, you can't search by sold type (cash, FHA, conventional, etc.), so you will have to do our best to approximate who it was sold to.

In this example, you will be searching for single family residences (SFR), excluding those pesky condos and townhomes (and land, of course) for now. Since these aren't perfect systems and you are trying to get to know the areas, there will be some trial and error here. Start with low prices to see what has sold the cheapest and work from there. These systems will also have different ways to search the same thing. Some have a map search, and others have zip code or area searches. Let's search using the map search to start. Bring up your city, zoom in on an area, and get started. To make this process easier, start off in your own neighborhood or an area that you have an interest in and are familiar with. Once you know what you're doing, you'll be able to expand your search area to other parts of town. Please note that these instructions are for the following programs as of 2017, they may change their websites down the road but these directions will help you get started.

MLS

- Within search criteria, filter by "Sold" and enter the last three months as a search criterion.
- Filter by "Property Type: Single Family."
- Filter "Price." Leave minimum at "No Min" and select your maximum at $50,000.
- Filter by "Sale Records" and "Last Three Months."
- Filter by "Property Type" and unselect everything but "House."

Redfin

- The home page will let you enter in a zip code, address, or city. Start by entering a zip code and narrow it down from there.
- On the far right will be an option for more filters. Click that and then select "Sale Records." The default sub-option is "Last 3

Months," which is perfect.

- You can check and un-check each property type here as well—house, condo, townhouse, etc. To see just single family houses, just select "House," and it will eliminate the rest.

- After closing the "More Filters" menu, select your price point. For price, enter $1 to $50,000 to start. If you don't get any hits or you know the neighborhood averages $250,000 houses, simply increase the price points until you get results.

Zillow

- Start at the top menu bar.

- Filter by "Recently Sold." Beware, Zillow considers recently sold to be anywhere within the last eighteen to twenty-four months. When testing this out, I found records that were nearly three years old.

- Filter by "Home Type." Unselect everything but "Homes." Remember, we are only interested in SFRs.

- For price, enter $1 to $50,000 to start. If you know houses usually sell for $300,000 or more, you might want to start off at $100,000, or $150,000 on the high end. Play with the sold amounts until you start finding the lowest sold comparables in the area. Those are what we're after.

This is where everything besides the MLS gets pretty ambiguous and will take more work on your part. The MLS will give you better data, even the ability to export searches into spreadsheets you can download and manipulate at will. Zillow and Redfin take a lot more hunting, messing with filters and settings, and taking notes until you get a decent feel for the neighborhoods. Finding the largest concentration of recently sold properties that were sold at a low price on these systems isn't easy, but with some time and effort, you will start getting the hang of it. I'd go through each home that was sold cheaply, even in my area where median home prices are $250,000 or so. There were some sales just under $100,000. Those were most likely bought by investors (and if you have access to the MLS, you will be able to confirm if that is true). Not many John Q. Public homebuyers would take on a beat-up property. Look through the pictures and description if available. You are looking for badly outdated properties or pictures that show the property in bad condition.

You are hoping to find descriptions that mention:

- Investor special
- Fix-and-flip
- Needs TLC
- Has potential for the right buyer
- Great investment
- Great rental
- BYOB (bring your own bulldozer)

Do this for several areas, neighborhoods, subdivisions, suburbs, zip codes, etc. Take notes or screenshots. You are looking for a trend—the highest concentration of properties recently sold to investors. Find the average price that distressed properties are selling for in the neighborhoods you are researching—this is called finding the "baseline" or "baselining". For example, find the lowest sold properties that are three bedrooms, two bathrooms. Try to figure out *why* they sold for so little. Did they need a ton of work? If you can find five to ten properties (three bedrooms, two bathrooms, two-car garage, 1,500 square feet) that need a bunch of work that all sold around $100,000 in a neighborhood, that's a trend you should note. Do similar searches on each platform to try to find what those same properties are selling for all fixed up.

The description for fixed up properties includes:

- Remodeled
- Refinished
- Rehabbed
- All new
- New carpet
- New paint
- New kitchen
- New bathrooms

Look at the pictures. Everything should be all new—tile, carpet, and bathrooms—looking like it's straight from HGTV. Let's say you found three to five of these and they sold between $200,000 and $215,000. This is a great sign. You just performed a baseline evaluation of this neighborhood and found that investors are buying for $100,000, with fix-and-flip investors reselling these same houses all fixed up for around $200,000. If you were to find a deal that is three bedrooms, two bathrooms, with a two-car garage and 1,500 square feet in this area for around $100,000, you'd know from your prior research that it is most likely a deal.

Let's say you search ten of these areas and find the following numbers for the last three to six months:

- Neighborhoods 1–2: fifty possible investor sales each
- Neighborhoods 3–7: twenty possible investor sales each
- Neighborhoods 8–10: five possible investor sales each

You will want to focus on neighborhoods 1 and 2 to start with because from our market research, we know there's more investor activity in these areas out of the ten. Wholesalers, as well as fix-and-flip investors, will do well in 1 and 2. Neighborhoods 3 through 7 aren't bad backup neighborhoods to expand into once you're ready, but neighborhoods 8, 9, and 10 look like duds. That's not to say you can't find a deal in 8, 9, or 10. They're just not hot areas that we will focus on to begin with.

Don't skim over this skill. Being skilled in finding comparables and evaluating baselines makes a big difference. I want you to put in the work now because it's an invaluable asset to your tool belt of skills. If you can take the top-down view of an area, drill down into it and figure out where investors are buying, you can, in theory, apply this skill to any market. I've used this skill to invest in properties I've never seen, several states away. With MLS access and an Internet connection, you can get good enough at this to find and then sell any property across the country. Whether you want to invest in properties five minutes away or five states away, move across the country and start in a new market, buy your rentals from wholesalers or start finding your own direct deals, this skill is invaluable.

Now let's take a look at ListSource.

ListSource

There are a few outside-the-box ways to use ListSource, including using it as a workaround to figure out investor sales in non-disclosure states. What you are going to do here is build a list with certain criteria and then let ListSource give you the number of investor-bought properties per zip code. This will let you know which areas in your given market are hotbeds of investment activity.

- Go to ListSource.com and set up a new account.

- Click on "Create Your Own." You want to customize our options here for best results.

- This lands you on the "Geography" tab. On the "Select Criteria" drop down, select "Zip Code."

- Select the state of your target market, then select the available zip codes you want and "add" them—at least ten or fifteen zip codes for best results.

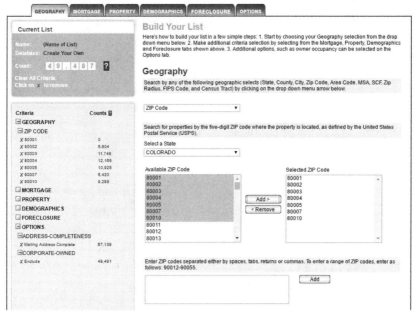

- If you need help selecting zip codes in your area, Google your city zip codes and then enter those into ListSource.

- Now that we have our geography criteria set up, let's go to the "Property" tab.

- Select "Property Type" in the drop-down menu, then "Residential: SFR" and "add" it. This will only select freestanding single-family residences in your areas. If you are targeting townhomes or condos, you can change this selection.

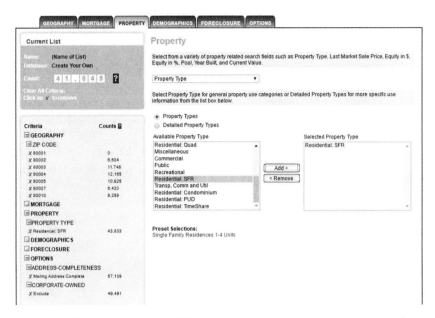

- While still in the "Property" tab, change the selection from "Property Type" to "Last Market Sale Date." You want to make sure you only select properties that sold in the last three to six months.

- Toward the bottom of this page, you will see "Preset Selections." Select "Last 3 Months" or "Last 6 Months," which changes the dates above, then "add" it to the selected box.

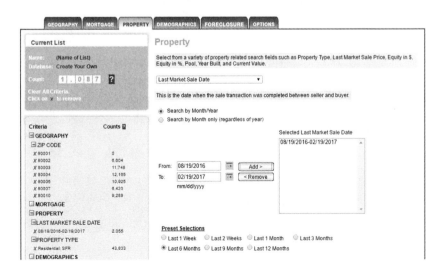

- You now have your geography, your property type, and your sold date criteria in there. Now go to the "Options" tab.

- In "Owner Occupied Status," select "Absentee Owned." This is the closest you can get to cash buyers; these are all buyers who did not intend on living in the property when they bought it. Therefore, there's a high likelihood that these are investor buyers.

- For "Corporate Owned Properties," select "No Preference." You don't care if an LLC was the purchaser of the property. It's more likely an investor with their investment company purchasing the property.

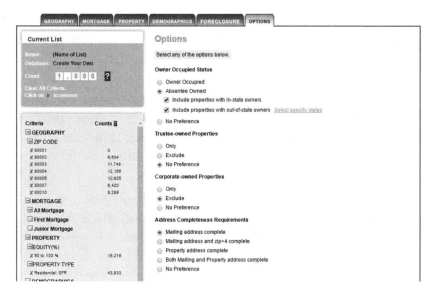

- At the bottom of the page, there is a blue button that says "Purchase List." Don't worry, you won't be buying anything.

- Click the yellow tab at the top that reads "Purchase Partial List."

- Select "Custom Selection."

- On the drop-down menu that appears, select "Zip Code."

- If at any time you want to change the parameters of your search, in sections 1-6, there is a "Refine Search" button that will take you back before Step 7.

Append Output Fields	**Purchase Partial List**	Suppression

Select Number of Records

○ All **174** Leads

○ Only [   ] Leads

○ Every [1 ▼] nth lead, max, [   ]

◉ **Custom Selection**

Group properties by: [ZIP Code ▼]   Prev 1 - 6 of 6 Next   [Export]

State / GroupBy field	Records	All	Only	Every Nth	Maximum
CO	174				
80002	24	☐	[ ]	[-- ▼]	[ ]
80003	32	☐	[ ]	[-- ▼]	[ ]
80004	47	☐	[ ]	[-- ▼]	[ ]
80005	26	☐	[ ]	[-- ▼]	[ ]
80007	9	☐	[ ]	[-- ▼]	[ ]
80010	36	☐	[ ]	[-- ▼]	[ ]

This now gives you investor buyer purchase numbers by zip code within the timeframe that you set up. You should see a list of the zip codes you entered at the beginning, and next to that in the "Records" column, you will find the number. If you perform a quick search down the list, you will see that certain zip codes have five to ten times the number of absentee sales as the others. This is a good place to start your targeting.

In this screenshot, see how 80007 only has nine target properties that match our criteria, while 80004 has forty-seven? While using this ListSource trick, I would concentrate on the following zip codes since they have the highest number of target properties that investors are buying: 80004, 80010, and 80003.

What Is This Magical MLS System Anyway?

As previously mentioned, MLS is short for "Multiple Listing Service" and is a website platform where licensed real estate agents who are listing a property for a seller will market the properties they have for sale. This is a one-stop shop for agents, their main bread and butter where they list (market) the properties they have and where a buyer's agent goes to search what is available on the market for their client. This is the main information platform. It's where websites like Zillow and Redfin get their property information (albeit secondhand). The MLS is always a regional platform, and some cities or areas have two or more MLS systems overlapping in the area.

Unfortunately, there is no national platform. As nice as it would be to have countrywide access and the ability search for properties across the nation, it's never going to happen. So, when your neighbor wants to sell his property, he will usually call a real estate agent. The real estate agent will sign a contract with your neighbor to list his property on the market, and the first steps of this would be for that agent to enter the property into the MLS system for other agents to find. All kinds of properties are listed on the MLS—your neighbor's, certainly, but also bank-owned foreclosures, short sales, auction properties, investment properties, even multifamily and apartment buildings. The barrier of entry to have direct access to this system is usually the following: obtaining your real estate license (classes, tests, fees), hanging your license at a real estate brokerage (fees, contracts), paying into either a Realtor board or the MLS board (more fees!), then paying a monthly fee to use the darn thing. MLS information is heavily protected by the regional boards and, of course, the Realtor association since direct listing information is almost all that agents have left these days, thanks to the Internet. However, there are great ways to have mutually beneficial relationships with agents. You can be a great asset to them—and, of course, vice versa.

If you don't want to get your license yourself, cultivate a relationship with an agent who will actively search the MLS for you. You could certainly network with an agent or three and ask them to send a spreadsheet or list of cash sales in the last three to six months. On most MLS systems, this takes roughly three minutes to complete. You are certainly able provide enough value to a real estate agent for three minutes of their time if you make the effort.

What Can an Investor Offer an Agent?

Wholesalers and other investors market for leads, and sometimes those leads don't work out for them. The seller might owe too much on the house or be at the break-even point on price, and sometimes the seller simply needs an agent to list and sell the house. This is where you can reciprocate with your go-to agent, who has been doing you favors, by giving them a seller who does not work for your business model. When leads are short sales (where the seller owes more than the house is worth), the agent can usually work the short sale and represent both the seller and the investor (you). I don't know many agents who wouldn't run some reports for an investor in exchange for leads.

If you want to get your hands dirty, you can also offer to do some grunt work for the agent. This is pretty much how I started off in the business. As soon as I got to Phoenix, I had more time than money and more energy than experience. I networked with some investors and investor-friendly agents and told them I'd do anything to get some experience in. They had me run signs across town, put up lockboxes, check on properties, and perform menial work. In exchange, I was taught how the local MLS system worked, I received printouts of cash sales, I got pocket listings sent my way, and I built great relationships and friendships that continue to last today. Later, I did the same thing when I moved back to Colorado. To learn as much as I could in this new market, I delved into the MLS system, informed myself on BPOs (broker price opinions—think of it as a less detailed appraisal), and I drove by properties to take pictures. Soon enough, I was doing all of the BPOs for the office and running all of the short sale leads. In 2006, before short sales were well known, I was an expert thanks to this experience. If I hadn't done BPOs for eight hours a day, I wouldn't be an expert at valuation today.

The golden rule of networking is to first seek to add value to a relationship before you ask for favors. It goes a long way in business. A simple cash sales report or setting up the MLS to send you new listings might only take a few minutes for an agent. But if you ask for help with after repair value, for BPOs, or for a laundry list of other things, start by being of service to the agent first. Then when you are stuck with an ARV and need an agent's opinion, they will be happy to give it to you since your relationship is give and take—not take, take, take.

Market Analysis for Reverse Wholesaling

When analyzing a market, it can be easy to rely on the raw data from the above exercises. However, the data itself can only tell you so much. Getting the details out of cold, hard numbers you see on your screen is impossible, and there is always more to every story. What if you could analyze a market based on not only where investors are buying, but also what they prefer to buy, down to the last detail. Reverse wholesaling slays two dragons at once: getting firsthand knowledge of a market from experienced investors and finding possible buyers to wholesale to or partner with. Let me explain.

Wholesaling can sometimes be difficult if you aren't familiar with the local market and what types of properties investors are buying. You think you have a great deal in your hands, but you start shopping it around and get no takers. There must be a better way! What if instead you talked to investors and learned what they really were looking for in a property? Now you can take their orders, fill them, and give them exactly what they want. This is the concept of reverse wholesaling. They tell you what they are looking for and where, and you go find it.

It makes life so much easier when investors tell us where they like to buy, the type of properties they're looking for, and the price formula they use? Instead of just throwing a dart at the dartboard, finding deals in that area, then shopping the deal to buyers, we want to talk to the buyers and fill that order. Investors might tell you, "I buy three bed or more, two bath or more, 1,500 square feet or more, in the 80205 zip code for no more than $90,000." You might start with two phases: using online tools and networking with agents to find investor sales. You'd start to notice where big concentrations of deals happen. That's a great place to start. You could likely begin marketing efforts based on that information alone. But I ask each of you to make sure you are using the reverse wholesaling technique as well, as often, and as much as possible. Let's get out there and meet some actual investors, build rapport, and bring them into our business circles.

When networking with investors, I always ask them to tell me about the details of their last few deals. When I get an idea of what the buyer is buying and where, I know if I find a deal within those numbers that if I'm wholesaling, I likely have a buyer. Even if I'm not wholesaling, I'm doing the homework of finding out where people are finding deals and what their numbers look like. When starting from zero, this can be a shortcut to figuring out good areas.

The more you network, the more you'll find that a lot of people you meet during your research in phases one and two will surface in phase three, reverse wholesaling. You will see that in active areas, there are prominent investors who generally buy there. Take these three steps—using online tools, networking with agents, and reverse wholesaling—and mash them together. Work each one until you have a pretty good idea of one to two neighborhoods or areas in which to start. After you have your targets selected, it's time to start trying to find deals in those neighborhoods. Remember when I said that an investor with no deals isn't an investor? Okay, then let's start analyzing what kind of sellers we will target and how to reach them—then we'll focus on getting deals in our pipeline.

Case Study—Virtual Wholesaling Is Real!

Type of Deal—Bank Owned
Investment Strategy—Wholesale

This deal was special for me; it was the one that opened my eyes to the possibilities of wholesaling from *anywhere* using the skills I'd picked up over the years. With an Internet connection, access to the MLS or something similar, and a few buyers in an area, you can potentially wholesale deals in any state while sitting on a beach in Singapore.

In this particular instance, I found a bank owned (REO) property listed on the MLS that was about fifteen to twenty minutes from my house in an area where I had wholesaled before. Since I already had a baseline for that neighborhood, I knew it was a deal by looking at the price and the pictures. I immediately called the listing agent and offered to run him over an earnest money check. I also offered to let him double-end the deal (take both buyer and seller commissions). I ended up getting it locked up that day for $50,000.

The problem was I hadn't actually seen the property yet. But, I decided to try something new, so I sent out a buyer who I knew liked to buy in that area to see if he would buy it for $55,000. He was hungry for deals and called me two hours later to work up a contract for the property. I made a quick $5,000 and learned a valuable lesson: If I could wholesale a house I'd never seen fifteen minutes from me, I could do it pretty much anywhere.

CHAPTER 3:
Reaching Your Market

Yoda: I am wondering, why are you here?

Luke: I'm looking for someone.

Yoda: Looking? Found someone, you have, I would say, hmmm?

–Star Wars: The Empire Strikes Back, 1985

There are many kinds of sellers and many types of properties for sale out there. Just like there are all kinds of people out there, there are all types of sellers who are selling for all kinds of different reasons—from distress to divorce, from hoarding to simply moving out of town. This will be your crash course in all kinds of seller situations—why they might sell and how you can be there to help them.

In this chapter, after I offer a quick definition of different types of sellers, as well as where sellers can be found and how much competition you will have from other investors and agents for sellers, I'll review deal-finding strategies. I also break down potential pros and cons of working with each type of seller and deal. By the end, you should have a good idea of what sort of seller you'd prefer to work with and the methods you'd like to start using in your market to get deals flowing.

On Market

With these properties, the seller has contacted an agent, and the agent has listed the property for sale on the local MLS for other agents and private homeowners to find. (Realtor.com is the national public side of MLS systems; most MLS systems will also post on Realtor.com.)

Competition level: highest. Danger, Will Robinson! Since MLS-listed properties can be seen by every agent in town—and every client the agents have on an automatic email system, and the public via Realtor.com/Zillow.com/Redfin.com—it's safe to say that the most eyeballs possible are on these properties. That's great for sellers. That's exactly why people list their property—to get maximum exposure. That must mean it's a waste of time for wholesalers or investors, right? I say no. The MLS might have the highest level of competition, but that doesn't mean you won't find deals there.

Off Market

In these instances, the sellers haven't yet contacted an agent, and in some cases, they may not have even considered selling. These sellers can range from those offloading highly distressed properties to those who just haven't gotten around to contacting an agent yet and who may want to see what you're offering first.

Competition level: low. Since we, as investors, are actively seeking these people out, it goes without saying that competition is low, but you need to know that "low" is relative, at least compared to the MLS. That does not mean there aren't a ton of other investors who are marketing to off-market leads and trying to do exactly what you're doing. The more specific, creative, and clever you are as an off-market investor, the lower the competition gets. If you go online or talk to local investors and see that seemingly everyone is mailing white postcards to absentee homeowners (landlords, mostly), you will know that there will be a ton of competition in that specific niche. Will you just blindly do the same thing and hope to elbow your way into a landlord's already full postbox to get their attention? I certainly hope not.

Auctions

For a variety of reasons, some properties may be put up for public auction, where potential buyers vie to outbid each other to get a deal. Do you like fast-paced action? Do you enjoy split-second, hundred-thousand-dollar decisions? Do you long to associate with the largest players in your market? Do you thrive on drama? Do you crave Count Chocula? (Seriously, when will they keep that on the shelves year-round?) If you answered yes to any of those serious questions, then boy, do I have the place for you! Auctions!

Not just any auctions, but a place where they are selling houses, condos, townhomes, commercial property (think strip malls, apartment buildings, office buildings), and land to the highest bidder.

Competition level: medium. There are a few caveats to auctions—there might be fewer bidders present than there would be on an MLS listing, and the barrier to entry for the average investor is quite high. This is due to usually having to pay the full cash amount of the winning bid on the spot or shortly after the auction. Most auctions are publicly advertised, so as with the MLS, there are high amounts of people who know: a) there's an auction going on and b) the properties that will be for sale. Mix in the grizzled veterans of your market and big players like hedge funds who buy at auction with seemingly limitless amounts of financial backing, and you can see where a run-of-the-mill investor won't even have a ticket to ride the auction train.

Now, as for the various types of properties:

Distressed Properties

Distressed properties are found on market, off market, and at auction. You'll hear this term often in this business, but what does it actually mean? A distressed property might mean that either the seller is in distress or the property itself is distressed. If you find both at the same time, that usually means the stars have aligned to make a great deal. Either way, it is likely that the property will sell well under market value. That's why we're here, right? To solve problems and negotiate for inexpensive properties.

What kind of seller distress situations will cause a property to be sold under market value? Good question!

Financial Distress

People have issues, and when they have money issues, it usually spills into other areas of their lives. When the economy, real estate market, or stock market tanks, you will likely find high levels of financially distressed sellers who are no longer able to afford their homes.

- Personal Financial Distress. This refers to actual money issues of the seller. They can no longer make their mortgage payment due to job loss, mismanagement, gambling, or many other reasons. When a homeowner stops paying their mortgage, they only have a small window of time during which to sell their property before the bank initiates foreclosure proceedings. Foreclosure is when the lender legally takes the property back since the current homeowner can no longer make payments. Another cause of distress is when a homeowner gets an adjustable rate mortgage, or ARM, and the loan does just what the acronym implies: It adjusts. This can turn a $1,000 payment into a $1,800 payment or more, making the mortgage no longer affordable to the homeowner.

- Property Is Underwater. In this case, the amount of the loan is more than the house is worth. If the homeowner is underwater and they try to sell the property, they will have to bring the difference between the loan and the sale price to the closing table. For example, the seller's loan is for $150,000, but the market has gone down and the property is now worth $125,000. If they try to sell, they will have to bring the difference, or $25,000, in cash to closing. You can see where this might be a problem, as people generally do not have this kind of money just sitting around. In the last market crash, many homeowners just stopped paying their mortgages, knowing they could never sell their homes.

Personal Distress

Homeowners aren't just bound by financial issues. Usually, many factors add up to create the perfect storm. These life circumstances are mostly out of their control, but create a ton of stress when an unwanted home is involved:

- Death
- Divorce
- Employment change
- Elderly homeowner making transition
- Investor tired of being a landlord

This is where our mission to help homeowners meets an opportunity to buy properties at a discount.

Distressed Property Condition

Homeownership, while part of the "American dream," is actually pretty darn expensive and can cost you a lot in the long run. Deferred maintenance is like a ninja—if you avert your eyes for a second, he will pummel you with costs that'll add up heavily over time. "Deferred" means put off until later. This refers to all the little things that break or need attention over time. Many homeowners ignore these things until they have gone from a few small things to a huge laundry list of items that have gotten worse over time. Where once the paint was chipped, it will eventually peel, then a few years later the wood is rotted, and after a few more, there's a water leak that's destroying your basement. These things add up, and when an owner won't or can't address these issues, they will eventually drag down the home value to the point where only someone like you or me will come in and buy it for a discount.

Retail buyers who buy houses don't want to deal with a ton of big, medium, or even small problems. They want a house that's move-in ready—and so does the bank that's lending that buyer the money. Many times, depending on the loan type, a house can be in such bad condition that a new buyer may not even be able to get a loan on the property. With our friend Deferred Maintenance comes his cousin, No-Updating. A badly out-of-date house is not only unsightly and undesirable, but can be dangerous. It costs a ton of money, time, and energy to keep the cosmetics up-to-date with new design trends, bathrooms, kitchens, flooring, paint, etc. It's even more costly to keep up the electrical, plumbing, and heating systems. An old electrical system in a home can be deadly, and there are certain electrical types that cannot be insured. In these instances, a bank wouldn't loan on the home.

Foreclosures

There are a ton of misconceptions when it comes to this area of real estate, and most do not realize that there are three distinct heads to this beast. I wanted to initially file this section under "Financial Distress," but it really deserves its own section. Most of the time the process starts with financial or personal distress—loss of job, reduction in income, death, medical issues, or one of a hundred other reasons. The homeowner can no longer pay their mortgage, which starts this entire process. Once the process starts, there are different levels of motivation to sell the property as it moves along in the three phases of foreclosure.

Let's look at these three phases of the foreclosure process and where each buying opportunity exists: pre-foreclosure, public auction, and real estate owned. ***Important Note:*** the foreclosure process can vary widely in each state. From here on out, we are going to be using Colorado as an example, but it is important that you understand the rules will be different in other states. Make sure you do your homework and fully understand how the process works in *your* state.

Pre-Foreclosure   **Public Auction**   **Real Estate Owned**

What is a foreclosure, you might be asking? Here is the simple version: Foreclosure is a legal process, where the lender on a property has the right to gain ownership of the property through a lawsuit or legal action if the borrower stops paying the lender; this is called defaulting on a loan. There is public notification of the default leading up to the sale date (pre-foreclosure). On the sale date, the property is sold at auction (public auction). If the lender is the winning bidder at the auction, they will then try to sell the property on the open market (real estate owned/REO).

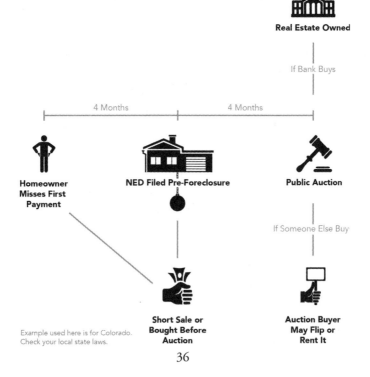

Pre-foreclosure

Where They're Found: On Market, Off Market

Competition level: high. Think of competition this way—if the information or people are easy to find and publicly advertised, then there will be the highest level of competition. Other investors, real estate agents, the bank, the mortgage insurance company, bankruptcy attorneys, loan modification companies, everyone and their mom will be mailing and calling about pre-foreclosures. The kicker is, most homeowners who are facing foreclosure have their head in the sand, ignoring calls or disconnecting their phones, and throwing their mail away without even opening it.

Homeowners who stop paying their loans usually have a grace period before the bank starts to take legal action against them. As soon as the homeowner has missed four months of payment (this varies by state, but we are using my state of Colorado as an example here), the bank will then make the legal action public. This is called "notice of default," involving a public notice that the homeowner is in default, with paperwork filed at the county courthouse and advertised in a newspaper. The homeowner and the public are now notified of the pending foreclosure/sale date. In Colorado, this occurs four months from the notice of default and includes the amount owed by the lender. They are nice enough to tack on a ton of late fees and lawyer/filing fees to that amount owed.

Basically, there are four months of missed payment and a notice of default is given. Then there are four months until the auction/sale date. That means a minimum of eight months of no payments, though I have heard of cases where this process can be delayed two or more years. During this time, the homeowner still owns the property, and they can sell it at any time leading up to the sale date—and most of the time they are very motivated. If they sell the property before the sale date, there is no foreclosure proceeding, and therefore no record of a foreclosure on their credit report. Whether you can make a pre-foreclosure deal work will depend on whether the homeowner has any equity and whether you have enough time before the sale date to make a deal work. I've been contacted a few days before the foreclosure date, but be wary of these deals. While possible, it takes experience to pull off a sale in just a few days.

Pre-foreclosure with equity. Let's say that when Mary contacts Joe that Joe falls into this category. Joe still has a mortgage and owes $50,000 but can no longer afford his mortgage payment. When Mary contacts him, he's in pre-foreclosure and motivated to sell. He wants to avoid a foreclosure on his credit report. Since Mary ends up buying the property from Joe for $70,000, the difference between what Joe owed his lender and the purchase price is $20,000. That is the amount of equity that Joe had in the property. He'll walk away from the closing table with roughly $20,000 and avoid foreclosure ($70,000 purchase price − $50,000 lender payoff = $20,000 equity).

Pre-foreclosure with no equity. Back to our Mary/Joe example, let's pretend that Joe owes his bank $100,000. This would make that last equation look more like this: $70,000 purchase price − $100,000 lender payoff = -$30,000 equity. That is a negative number, and Joe cannot make up the $30,000 difference by pulling money out of his bank account. You might say, "Well, that's the end of the road. There is nothing that we can do for No-Equity Joe." I say, "Wrong! Ever heard of a short sale?"

Short Sales

Let's work with the version of Joe the seller who owes more than his house is worth. He owes $100,000, and Mary can only buy the house for $70,000, like in the above example. What they can do is start the short sale process with Joe's lender. It is still common in many areas for homeowners to be underwater on their homes because of buying at the height of the real estate market before prices plummeted. This caught many homeowners upside down, unable to sell now that their homes were worth less than they owed their lenders. With a short sale, the homeowner still has the rights to sell the property, but the lender now gets to say, "I'm going to reduce the amount that Joe owes us, but I get to approve the shorted payoff [short sale]." Here are a few quick tips to know about the short sale process:

- The seller needs to be in default for a bank to move forward with the short sale process. Joe has missed four payments so far, so this is a good candidate for Mary to pursue.

- The seller must have a documentable hardship or reason why they are missing payments and need a reduced payoff to sell the house. Look under "Financial Distress" above—it could be any of those reasons. The bank also needs reasonable proof of the event or situation, so they proceed to dig into the seller's private information. I always aim to be up front with a homeowner about this.

- The bank likes to see a real estate agent involved. Many banks will not consider a short sale without the property being listed. In this case, Mary has networked with a local agent whom she trusts to bring into the transaction to help with buying Joe's house.

Short sales have serious tax and possible legal consequences for the homeowner. I'm not a lawyer, and most likely neither are you. Therefore, you shouldn't directly consult the homeowner on any tax issues but you should still be aware of them. Usually, the bank has a form the homeowner signs that lays out any tax or legal consequences in effort of full disclosure.

- Deficiency Judgment. One piece of that huge stack of paperwork Joe signed when buying his home was the bank's right to sue or recoup any losses the bank takes if Joe were to accept a short sale payoff. It used to be that the bank would try to get Joe to sign a note or a judgment before closing stating that Joe owes the bank the difference between the sale price and the amount left on his loan— in this case, $30,000 ($70,000 purchase price – $100,000 lender payoff = -$30,000 equity). I've only had one or two banks try this, and we fought back on it. But just because it's not common these days doesn't mean that the bank doesn't have the legal right to enforce this.

- Tax Filing. Who loves the IRS? Not homeowners kicked while they're down by having to do a short sale, then owing taxes because the lender filed paperwork with the IRS showing the balance owed ($30,000 in Joe's case) as forgiven debt. What does this mean in tax-speak? It means the $30,000 is now shown as income to Joe for the year he completed the short sale. This can have some pretty serious tax consequences, as now Joe, on paper, made $30,000 more that year and did not pay taxes on the increase. This can make Joe go from getting a return to owing several thousand dollars in taxes. Surprise! But thanks to the Mortgage Forgiveness Debt Relief Act of 2007, if the owner lives in the home when the short sale closes, the IRS waives this tax. The bill was extended in 2014, but is no longer in effect as of 2016. However, it is a good idea to be aware of and actively look for programs like this.

- Credit Report. While Joe dodged the bullet of a foreclosure haunting him for seven years, he will still take a big hit on his credit report. This is due to the combination of missing payments and the bank possibly reporting the debt as being paid off, but not in full when the short sale closes. While not nearly as bad as a foreclosure or bankruptcy, Joe's credit is going to suffer through this process.

Here is a quick short sale story, so you can understand the process a little more.

Mary and Joe agree to a price for Joe's house. Congratulations! Mary is going to negotiate this short sale, so she contacts Joe's bank with Joe's permission and gets a list of paperwork that Joe will need to show a financial hardship. Joe gathers all the documents requested—W2s, tax returns, bank statements, and a hardship letter from Joe to the bank stating why he is in distress. Mary collects these from Joe and submits them to the bank, along with the signed offer and any paperwork needed from the agent. Joe's bank will now review each document and likely kick them back to Mary for anything missing or needing correction.

During this time, Joe's bank will order either an appraisal or a broker price opinion (BPO). The bank is trying to determine if the market is now supporting Mary's offer of $70,000. Once Joe's paperwork is approved, and the valuation comes in at an acceptable price, the bank will either approve the short payoff, decline the short payoff, or counter Mary's offer at a higher price.

If the short sale is accepted, the bank will issue an approval letter. This states the new payoff amount and any terms attached to the acceptance. Terms include the seller having to sign a deficiency judgment to avoid a deed restriction on the property. Deed restrictions restrict what the *next* owner can do with the property, and the favorite one of a few big banks is to say that the new buyer cannot re-sell the property for ninety days after closing. As a wholesaler, this is no good—and I'd fight it. This shouldn't affect other investors such as flippers and landlords as much, if at all. Mary submits the approval letter to the title company, and Joe and Mary head to closing.

You might say, "But isn't the bank taking a huge loss on these?" The answer is yes, but they mitigate these risks with the deficiency judgment, creative bank accounting, and mortgage insurance. Mortgage insurance is mandatory insurance the homeowner must pay if they didn't put a big down payment on the loan when they bought the house. It insures the bank against loss if the homeowner defaults on the low down payment loan. The bank carefully considers if they will take a bigger loss with a short sale versus going all the way through to foreclosure auction and re-selling the property. Many times, the loss on a short sale is less than all the lawyer fees, repair costs, agent fees, and cost of taking back the property. Banks are not in the house-owning business, and they will try to avoid taking back a home if possible.

There are some serious pros and cons to short sales. I don't mind short sales now that I have eight years of experience with them, but to other people, short sales are a torturous process.

Pros:

- Less competition. If you see short sales on the MLS, it's highly unlikely that a retail buyer is going to wait out the three-month to two-year process of closing a short sale. Many investors shy away from them for the same reasons. Not many want to wait that long before getting a payday.

- Great deals. With a short sale, you are essentially negotiating with a bank for your own profit margin.

- Patience is your friend. I will chronicle a deal I did at the end of this chapter, where I discovered that a short sale is like putting a property in a time capsule. In this case, the bank was still using an appraisal from two years before we actually closed, and the market shot up in the meantime. If you have a good team around you, you can stack up as many short sales as you can handle, and as they get approved or denied, your pipeline stays relatively full and you are moving deals.

- You are truly helping someone. This is my favorite part—helping an individual or family avoid foreclosure. They'll steer clear of a stigma on their credit report, and they won't have the bank knocking on their door telling them they have to be out in as little as two weeks.

Cons:

- Patience is not your friend. Like I said above, my longest short sale was over two years. This wasn't passive; there would be days I was on the phone for hours with the bank. This process is not for the newbie or the faint of heart.

- A tedious process. If I had a dollar for everything I've had to re-submit to the bank, let's just say I wouldn't ever need to do a deal again. The banks will lose your paperwork, then lose it again, then lose your number, then your negotiator at the bank will be transferred or fired, then you will start all over with a new person—on and on it goes.

- Deed restrictions. I don't like being told what I can and can't do with something I own, even if I own it for ten minutes. The ninety to 120-day deed restriction can throw a huge wrench in your machine when it comes to wholesaling or fix-and-flips.

Agents

Many banks require there be an agent involved. If this agent is not your preferred agent who you know and trust has short sale experience, you could be in for a ride. Many agents have never attempted a short sale, yet are listing them on the MLS and acting like they know what they're doing. This has caused more than just a few homeowners to lose their homes to foreclosure after the inexperienced agent botched the entire process.

Pre-foreclosures can be a great and very profitable deal source. I always say this to new people I meet: If you are there to truly help and solve their problems, you will do well in this business. You will be part investor and part therapist. Since most people in a pre-foreclosure situation have a distressed situation, you might be the only one they have told. You will likely hear the entire sad tale. I've lost count of the number of hands I've held, people I've had crying on my shoulder, and doors I've found slammed in my face. If you don't like people and can't handle these situations, this might not be for you. If you can get in front of these people, build trust and rapport, and exhibit a genuine attitude to help, you will do well in this niche.

Pros:
- Chance to help people. I know you aren't in this business for charity reasons—but you will be able to provide expertise and direction in someone's situation and give them a viable solution to

their problem. You can help them avoid the big foreclosure stigma and make some money in the process. Win-win.

- Motivation. Sellers who are in pre-foreclosure are some of the most motivated sellers out there.

- Good deals. There can be plenty of equity or room to create equity through a short sale to make a deal possible.

Cons:

- Time crunch. You only have a matter of months to identify, contact, research, contract, then sell a property. When a seller calls you with a screaming deal that is two weeks from the public auction date, you'll have to move extremely quickly. You are usually up against the public foreclosure auction date; no wonder these sellers feel like their backs are against a wall.

- Highly personal. Most sellers facing pre-foreclosure will air out their entire situation to you. If you can't handle this, it might not be for you.

- Special protections. Some states, like mine, have laws that were passed to try to protect those in pre-foreclosure from scammers and agents or investors who want to trick or cheat a homeowner out of their equity. Research whether your area requires special contracts, special verbiage, or anything out of the norm to purchase directly from a homeowner late on their payments. Here in Colorado, we have a special short sale/pre-foreclosure addendum that states the seller can walk away from the contract at any time, for any reason, up to a certain date. There is also special verbiage in the contract that spells out what a short sale is and the possible ramifications of completing one.

Public Auction

When someone tells you that they "bought a house on the courthouse steps," this is usually what they are talking about. Each state and county uses this procedure when dealing with foreclosures.

First, let's get the two foreclosure types out of the way. This will vary by state, with some areas allowing either one or the other, though the result is the same:

- Judicial Foreclosure: In short, the foreclosure proceedings are brought through the court system much like a typical lawsuit.

- Non-Judicial Foreclosure: Foreclosure proceedings are brought through the county, with a public trustee or other office in charge of the process.

The notice of default is served, putting the homeowners on notice that they need to either make arrangements to pay back what is owed and start making payments again, prepare for a short sale, get a loan modification, or face the foreclosure date. Many states have a "cure date" before the foreclosure auction date. This is the final day the homeowner can bring the loan current. After that date, the homeowner could have a suitcase full of cash to pay their default amount, and the bank wouldn't care. In other states, the homeowner has six months *after* foreclosure to redeem the full amount owed and get their house back! When the auction day comes, there is always a minimum, or reserve, bid, where the price starts, and it can only go up from there. Who sets this reserve price? The bank will *always* put in a bid on their own property. This could be the amount owed by the homeowner plus lawyer fees and late fees, but in a depressed market, it could be less than what is owed. When the market is down and there are a ton of foreclosures, the bank is smart enough to know nobody will pay more than a property is worth. They set the bid lower, hoping that an investor will buy the property so the bank won't have to take ownership of it and sell it on the open market. They take their losses up front, so to speak.

Let's say Mary is now at a point in her business where she can play with the big dogs at the county auction. The list is usually released a few days before the auction date, giving anyone interested in buying a property on the list time to do their homework, pull title reports, drive by the properties, etc. On the day of the auction, Mary knows she must bring a cashier's check for a deposit amount in case she wins the bid on the property she is interested in. Investors usually convene in a conference room or office at the courthouse, and the auction begins. Each property up for sale is called off, one at a time, and the auctioneer then goes through the auction process, calling out the reserve bid, and seeing if anyone else is willing to pay that or more for the property.

Sometimes this can get heated, with investors fighting to up the bid. Most of the time, however, the reserve bid is called, and nobody in the room wants it. When this happens, the bank essentially wins the bid, and the property will then become owned by the bank. Mary is interested in one or two properties. The bid opens, and she bids $50 more than the opening bid—and miraculously there are no other investors interested. She wins it! Now what? Well, Mary signs something from the county stating she is the winning bidder, she hands over her cashier's check, and then she works to line up the rest of the funds immediately. In Colorado, you have until 2:00 p.m. to come back to the county with a cashier's check for the balance owed, but make sure to check your local laws in advance of attending an auction. This is why bigger investors usually play at auction; most people don't have hundreds of thousands of dollars sitting in a bank account available the same day as the auction. Mary does, so she pays the balance, and in a few days, she will hold title to the property. What next?

Redemption Period

This timeframe happens after the foreclosure sale and allows junior lienholders a chance to buy the property after auction. To understand this section is to understand lien order. When Bank A loans Joe the money to buy his house, they are in a first position lien. This means they have priority rights documented by a deed of trust that Joe signs. If Joe goes out and gets a home equity line of credit (HELOC), this would be filed in second position, behind the first loan. Second position does not have all the same rights as first position, but still grants decent security to the bank. When Joe does not pay an air conditioning repair company for replacing his A/C unit, they file a lien on the house to recoup their money if the house ever sells. Which lien position will they be in? You guessed it, third position. This just keeps going for those people or loans that wish to ride Joe's lien train. The only exemptions are taxes and home owner associations (HOAs). If Joe owes the IRS money or has not paid his property taxes and they go to file a lien on the property, do you think the IRS or government tax lien will just get in line? Nope—they go to the front of the line, even in front of the primary lender, who first loaned Joe the money to buy the house. Say Joe lives in a super lien state like Nevada (be sure to check if your state is one too). This means when he doesn't pay his HOA dues and the HOA puts a lien on his house, they also do not get in line. Do not pass go, do not collect $200, go straight to the first position lien! What happens if Joe owes the IRS and his HOA? Well, IRS/taxes are always first, HOA would be next, then his primary lender, then his HELOC, then his A/C repair company lien, etc.

What does this have to do with anything? During the redemption period, the junior or lesser lienholders have the right to "redeem" the next highest position lien and take ownership of the property. Say the A/C repair company *really* wants to get paid. During the redemption, they have every right to pay off everyone in front of them in order to take possession of the property. This means they would pay the full amount owed to the IRS, the HOA, the primary lender, and the HELOC company. Why would they want to do this? Well, if the amounts of all those entities paid off is still less than the property is worth, the A/C repair company could sell the property to recoup their initial loss. The fifth position lienholder is not likely to redeem the property due to the small likelihood of there being any profit in the deal after everyone is paid. But the second or third? Sure.

Why would they do that, you ask? Liens get wiped out during the foreclosure process. Meaning, if no investors bid at auction and the lender wins the bid by default, anybody behind them in line gets zero dollars for their liens, and they get completely wiped out. This is the risk of second position and beyond, and this is why second loans and HELOCs usually have higher interest rates—to mitigate the risk of being wiped out. This is also why redemption periods exist—to give junior lienholders a chance to recoup their potential losses. The opposite is true as well; if the HELOC forecloses on the property, the first lien (or liens in this example) would remain in place, and the junior liens would be wiped out.

If you're reading this book, you're probably smart enough to ask, "But what happens if this goes into a bidding war with investors and gets bid way up, over the primary lender's reserve price?"

States vary by policy, but the amount is either divvied up between the junior lienholders or solely goes to the next lienholder. A lienholder cannot be paid more than the amount of their lien, so if Joe's property is purchased at auction for $150,000 and he only has one lien for $70,000 (also the opening bid), Bank A does not just pocket the overage amount. Since Joe has no junior liens, Joe gets a check for the difference—even at foreclosure auction. Think of Joe as the last lienholder—if there is any money after everyone is paid, he will get a check. In some states, Joe has the right to redeem the property, just like any lienholder. He could come with the full $70,000 and redeem the property out from under the foreclosure auction winner. The winner would then get their money back and no property, and the redeemer would take ownership of the property.

Pros:

- Good deals. Due to a very high barrier of entry, most investors in your market are not attending auctions and bidding on the properties.

- Instant gratification. When a bid is won and money is paid the same day, you should have title in hand faster than most closings you could set up.

- Networking with big players in your market. Attend auctions if you want to associate with the heavy hitters in your area, whether they are bidding or just watching.

Cons:

- The aforementioned high barrier of entry. Even most experienced investors don't have a ton of liquid cash to bid on properties at auction.

- Not for new investors. I would recommend new investors find other local market opportunities. The chances of being burned at auction are very high. I've witnessed investors buying at auction who thought they were getting an amazing deal, only to discover that the second lien was the foreclosing lien and that the investor actually bought the second position. Maybe in this case the first lien was still in place, leaving the investor title to a property with the first loan still attached! Ouch.

- Title not clear. In many areas, the title to the property is not guaranteed to be delivered to the winner free and clear of any issues or problems. This can cause huge problems for the winning bidder, usually after anything can be done.

- Limited due diligence. Title issues aren't the only things that come up. Most investors cannot gain access to the home during the few days of due diligence they have. This could mean the property is full to the ceiling with something fun like marshmallows and glitter—or something less fun like a meth lab or black mold. That brings us to the next point.

- Occupants. When you buy a property at auction, whoever or whatever is currently in the property is now your problem. Many states grant rights to occupants, especially renters, of houses that go into foreclosure. Whether a disgruntled homeowner who trashed the property before moving out or a renter who can by law enforce the rest of the terms of his valid lease, you never know what you are going to get. Many investors are prepared to offer "cash for keys" to occupants, meaning if the renters leave the property in as-is condition, the investor will pay the occupants money to move out to avoid the hassle and expense of eviction. This could be $500, or it could be $5,000. It simply depends on the occupant and the area. If you are in a state like Colorado where a valid lease (even if signed by the landlord who stopped paying his mortgage and let it go to foreclosure) can be legally upheld, you might have just inherited a tenant for the remainder for their lease. Are you having fun yet?

- Small number of deals. While the deals that do come through can be great ones, in most areas, 70 percent or more of properties go back to the bank since there are no interested investors at that price. That means all the investors who are fighting for the properties are sometimes fighting over three or four out of twenty or so up for auction that week.

In short, the public auction section of the foreclosure process is best left to advanced investors who boast years of experience, are extremely savvy, and have deep pockets.

Other Property Types and Their Owners

Real Estate Owned

Where They're Found: On Market, Auction, Off Market
Competition level: medium-high. Since most REO properties are listed on the MLS for sale to the public, a bunch of eyes are on these when they get listed or their prices get reduced.

REO is an acronym for "real estate owned," which actually makes little sense. Another name is "bank owned," or "properties taken back by the mortgage lender after the homeowner stops making payments and the bank foreclosed and now wants to sell the property on the open market" (or PTBBYMLATHSMPATBFANWTSTPOTOM). When a bank buys a property at auction, they take it into their inventory of properties. The bank will buy the property back at auction to protect their investment. Remember, they loaned the money to the homeowner. When the homeowner stops making payments, since the loan is collateralized by the property (basically, the property itself is on the hook for the loan), the bank will try to sell the property to get some of or all their money back. Banks are not real estate-holding companies, so the next steps are to find out what the property is worth and then try to sell it where the most people will see it: the MLS. The entire process of pre-foreclosure, foreclosure, and selling the property as an REO is not cheap. The bank loses money every day the property sits empty on the market. Just so you understand the process on the bank side, before the property even hits the MLS, I'll give you a quick timeline:

Assigned to Asset Manager   Valuation   Marketing Property on MLS

Bank Buys at Auction   Occupancy Check   Repairs Made or Sold As Is   Sold to Homeowner or Investor

Cash for Keys   Price Reduction

Eviction   REO Auction

No timeline here, this can take as little as 14 days or 2–3 years!   Sold in Bulk REO Package

As you can see, as soon as the auction is over, the cogs in the machine start turning.

- Assigned to asset manager. The asset manager is either an employee of the bank or employee of a company the bank contracts to dispose of their REO assets. The asset manager oversees the entire pre-marketing and sales process.

- **Asset manager assigns to real estate agent.** Banks need local boots on the ground to get the properties ready for sale and then sold. They hire real estate agents to do many of their tasks for them since the agents know the market, as well as local contractors and vendors.

- **Occupancy check.** The real estate agent drives by the property to see if anyone is living there. They post a note or notice on the door to have anyone in the property call for more information. If vacant, they secure the property with new locks and board up any broken windows. If occupied, they post the note, knock on the door, or otherwise wait for the occupant to contact the agent. If the occupant is cooperative, the agent will negotiate a cash for keys arrangement, so the property is left in as-is condition in exchange for some "walk away money" for the occupant. If the occupant is not cooperative, the agent contacts the bank and the bank initiates the legal eviction process.

- **Valuation.** There are three valuations in the first few weeks after the public auction, usually all done by agents. The agent assigned the property does what is called a drive-by BPO for the bank within days of assignment. "Drive-by" means exactly what it implies— the agent is only evaluating the outside condition of the property, assessing the property against comparables, etc. The agent does not get inside the property until the property is vacant or there is a cooperative occupant. This is when the agent completes a full BPO, taking into consideration the interior condition. The bank will also contact another local real estate agent to conduct a second opinion BPO so they don't only have data from one source. They take into consideration the two BPOs when determining price and whether they will fix up the property at all.

- **To repair or not to repair.** The bank now weighs whether the cost to do any repairs will net them more money in the sale or whether they need to just sell as-is for a discount. Even if the bank repairs or updates the property, they are usually not worth it. The quality of work is usually so-so, and the actual materials are the cheapest available. The appliances are low-end, the paint is cheap, and the carpet is thin. Putting in money is rarely worth the exit price; it's like trying to put lipstick on a pig. In the end, there are still a ton of updates to be done, and the actual work done and materials used need to be replaced.

- Marketing. Soon after valuation and once the title is clear, the real estate agent gets notice from the asset manager that the property is ready for sale. The agent gets their listing price and puts it on the MLS system. The asset manager takes the two BPO prices and figures out what the starting price will be. Most of the time, the initial market price will be on the high end. The asset manager is optimistic and tries to get as much money as possible for the property. Sometimes, they start medium or low, hoping for a fast sale. The offer range that the asset manager will accept is usually within 5 percent of the list price for the first month. This means that lowball offers won't fly. The asset manager is optimistic, after all.

- Price reductions. Every thirty days on the market, the agent must do either a MMR (monthly marketing report) or an updated BPO. The bank is looking for any market changes and to justify a possible price reduction. Like clockwork, every month a property is on the market, it will get a price reduction. This can work to your advantage. If you see an REO that has been on the market for eighty-eight days, you can be sure in the next week or so, it will be getting another price reduction!

- Under contract. If you are the lucky buyer of an REO, you'll always have to sign bank addendums as well as the pertinent state contracts. Notice I said "state contracts"—they don't accept those one-page guru contracts. This contract must be on state-approved real estate contract forms. Oh, and nine out of ten bank contracts are not assignable, so keep that in mind if you are wholesaling, you likely should choose another exit strategy besides assignment.

After the bank has tried to sell the property on the market for a certain amount of time (usually four to six months with no sale), they try to dispose of the property by holding an auction. They hire an auction company to advertise the property for auction and hold the pre-auction, then the auction itself. Keep in mind, the entire time the property has pre-auction status (leading up to the auction), it's still listed on the MLS. Many companies will accept offers before the auction. So, if you put in an offer before the auction and the bank likes it, they will then remove it from the auction date list. I've won several properties this way.

Many times, the auction company will take all the auction properties in a certain city or geographical area and auction them all off on the same date. The property information is listed on their website, and they hold the auction in either one central location or at the homes themselves. Most of these auctions require you to bring a cashier's check for your earnest money amount. If you are the winner, you will sign their addendums and contracts, then you get to go home while the auction company submits your offer to the bank for final approval. Sound a little strange for an auction? The truth is, these are far from true auctions like those we described previously.

In an actual auction, the winning bidder is the winner and walks away with an item or moves forward under contract. In REO auctions, they take the highest bid and submit it to the bank just like a real estate agent would. The bank can decline the offer, counter with a higher price, or just ignore you for weeks. Many times, the offer goes to the asset manager at the bank for approval. The asset manager might send it to their supervisor, and the supervisor might send it to the bank investor for approval. (The investor is the company or individual who lent the bank the money for a pool of mortgages.) Sometimes the offer must go to a mortgage insurance servicer for approval. Now you can see why if you win the auction, you might not actually go under contract for weeks. Or they might decide to ask for more money.

If you are the winner and the bank accepts your contract, you then move forward under contract toward closing. With these types of auctions, you still get an inspection period to decide if you want to move forward with the purchase of the property—whereas with actual foreclosure auctions, you get no such leeway. Pre-auction is a blind bidding system; you won't know the amount of anyone else's bid. In person auctions, the auctioneer starts the bid at the advertised price and then lets the bidders up the purchase price of the property. Let's visit a few of the most popular REO auction sites:

- Auction.com
- HudsonandMarshall.com
- WilliamsandWilliams.com
- Hubzu.com

Hubzu.com is a different beast. It's owned by a bank (Ocwen) that uses the site to dispose of its assets and has no live auction. Ocwen lists all its available properties on its site and then employs a bid system where you can see the last highest bid. This turns into a mess. While I have bought plenty of Ocwen properties in the past (pre-Hubzu.com), I can't wrap my head around how anyone gets a deal off this site anymore. But, it might work for you if you are in a smaller market with less competition.

Pros:

- Listed on MLS. There is no secret to finding these properties; they are required to be listed on the MLS by the bank. Any investor or agent—or anybody with Internet access—should be able to find these.

- Price. Thanks to the asset manager pricing the property low initially to unload it, as well as frequent price reductions, REOs can be great deals. Since the banks are the only sellers who don't care as much about losing money on the sale or selling for less than what is owed, REOs can be bargain basement steals.

- Negotiation. The nice thing about REOs is that you are dealing with an experienced listing agent who lists dozens or hundreds of these properties a year and an asset manager who might be managing 500 or more properties at once. This removes emotion from the equation. The asset manager or listing agent will not get personally offended by a lowball offer. It either works for the bank's pricing matrix or it doesn't. You simply submit your contract with your price and maybe a justification for that price (repairs needed) and wait to hear back—yes, no, or counteroffer. Let's say inspection turns up something major and you need to re-negotiate the price on the property. If you submit a price reduction to a normal seller, they will get offended; they "thought the price was agreed on" and other such grumblings. Not the bank—they just process it like a computer would. Does this price work for their bottom line? They'll answer either yes or no. It removes a lot of drama from real estate transactions.

- Due diligence. Unlike in public foreclosure auctions, you still get to inspect the property and have time in your contract to back out if the inspection turns up anything you won't deal with.

- Steady inventory. This would be a totally different chapter if written in 2008; I'd be running around trying to dodge the foreclosure properties raining down from the skies. There was a glut of inventory, with dozens of foreclosed homes in every neighborhood. Now foreclosure numbers are down across the board, but every week in every county across America, there are foreclosure public auctions still happening, feeding the REO machine. Sure, the numbers are fewer, but there will never be a time where the foreclosure rate is zero.

Cons:

- Listed on MLS. Remember my mantra that more eyes mean more competition? Being easy to find is both good and bad. Homeowners, investors, agents, and everyone else have their eyes on the MLS and want a piece of the action.

- Deed restrictions. Much like in our short sale con list, there are certain banks out there that want to restrict investor activity on their properties. By restricting the resale of the property for ninety to 120 days after the initial closing, they believe they can stop us from doing what we want with property we own. Since they cut out assignments on the contract and then put in a deed restriction to block a double close, they are targeting wholesalers pretty much exclusively.

- "First look" periods. In their valiant quest to thwart investors at every turn (even though we buy most of their crummy inventory), certain banks now only allow owner-occupant homeowners to submit offers on REO properties when first listed. Some banks have a fifteen-day first-look window; some have a twenty-five-or-more-day first-look window. The listing will almost always advertise this fact, usually saying "no investor offers until after xx/xx date" or "homeowner first-look until xx/xx date." I wouldn't suggest putting in an offer as a homeowner just to lock up a property. Not only will you have to sign an owner occupancy affidavit; it's just not how we do business.

- Title company. Owner's title insurance is a policy that the seller customarily pays for on behalf of the buyer. Why am I telling you about this? While most states have a law or rule saying that the seller cannot force a buyer to use the seller's title company, banks have decided to do the following: They will allow you to use their title company and will pay your owner's title insurance policy, or they will allow you to use your own title company and will not pay this closing cost for you. This expense can be $1,500 or more on some closings. The bank's title companies are contracted by the bank during the foreclosure process and can severely lack in customer. Where other title companies rely on referrals and repeat business, they have steady bank business, so they don't care if you, the buyer, are treated right. The bank title companies know you will be back if you buy REOs regularly, unless you want to pay your own owner's insurance policies repeatedly. Personally, I don't like being out of control on deals, which means I don't like using unfriendly or unfamiliar title companies. Now I just suck it up, pay the cost of the title policy, and close with a company I know will take care of me.

Absentee Owned Properties

> "Bueller . . . Bueller . . . Bueller . . . "
> —*Ferris Bueller's Day Off*, 1986

Where They're Found: On Market, Off Market

Competition level: low-medium. Who are these owners, and why are they absent? Answering questions and helping these owners out can easily make you some serious money. This term, "absentee owner," means that the owner of the property has a mailing address different from the property address, i.e. they don't live at this property. Usually these owners are landlords or other investors who bought the property intending to rent it out. Sometimes it can be a homeowner who lived in the property for a time, then moved out and kept it as a rental. Maybe they moved across the country and couldn't sell it, so now they cover the mortgage with a tenant. Maybe the owner inherited it from a now-deceased relative. They may have never visited or ever laid eyes on the house. Some absentee owners are not distressed sellers; they are savvy investors who have multiple properties that are well-managed, well-maintained, and full to the brim with paying tenants. Some are tired landlords—they just evicted their fourteenth straight deadbeat tenant who trashed the house, or the city is compiling fines or tax liens on grandma's old house that the granddaughter has now inherited. Some are happy, while others are miserable and want out.

Pros:

- Motivation. Sometimes even the distance between the owner and the property is motivation enough for the seller to get rid of the property. Many have not been back to see their property in years and have no idea of the current condition. These can be huge opportunities to help absentee owners out of their bad situations.

- Opportunity to help. Absentee owners can have crazy stories and be near the point of giving away their properties. They might be dealing with tax liens, city code violation liens, tenants who trashed the property, vacancy for years, inability to find a new renter, issues with paying the mortgage and taxes, and confusion over what to do with a property two thousand miles away. This is your chance to help them with their situation and make some money in the process.

- Easy to locate. Since most states have public property records, it can be as easy as seeing if the owner's mailing address is the same as the property. ListSource is a great tool to grab every absentee owner in your area within minutes. You can decide which ones to market to by finding out how long they have owned the property and the potential equity amount.

- High equity. The last few leads I've had from absentee owners have involved properties where the owners have owned since the seventies and are free and clear. Since many landlords pay cash for their rentals or put 20 to 40 percent down, there will be some amount of equity in the property most of the time. Inherited homes, gifted properties, and properties where owners moved out and rented all tend to be good, high-equity candidates as well.

Cons:

- High number of landlords. Many landlords looking to sell want or need to keep their tenants in place, so unless you want to inherit tenants or like the numbers a rental purchase price can bring, these can be difficult to wholesale or flip.

- Smarter sellers. The long-time landlords and other savvy investors you might be contacting have been in this game since you were in diapers. They keep tabs on their portfolio and have agents send them an updated yearly BPO for their properties. They sometimes have MLS access and know how to run their own comps. These savvy men and women know what the property is worth and aren't looking to give away the farm to a young buck like you.

- Higher competition. Most gurus and real estate training information online have you start marketing to absentee, high-equity owners in your area to start getting deals. As soon as a seminar ends or big program opens online, the newbies go get their lists and start badgering the absentee owners. On the absentee owner side, it must be interesting to get waves of mailings asking to buy your property. This does not mean you as an investor don't have an opportunity to stand out, provide better service or information, and profit from this niche; it just means the minute the latest traveling seminar leaves town, you must stand out from the noise of more competition.

Owner-Occupied Properties

Where They're Found: On Market, Off Market

Competition level: low-medium. We went over the reasons for financial, personal, and property distress. These can apply to easy-to-find properties, such as listed REOs or absentee owned. Without seeing every property in an area, it can be hard to pinpoint which homeowners are having trouble and might need your help. A few clues that can help determine the possibility of distress are: amount of time the property has been owned (deferred maintenance perhaps) and remaining mortgage amount (financial distress). Of course, you could also drive up and down the street looking for obvious signs of neglect or problems (see the "driving for dollars" section). Most of all, you should listen to the homeowner, figure out what their problem is, then solve it. Some just want to move south to never experience another winter again and need $40,000 out of their equity to do so. Some need money to get to an assisted care facility or are overwhelmed by the deferred maintenance and know the property won't sell on the market with shag carpet and mustard yellow wallpaper.

Pros:

- No agents. You can incentivize these sellers by letting them know they do not have any agents to pay in the transaction. This is a bonus for the investor because an agent has not advised the seller to list the property at a sky-high price.

- Flexible closing. Some homeowners want to be out yesterday, and some need five months to move. You can offer peace of mind by letting the seller know you can close whenever they are ready. The seller is always grateful when you either close quickly or let them stay a few months more. They could not get this flexibility by listing it on the MLS with an agent.

- Low competition. If you hit the right marketing channels, you might be the only buyer the homeowner is talking to. They might not consider calling anyone else, including an agent, if you build great rapport with them and solve their problems. People often trade cash for terms, meaning they give up money if the terms make more sense.

Cons:

- Personal situations. When the distressed homeowner lives at the property, it can cause extra drama and stress in a deal. Sometimes a week or two before closing, the seller realizes they have to be out and starts dragging their feet or trying to change their mind. Their attachment to the property begins to overtake their motivation. Maybe there's a death in the family and they have to sell. It can be an emotional and crazy time for them and by proxy, you.

- Ownership. This usually gets complicated in a situation where one of the owners died and the correct procedures were not followed to ensure the remaining spouse has full ownership rights to sell. Or maybe someone died, and now there is an unruly one-sixth owner who lives in the property and refuses to move even though the other five people want to sell. These situations can get hairy, and knowing how to handle them is part of *your* job.

Pro Tip: Let them leave their stuff. This is a great incentive that has won us deals over our competition. Some people are overwhelmed by their stuff and can't imagine moving everything. They plan to throw a bunch of stuff away. This can be burdensome for the owner when they have furniture, mattresses, or exercise equipment to get rid of. I tell them they can take whatever they want and leave whatever they don't. Offering a solution can get them to say yes much faster.

Non-Distressed Sellers

Where They're Found: On Market, Off Market

Competition level: low, medium, and high. We've covered the distressed and the absent. What does that leave for investors? Not much, really. Sure, you might be able to knock down the price on a non-distressed property, but that is the exception rather than the rule. Pareto's Principle tells us that 80 percent of the results can be gained by 20 percent of the right effort. That means we should go after the more likely deals, which would include those involving motivation or distress. Spending a ton of time for small results is crazy, and we don't want to disappoint an Italian economist who died 120 years ago, do we?

Do you remember those commercials in the 1990s, where some TV star would tell you not to drive like a jerk, and then it would end with, "The more you know!"? This chapter is a lot like that, minus the bad actor stating the obvious. The more you know about all the different situations sellers are in, the more you will be able to help them. The more you help, the better you get. One day, you will get a call from a motivated seller where their grandma died and left the property to five grandkids. Maybe nobody paid the mortgage or taxes, so it's in foreclosure and has a tax lien. Perhaps two of the five grandkids are in bankruptcy. On that day, you will know exactly what to do. From REOs to private sellers with five of the above scenarios, each deal is different. The more you know about each situation, the better you will be as an investor.

Case Study—REO Auction

Type of Deal—Auction
Investment Strategy—Fix-and-Flip

An REO was being auctioned off. This house was in a decent area of a Denver suburb with which I was somewhat familiar. Still, I hadn't done many fix and flips yet in my career. I was looking for a distressed owner or bank to try to buy from, and after a few months of searching, I had my eye on this big old house that needed tons of love. I saw it up for auction with the price starting at $159,000, but knew that was way too high to make a profit. Sometimes you can put in an offer before the auction and get it, and that's what I tried. I didn't get it. The winning bid was higher than my offer of $116,000.

A phone call a week later from the auction company told me the higher offer backed out. They asked if I would like to buy it for my offer price. Why yes—yes, I would. Before it went back on the market and before it even went to the actual live auction, I scooped up this property for a steal. After $45,000 in renovations, I sold it for $220,000. Just goes to show you, sometimes if you make an early offer it can come back around to pay off for you.

CHAPTER 4:
Networking, Agents, and MLS

"Wait. I have an idea. Why don't you go over and introduce yourself? And that way, you can build me up so I won't have to brag about myself later."

—*Dumb and Dumber*, 1994

In our quest to master deal-finding, we would be remiss if we didn't include this chapter. Getting out in front of other investors, both more and less experienced than you, is crucial. Networking will help you find deals, link up with partners, and learn from the experience of those who have been in business longer than you. The importance of agents in your business is also detailed here—you'll want to learn how to find and work with them. And, of course, we couldn't talk about agents or finding deals without talking about the MLS. Like in your seventh-grade biology class when you dissected that poor frog on the lab table, we will take the MLS apart, revealing all its gory details.

Networking

Have you ever noticed how the words and phrases used to describe networking are the worst? Have you intentionally "rubbed elbows" with anybody in your life? I used to not put much stock in networking when it came to finding deals. I used it only to sell deals or get more information about certain areas. Boy, was I wrong.

BiggerPockets.com Marketplace

BiggerPockets.com houses the largest collection of real estate investing forums on the Internet, so naturally it's a great place to meet and connect with investors all over the nation—and in your backyard. I owe a big part of my real estate career to BiggerPockets. When searching for information online back in 2005, I could only find bad sites and poorly designed forums. When I found BiggerPockets.com and started contributing on the forums and later the blog, the quality of people I networked with changed dramatically. I've easily completed twenty deals with other BiggerPockets members. One important part of this site besides the networking portion is the marketplace. This is a place where pro members can post properties for sale—some are rentals with tenants in place, some are wholesale deals, and some are simply homes other investors are looking to offload. Whatever the deals it offers, the marketplace a great place to keep tabs on.

Pro Tip: Setting up keywords on the site for your local area ("Denver, Colorado," for example) will allow you to keep tabs on the conversations of over 500,000 members as they pertain to your interests. If someone posts the word "Denver" and I have the keyword setup on the site, I will get an email. If someone has a hot deal in Denver and posts it on the Marketplace, I can potentially see this deal before many others in my market.

Real Estate Investor Association (REIA) Meetings

What is REIA? It's a group of investors who meet up in most cities and states to learn, connect, network, and trade deals—at least, that's what it is in theory. I'm not the biggest fan of REIAs, but they do have their uses. They usually meet once a month, and most of the time, you have to pay to get in or buy a yearly membership to attend. Who shows up to these? It's usually a good mix of new and veteran investors, as well as some vendors like lenders, agents, title companies, contractors, etc. This is a good place to get the word out about your investing niche and to figure out where investors are buying and what their last few projects are. You can schmooze with the vendors and get to know some professionals who might come in handy during closing.

Why am I not a huge fan of these overall? A REIA is often headed by a local guru-type. The business funnel is to get you in the door (for a fee), then upsell you on boot camps and coaching, which can cost $300 to $10,000. The speakers each month are usually travelling gurus who give you 10 percent information, 40 percent hype, and 50 percent sales tactics to get you to buy a program or coaching. The traveling guru cuts a portion of his sales to the local guru, and that's how everyone makes money. Are some of these guys helpful and legitimate? Absolutely. I know a few investors who have gone through these and ended up doing well. But I also know plenty who have been suckered into programs with no support or even worse, poor information.

REIAs can be great, or they can be a nightmare. It just depends on who runs them and who shows up to network. Absolutely go check yours out and judge for yourself whether it's worth your time and money to attend. I started off with two REIAs in Phoenix, but stopped going as I outgrew the model. Still, many attend these meetings because most REIAs are full of investors looking for deals to buy and sell. Networking puts us in front of many types of people; you might find a landlord ready to sell due to an eviction or a wholesaler with a few unsold properties. Many meetings have a "wants/needs" section where people can post on a board or get up in front of the group and pitch properties to buy or sell. Take out a notepad and start writing down what these people are seeking to obtain or offload. It can be a great way to find deals!

BiggerPockets.com Meetups

These are similar to REIA meetings, but they're put on by BiggerPockets members who want to connect with other BiggerPockets users in their areas. Let's say Mary used to live in Chicago and used to attend a BiggerPockets meetup monthly. She likes that she got to put faces to the names she interacts with online and that she was able to network with like-minded individuals. This is the power of the local meetup.

Usually there is no selling at these meetings; it's mostly networking with a market update presentation. Now Mary had to move for family reasons to Denver, and she searches online and finds no current BiggerPockets monthly meetups. Mary can accept this. Or she can do what I did—start one! I started the first BiggerPockets meetup after talking with Joshua Dorkin,

BiggerPockets's CEO and founder, about hosting a laid-back networking group that I could advertise on the forums. He gave me the go ahead, and it's been going now for three years strong! The quality of networking and people has blown me away, and I've easily completed over a dozen deals with people I've met in this group. There have been wholesalers I've helped sell deals (co-wholesale), deals I've bought, and deals I've wholesaled. It's a great place to meet buyers and those selling great deals. Get on the forums and search the events section, and if you find a group, great—go join them! If you can't find a group, create one; it's one of the best decisions I've made.

Meetup.com

Think of this as a central directory for anyone who wants to meet other people with likeminded interests. If you are into knitting twelfth century-era armor for cats, you will likely find someone who set up a group for that. Naturally, Meetup.com features plenty of REIA-type groups that you can check out.

Investor-Friendly Title or Real Estate Agent Events

In the long search for reliable investing information on the Internet, the topic of "building your team" will inevitably come up. You may notice much whining and crying regarding finding investor-friendly agents, title companies, or closing attorneys in the real world. It sounds good on paper, but these people aren't exactly raising their hands, promising to play nice with investors. Or are they?

As double closing, wholesaling, and assignments become more and more common, there are more and more real estate professionals who advertise that they are investor friendly. How convenient! In my market, the high desert cow town of Denver, there are no less than three good-sized real estate brokerages and a handful of title companies who put on investor events and come right out and say "investors welcome!" At these events, you will no doubt encounter other investors who frequently use the services of those who invited them.

It's always in the best interest of a good title representative to introduce repeat customers (read: experienced investors doing a good amount of deals) to new or potential customers (you, the novice investor who hasn't done many deals) to generate business from those relationships. Think about it— if you meet a player in your market who's buying flip properties and you start selling deals to them, do you think you might use the investor-friendly title company to close that transaction when they were the ones who introduced you? The title rep is banking on it. It's in everyone's best interest, including these third-party vendors.

Real Estate Auctions

As I said earlier, auctions are exciting, fast-paced, and are usually attended by the biggest players in your market. Why is that, you say? On a scale from green newbie to Clint Eastwood, these guys are the Clint Eastwoods of real estate. Many times, they are bidding on these properties without the benefit of full due diligence, meaning they likely have not seen the inside, there might be hostile tenants still in the property, they did no inspections, and they, of course, have to pay cash—many times, right on the spot.

This is not a beginner's game; this is for people who have been in the business for years, who have bought dozens of houses. I'd say a grizzled, sunbaked, poncho-wearing veteran investor with a week's worth of stubble and a horse named "Killer" is a good person to get to know. Meet them. Ask them where they prefer to buy and whether you can contact them about deals. Even the hedge fund buyers like to buy from wholesalers, and they can often be found at real estate auctions. These auctions can be either foreclosure auctions or REO auctions (bank owned foreclosures).

Agents

Who are these agents you need on your team? Why do you need them? Why would they want to work with you, an investor? These are all great questions. Remember how I said that agents and investors are seemingly natural enemies? While people on both sides believe this, I know that we can all get along. Since they have market knowledge, agents can be a great asset for finding deals, and, of course, they have coveted MLS access. The main hurdle for investors is to find an agent willing to find good investment deals.

There are two types of agents you will work with in this business—the listing agent and the buyer's agent. The listing agent typically represents a seller, either private or a bank, while the buyer's agent represents you and finds you deals. The former is common, and the latter is like a unicorn at the end of a triple rainbow. In all cases, when it comes to agents, you want to make sure that you do the following:

- Be professional. Agents work with real estate all day, every day for a living. They're able to sniff out a faker or someone who is all talk quickly. When you are honest and professional, you will stand out and build rapport with the agent, which always goes a long way.

- Perform. Not a song and dance from the Broadway hit *Spamalot*, but do make sure you aren't a typical flakey investor mucking up deals, ruining transactions, and complicating situations. When you mess with agents' commissions, you are messing with their paychecks and their emotions. You will certainly get blacklisted fast. Once you get a reputation for backing out of deals and messing with agents' incomes, you have two options: You can change your legal name and continue investing, or you can keep your name and cut this deal method from your repertoire. Agents will cut you off because word travels quickly, like it or not.

- Add value. Like I mentioned in the networking section, most people are more willing to go out of their way to help only after you have helped them. To most agents, providing values means being a consistent deal closer, quick to evaluate deals—someone who doesn't throw a wrench in their cogs. This makes them the hero ("I sold that problem house in two weeks, Mr. Seller!") and makes them money. If you are a consistent and easy-to-work-with buyer, agents will start bringing you deals left and right. If you take care of them, they'll act as the best bird dog you will ever have.

A listing agent is a licensed individual hired by a seller, who then lists the property for sale in one of the following ways:

- On the MLS. The agent markets the property directly to all other agents and the public.

- Using a pocket listing. The agent markets the property directly to other agents within their own company and to individual buyers they believe will generate a quick and easy sale for the seller.

Wait, they represent the seller? You might be asking yourself, "Why would an agent who represents the seller be a good asset for me, the investor, to find deals?" Good question, self. When you find a property through your own MLS login, Realtor.com, or Zillow.com that you might be interested in, you will have to pass the gatekeeper in order to see it, submit an offer on it, and get it under contract. The listing agent is the intermediary between you, the buyer, and the seller, whom they represent. Talking directly to the seller is possible, but most of the time, they will just refer you right back to their agent.

Multiple Listing Service (MLS)

MLS properties are found on market and at auction. Again, the MLS should equal "high competition" in your brain, and while there are deals to be found, I would never advocate this to be your sole deal source. As an investor, it certainly pays to have multiple sources for getting deals, and the MLS can be spotty when it comes to consistency.

There are three main plans of attack when it comes to finding MLS deals.

1. You are an agent. Well, that's easy. When you are your own agent, you can look at the MLS all day long if you want. You can write up one offer a week or a hundred offers a day. Sure, you have to disclose that you are an agent in all of your real estate deals, but that is a small price to pay for the benefits. As a bonus, you may earn your share of the agent's commission on top of getting a great deal! *Pro tip*: Even when I am my own agent, I'm more than willing to give my commission away to the listing agent to get a deal. I'll let the other agent represent my company, so they get paid the full commission. I'm happy to incentivize agents to bring me more deals; they get paid twice, and I get the deal.

2. You have an agent. If you form the right partnership, your agent may be the only source of deals you will ever need. While your agent is there to get paid on deals you close, the work leading up to those deals is all done for free. They perform showings, search the MLS, write offers, negotiate, and handle the entire process leading up to closing (inspection, negotiation, title work, etc.) on your behalf. What I'm saying is that you should respect your agent's

time and make sure you have your ducks in a row to make the transaction go as smoothly as possible. The easier you make it on your agent, the more he or she will work to find deals for you.

3. You use the listing agent. This is where you find the properties yourself and then contact the listing agent to also represent you as a buyer for the deal you found. To succeed here, you should be good at finding your deals yourself. There is nobody working for you to mine the MLS. Still, one of the best calls a listing agent can get is from a buyer who is serious about buying a property and wants to use the agent for the transaction. The listing agent in this situation then gets the full commission instead of their usual half share when two agents are involved. You can see how that would incentivize an agent to push your offer a smidge harder to their seller.

I personally use a combination of methods one and three, but your approach might be different. Here are some pros and cons to using the MLS to connect to the right deals with the right sellers.

Pros:

- No marketing effort needed. Sellers contact agents, and agents list the properties on the MLS. There is no effort needed on your part to contact sellers directly.

- REO properties live here. When banks hire agents to dispose of their unwanted assets, the properties, 99.9 percent of the time, get listed on the MLS.

- Short sales live here, too. Many banks require short sales to be listed, so naturally this would be a good place to find most of them.

Cons:

- Proof of funds. When you make an offer on an MLS property, most often your offer will not be considered without proof that you can pay cash for or finance the property.

- Competition. I keep harping on this concept, but it's true. The downside here is how public these properties are and how many people see them online daily.

- MLS access. You either are an agent, you have an agent, or you buy through the listing agent.

- Highest and best. When there is competition, the sellers and agents will start asking the buyers to compete heavily with each other. If there are five offers on a property, instead of the seller simply picking the best and moving forward, they will now ask all the buyers to re-submit their offers with their highest and best price and terms. This means five parties will be blindly bidding up their offers. On the REO side, I've watched as four offers submit "no change"—and one go up $15,000. They ended up bidding against themselves and overpaying for the property by a wide margin.

MLS Decoded

Ever overhear a few agents or investors talking shop? Sometimes it's like a foreign language, and looking at an MLS sheet can be like trying to decipher the enigma code from World War II. If the agent has good common sense, they will advertise their listing in as plain of language as possible. But sometimes agents think that only other agents look at what they write in the MLS, and that can make our jobs tough. I'll break down what is important on your MLS sheets and then decode the language agents use in the remarks sections that will appeal to investors.

Having used twelve different MLS systems in my career, I know they can vary widely. What doesn't change are the basics:

1. Address. Well, without this, we would certainly be lost.

2. Price. Again, basic stuff here. This is the current listing price.

3. Status. This could read "active," "under contract," "pending," or "sold."

4. Bedroom and bathroom count. This should reflect what your county tax assessor has listed as well. As usual, double check everything because the agent might have included non-conforming bedrooms in the basement (which can't be counted legally) or may have put two full baths instead of the actual one full bath and one-half bath in the property.

5. Square footage. This gets input incorrectly all the time. Be sure to

double check the tax assessor records, and when in doubt, triple check by measuring the property yourself. For most areas, this is the livable square footage above the ground and does not include basement square footage or garages.

6. Basement. Does the property include a basement or not? Is it finished or unfinished? Is it permitted? What's the square footage?

7. Garage. What type of garage does the property have—enclosed or carport? How many spaces are there?

8. Year built. This tells you when the property was built per the tax records.

9. Type. This could be detached single-family, attached single-family, land, condo, townhome, etc.

10. Style. The property could be a ranch, two-story, bi-level, tri-level, etc. This is important to know immediately for when you go to find comparables and for avoiding the less desirable floor plans (I'm looking at you, bi-level).

11. Lot size. This is the size of the land that is included with the house, usually stated in square footage or acres ("9,627 square feet" or ".220 acres").

12. Zoning. This dictates what can or cannot be built on a lot. There could be missed potential if the lot can support two to four properties, but other structures besides the existing cannot be built on the property.

13. Agent remarks/public remarks. Here is the agent's area to write in any information or sales language they want, usually describing the condition of the property, including any special conditions. This is what the public can see, and this verbiage gets transferred to sites that pull from the MLS, such as Zillow and Redfin.

14. Private remarks. This is the agent's area to write in any information that they only want other agents to see. This can be full of gold as well. Sometimes it's special showing instructions, and many times it's information that cannot be published in the agent remarks section ("Enter at your own risk.").

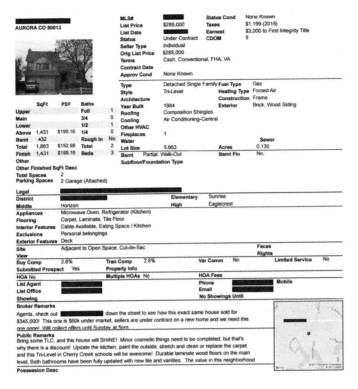

You might be saying, "Well, that's a whole lot of information. I'm overwhelmed!" You'll get used to it and know exactly what you're looking for in no time. It just takes experience looking at these regularly to weed out the information that is not important.

So, while the above fourteen MLS fields are probably the most important, here are a few more that I use quite regularly.

- Listing history/previous list price. This will tell you if the property has had a price reduction recently, as well as what the listing started at. If it started at $250,000 and is now listed for $175,000, you should wonder what is wrong with it for such a dramatic reduction.

- Construction/exterior/roofing/heating and cooling type. When the agent isn't too lazy to enter in all this important info, it can be a great snapshot of the property.

- Construction. Is it frame or brick? In my area, brick is much more valuable.

- Exterior. What kind of siding does the property have? Is it asbestos shingle (bad), or is it vinyl or wood cedar (good)? This field will tell you.

- Roofing. This is usually broken down into asphalt rolled (flat roof), composition shingle (industry standard), ceramic tile, or wood shake. If it's wood shake, I know the roof is old since they no longer use it for roofing. Also, if your area breaks it down into "composition roof 3-tab," for example, that will tell you the age of the roof as well, since they no longer make 3-tab roof shingles. You can bet the 3-tab and wood shake roofs are over twelve years old.

- Heating type. Properties are usually natural gas or forced air furnace, but when I see electric baseboard as the heat type, it raises minor red flags. Electric baseboard is more expensive and not common in my area; I know I'll have to knock some money off the ARV for any house that has it when I comp it out.

- Cooling. Does the property have air-conditioning, a swamp cooler, or none? In Colorado, you can get away with no A/C unit, but most buyers do want this feature.

- Sewer. Is it public or septic? Septic tank systems are an anomaly in a city, so a septic sewer would be a big negative mark on the property in those markets.

- Listing agent info. I usually scroll down first and see if I know the listing agent or if the name triggers clammy sweating from a previous deal gone wrong. Sometimes I will pass on a decent property if I know working with the listing agent will be a nightmare.

Agent Remarks

This is the area where the agent can write whatever the heck they want. Most of the time, the information is helpful; sometimes, it's totally useless; and many times, it's overly glowing. Many agents just want to sell you on the area, neighborhood, and schools—and use glittery words like "Pottery Barn perfect" and "sumptuous." No, I'm not kidding; a listing I came across this week used the word "sumptuous." This agent missed her calling in 500-character creative writing. Needless to say, as an investor, you will not likely be buying sumptuous properties anytime soon. Not entirely useless, that description coupled with the pictures can give you 80 percent of the picture.

In the agent's property description, we are looking—and hoping—for much more investor-friendly words. Remember back in the last chapter, when we talked about baselining your neighborhood and looking in the agent remarks for investor-friendly keywords? This practice can also be used to look for the best deals on the MLS. Look for indicators such as:

- Bank owned/REO/lender owned/corporate owned

- Foreclosure

- Must sell

- Fix up/handyman special/bring your tool belts

- Sold as-is

- All buyers must prequalify with Bank of America/pre-qualification letter must accompany all offers (pre-qualification verbiage)

- Cash only/will not qualify for FHA financing

- Estate sale/needs court approval; short sale/lender approval required

- No investor offers until 10/11/2017; seller will not accept non-owner occupied offers until 10/11/2017 (if there is no investor period, i.e. for Fannie Mae or Freddie Mac homes)

- Seller requires hold harmless agreement/waiver signed before buyer can enter property

- Enter at your own risk

- Bring flashlight/no showings after dark (no, seriously)

- _____ (yes, even blank can be good)

- For the love of everything good and holy, do everyone a favor and just burn this place down after viewing property!

Okay, that last one is made up, but I've seen some pretty funny ones in this business. Once you get used to the MLS and looking at a bunch of listings, you will be able to spot any REO, short sale, estate sale, or other form of distress or motivation. When the agent is basically telling you to understand the risks of entering a property with mold, a meth history, foundation issues, no floors, etc. before you can even step foot in it, you know the property is a potential candidate. The more combinations of the phrases above, the better. Someone should make "MLS Verbiage Bingo" boards and distribute them to investors. Even a listing with no verbiage and no pictures can be the sign of an agent who is lazy and doesn't care to put in the basics on the property. Maybe the condition is so bad they don't know what to say. Most retail agents will skip over these since there are no other indicators as to what is going on with the property.

While the fundamental formula for a deal does not change, getting deals from the MLS is very different than obtaining off market properties. Since there is so much competition, you have to hunt, peck, search, scour, and play games to get deals. Occasionally there will be a golden egg that falls right into your lap, but I find that to be the exception rather than the rule. Here are a few ways I have acquired MLS deals over the years:

- Price is Right Countdown. The listing history of a property can tell you a whole lot about what is going on without ever having to call the agent. An REO property is on a timeline, and every thirty days from the list date (or sometimes just the first of the month), the asset manager will ask the agent for updated market activity and recommendations for a price reduction. Like clockwork, the price will be reduced every thirty days until the property sells. You see a pattern for opportunity here? If you notice in the price history of the property that the price has been reduced every thirty days for the last few months, you can figure out the next potential drop. Timing on this can be tricky—there is usually a window where the asset manager has given the agent notice of the new price and the agent has two to three days to update the MLS and then send proof to the asset manager that the price was reduced in the system. If you can get your offer in during this magical window or even the minute the price reduces, you can pick up deals that others aren't looking at yet. If the property has been on the market over 120 days, it's considered an aged asset, and the bank will be much more likely to take a lower offer.

- Listing History Shuffle. A listing history can also tell you much about what is happening with the property. In this case, if you see the pattern of a property going under contract, then back active, then under contract, then active again when looking at a listing history, you can assume a few things:

  o Buyers like the price, but the condition is terrible and offers keep canceling during inspection.

o Potential buyers' financing keeps falling through due to condition of the property (remember, when a buyer gets an appraisal, the bank wants to know the property they are lending the money for is in decent shape).

o A potential buyer's financing has fallen through for other reasons. This has no bearing on the investor potential of this property; I'm just pointing out that some sellers have bad luck with buyers.

o In cases A and B above, there is great potential for a price reduction to make this deal work and the opportunity to be the stable buyer who comes in and saves the day.

- Double-Ended Incentive. I want the listing agent to be happy and feel like I'm adding value by purchasing a property. If I can get them paid double what they would have been paid otherwise by letting them represent me and double-dip the commission, all the better. Who are they more likely to call the next time they have a deal? As an agent, I'm more than willing to give up my commission in favor of getting the deal, and if you're a non-licensed investor, the power of the double-ended incentive can win you deals even in today's tight market.

- Pending Blast Out. Different areas have different definitions on the "pending" or "under contract" status in the MLS. But for this purpose, let's just say another buyer currently has a property that you want under contract. They got to it first, they beat you out, and they won. Game over, right? Not always. I like to pull up all the "under contract" status properties in my target markets and go through them maybe once a week. You can't win them all, but you can sometimes get a second chance. I will send this quick email to agents who are listing properties I'm interested in that are already under contract:

Subject: 1234 Main Street
Hi John,

I see this property is under contract. Congratulations! If the current offer falls through for any reason, could you let me know? I'm interested in buying this property. I can close fast and pay cash. You can represent me on the buyer's side as well. Thanks so much!

Anson

You might be surprised how good of a return you get on thirty to fifty of these emails a week. Even red hot deals have cash buyers who simply don't show up to closing. These deals go back to active on the market. Maybe hard money financing falls through or any number of things happen to cause the deal to fall apart. Most of the time, the agent can swoop in with your offer and look like a hero to his clients.

- Pocket Listing Feelers. Many agents rely on their friends, family and acquaintances, as well as clients who refer their friends and family, for business. This can mean that the agent is talking to many people, all with different timelines—some want to list and sell now, some want to wait until the summer starts, some need until June 14th when their transfer is approved. What I like to do is contact previous agents I've worked with or agents heavily entrenched in my favorite neighborhoods (some agents heavily market in one to three neighborhoods and become the go-to for that area). I ask them if they know of any properties coming up that might meet my criteria. These agents often get a short sale, pre-foreclosure, estate property, or hoarder house they don't know how to handle. That's where you come in.

- Early Bird Gets the Deal. In a balanced market or a buyer's market, this can be a great strategy. In a tight seller's market, this is not so effective. You will need direct access to the MLS or an MLS system that sends out instant updates for new listings. Some MLS systems (including my main one) will take an agent's saved search criteria and then send an email at midnight regarding new listings in the target area. By then, the good deals are likely gone. Once you have baselined your target areas, when a new listing pops up in your neighborhoods, you should know with some accuracy if it's a potential deal or not. When I used to check the MLS, I'd see one or two hot properties, I'd set a showing to go see them immediately, then I'd jump in my car. After a quick walkthrough of the properties, I'd go straight to my bank to get a cashier's check. With paper money in my pocket, I'd rush to the agent's office, hand them the check as earnest money, and ask them to write up my offer. Eight times out of ten, I'd get that deal. In a tight seller's market, many houses go to a highest and best situation from the minute they go on the market—or sellers hold off on deciding until offers collect for a week.

- Knock 'Em Down a Bit More. This is an investor practice where they first get a marginal deal under contract. During the inspection period, the investor conducts his inspection and then asks the seller to reduce the price based on the repairs needed. Sometimes sellers don't realize how much work their property needs until it's listed out in detail with retail contractor prices. Maybe they don't realize the cracks in the basement are worse than anticipated, or perhaps the furnace is on its last legs. I've used this practice, mostly on REO properties or short sales, and I always justify it with a real bid in hand. Many investors get a property under contract and then attempt a price reduction at inspection no matter what. Becoming more widespread, this practice gives investors a bad reputation. The inspection period exists to give a chance to renegotiate the price based on the inspection, but it has lost it its effectiveness as agents have caught on to investor schemes. Agents are now sometimes resisting investors by asking them to waive inspections on the contract or provide a verified contractor bid to back it up.

Hopefully this section will help you get MLS deals in the future, if you choose to pursue them. I never think it's a bad strategy to hedge your bets and work the on-market deals as well as the off-market ones!

Case Study—Four-Way Deal

Type of Deal—Networking
Investment Strategy—Fix-and-Flip

Want to talk about the power of networking? I met two of the three people in this story, "Bob" and "Bill," at the local meetup for real estate investors that I run; the third, "John", is a lender I met previously on BiggerPockets. com.

I met John for coffee and lunch a few times after finding his profile on BiggerPockets. John is a transactional funding master. We struck up a friendship and did a few wholesale deals together, where I used him to fund my deals for a day or two.

As for the other players—Bob had money but travelled a lot, whereas Bill had tons of time but not much money to play with for marketing, so they teamed up. Soon, they found a deal. I got a call from Bob asking if I might be interested in buying it—they were going to wholesale it to me. The deal was great, so I put it under contract, and we all decided the best way to close would be a double close. The problem with double closing (without jumping through a hundred hoops) is that Bob and Bill would have to bring cash to closing or figure out another way. I, of course, had them contact John for some transactional funding "flash cash" to use for a day or two. We closed, and four BiggerPockets members who met through networking got paid.

CHAPTER 5:
Marketing Methods

Max:	So Sara tells me that you're a consultant, Hitch.
Hitch:	Yeah, mostly marketing, little advertising, brand management.
Max:	I have no idea what that means.
Hitch:	No one does. That's why I get to charge so much.

—Hitch, 2005

So now that we've found our target areas, the magical places where investors are buying. We've networked with as many agents and investors as possible, learning where these investors are buying and what they want to buy. Maybe we've implemented an MLS strategy and are putting that to work to find deals. We are now ready to go out and find sellers whose problem properties we can help with. Now it's time to start contacting sellers directly or advertising to them. This is an off-market approach; these people have not yet contacted an agent or raised their hands and waived them around screaming, "I need to sell my house now at 50 percent off!" If only it were that easy.

I take two approaches to marketing: targeted direct marketing and broad direct marketing. Targeted direct marketing is where I send out advertisements to a specific list of potentially motivated homeowners and wait for them to call. Broad direct marketing is where I put up real or virtual ads and make my services known and accessible, so when a homeowner searches for a solution, they find me and call.

I like to think of it like this: My dad is a hunter and took me to the shooting range when I was old enough to be smart around guns. There, I honed a directly measurable skill: Did I hit the target or not? If you are familiar with guns, you should know the difference between a rifle and a shotgun. The type of ammunition is a key difference; one shoots a single bullet in an arc, while the other sprays small round metal pellets in a wide area. You can aim them both at the same target and get very different results. The rifle will leave one hole in the center of the target, while the shotgun will leave a hundred tiny holes all over the target. The shotgun shot is wide and all over the place, hitting from the edges to the center, while the rifle bullet is a narrow shot and highly targeted, only able to hit one small section.

Direct marketing can be either a rifle or shotgun approach, depending on how narrowed and specific you handpick your leads. Both have a good place in your toolbox; it's just a matter of how you work and what makes sense in your market. Let's start looking at the types of each commonly used by real estate investors. An entire book series could be written about how to market, who to market to, what to send, what not to send, where to put bandit signs, whether a website is needed, what pay-per-click ads to buy, etc. Still, by the end of this chapter, you should have a solid idea of the common methods and how to use them. While targeted and broad direct marketing methods have a similar end goal, they are different in their approach and execution. As different as they may be, they are complementary, and employing both provides a very powerful deal-finding business plan.

Broad Direct Marketing

Bandit Signs

These just sound cool, like something a desperado in the Old West would have. In real life, these can be an investor's little moneymaker, working for you 24/7—or until code enforcement or the police pick them up. Like billboard signs high up on the side of the road, bandit signs are meant to catch the attention of a driver and give them a call to action. The goal is to get calls and leads into your business and deal pipeline. The reality is, almost nothing in this business garners as much of a love/hate relationship as these pesky little things.

A disclaimer before we continue: In many municipalities and cities, bandit signs violate code statutes and can result in a fine or a call from your local police department. Some areas can and will fine you for repeatedly posting these signs, and they can be tracked back to you. Other municipalities may have other penalties for posting bandit signs. So, reader beware! Check your local city code for use of bandit signs, and go from there. Don't say I didn't warn you.

Just as with direct mail, there is a medium and a message that go with bandit signs. The mediums I have observed are yellow or white plastic or corrugated plastic signs. Some people buy them in bulk cut to size; others buy large corrugated plastic sheets and cut their own signs. There are two main ways to then display the sign—the stake and the post. Some use metal H-stakes, and others simply staple the sign to a wooden stake (when they aren't hunting vampires with them). Once the sign is attached to the stake, it is inserted into the ground. See, I told you this wasn't rocket science. Stakes usually aim to catch the eyes of drivers at intersections or highway off-ramps.

With the post, the objective is to put the sign high up on a wooden telephone pole, so drivers can see it a bit more easily. This also keeps them out of reach of code enforcement patrols who don't have a ladder handy. A staple gun attached to a long handle usually does the trick.

Bandit signs are an interesting marketing device—they are portable, disposable, appealing to only a certain demographic of seller or buyer, and can only fit so much writing. Therefore, the message should be absolutely crystal clear, and the method used to contact you must be easy to read.

Most people employ the handwritten approach, where they literally write on the sign in a giant marker, "I BUY HOUSES CASH FAST 555-555-5555." Those who don't like to write on things order the bandit signs online with their message printed in a font or type that looks handwritten. These two methods would likely test the exact same since from a car, they both look handwritten and the same message comes across. Like the handwritten yellow letter, this approach appeals to a seller's psyche on an informal level. They might just call to see what the heck is going on or run their problem property by this company or person.

While bandit signs are great for finding sellers, you can also use these little marketing tools to find buyers for your properties as well if you are wholesaling. If you were a fix-and-flip investor and you drove by a bandit sign that said, "Three-bed, two-bath house CHEAP! Must Sell! 555-555-5555," would you call it? Being the savvy guy I am, I already know that a regular homeowner wouldn't put this sign up and that the person on the other end of the phone is likely another investor, but who cares? A deal is a deal, and this can help me network for deals.

So, you have the medium and the message of your bandit signs, but where the heck do you put them? Don't fool yourself—only a certain level of motivated seller in a certain area is likely to be desperate enough to call a handwritten sign to get rid of their property. This is why you won't find any bandit signs in high-end, affluent, well-kept neighborhoods. These types of homeowners are usually equipped with enough options to handle the property if it becomes a problem for them. A lower-end or entry-level neighborhood with good driving-for-dollars candidates is where you want to deploy these bandit signs. Choose popular routes out of these neighborhoods, major intersections, and highway off-ramps going in and out of this area.

Some people put them up near Walmarts and grocery stores—anywhere someone living in the area will likely see your sign and call you. Keep track of where you put them up and drive by weekly. I said "disposable" earlier because these bandit signs will disappear—kidnapped by police, code enforcement, or the roving bands of old men and women who target these to take down (not kidding!). The old man/woman gang will sometimes tail an investor putting up bandit signs, taking them down as they go. Easy come, easy go, I guess! So, keep this in mind, and treat the marketing expense like you would direct mail. Know that you will lose most of your signs. Just hope you get enough leads to make it worth your while!

Websites and Internet Marketing

Now we are digging deep, making our way through the muck and mire to find the pearl-filled oysters the sea has to offer. Since the medium is virtual and some ad accounts require you to hook up your credit card, if you don't know what you are doing, you could wake up with an empty bank account. Also, Internet-based techniques change very quickly; one minute, your AdWords are rocking and your website is the first on Google, and the next, Google implements some changes and your site can't be located on pages 1-100. This section could be a book of its own, but the broad strokes of the topic should be enough information to see if this is something you want to learn more about and incorporate into your business.

Let's imagine a seller in a situation where their house has become too much and they need to sell quickly. It needs repairs, and they know that if they hire an agent and get people through the property, it will be months before it sells. Let's say they live in Kansas City. They search for answers online; they might open up their browser and go to Google.com and type in "Sell home fast Kansas City." Now, Google will do its Google-y thing and decide what shows up on page one, what advertisements to display, and pretty much everything else the seller sees. The good news is that there are things we can do to show up on that first page. Another important consideration is to ensure your website is easy to navigate, inviting, has good information, and includes a call to action. It's important to have a website set up with information that a seller will want to act on. Like with old-school direct mail marketing, your message and your call to action need to be clear. You don't want them to simply visit your website; you want them to visit and then call you or fill out your contact form.

Your Website

To website or not to website, that is the question. Oh, wait. It's 2017. *Of course* you need a website! If you have a good landing page online for your company, I call this the "trust site." Basically, a seller who doesn't know anything about you will want to know that you are a real person, a real company, and that you aren't a scammer. A well-designed website with a video of you talking about what you do and why a seller should contact you builds trust and goes a long way in dispelling qualms a seller might have.

A frequently asked questions (FAQ) area is good to have, and you'll want to make sure there is an easy way to contact you. Websites aren't just for bringing in sellers. They can be used for wholesalers to find buyers, to show private money lenders a history of your fix-and-flips, and to showcase your realty company. I have three primary websites—one for sellers, one for my company in general, and one specifically for sellers in foreclosure. Not everyone who visits my website is a seller; some are private lenders, and others are simply checking out my credentials. The way you craft your online presence has to work within the frame of your business and must support your end goal.

Search Engine Marketing

Search engine marketing is offered via many platforms. AdWords is by Google, BingAds is by Bing (Microsoft), and who knows what the other search engines use. You want to put your billboard on the side of the busy freeway where hundreds of thousands will drive by it daily, not on the side of Country Road 10 where maybe a dozen people will see it. What are these AdWords and BingAds? This is where you insert money, set up parameters, and get your website to show up as one of the top ads on Google or Bing when someone searches "sell house fast [insert city]."

If you've ever searched for anything on Google, you may have noticed the top three results are actually advertisements. The ads look like part of the search results, and most people only stay on the first page of Google results, trusting that Google will show them the best results. When someone clicks on the search result that is an ad, it charges the company or person who set up the AdWords campaign. This is called pay per click, or PPC. Companies pay to be seen first.

One of the issues with AdWords is that there is a decent number of other investors in your town who are also targeting "sell house fast [insert city]." So what does Google do when multiple people want to buy ads for those words or that phrase? They raise the price on the pay per click. You might pay $1 for each time someone searches to sell their home fast in [insert city] and then clicks on your ad link. If multiple people are vying for that phrase, Google might make you bid on those words to where you might be paying $3, $5, or higher per click. Is it worth paying for those clicks to hopefully convert a seller to a deal? Some say absolutely, and some say no. It depends on how much money you have to test different campaigns and words, as well as whether you have a good enough site that will convert sellers.

So why do I say that you can lose your shirt in this marketing arena?

If you don't know what you are doing when you set up your words or phrases, you could be throwing money away on a useless and non-targeted advertisement. This, like direct mail, is a numbers game. If you correctly target the right search terms, you should see clicks through to your site, and if your website is good enough, you should see sellers responding. Poorly targeting words, areas, or demographics on AdWords is like randomly mailing letters and hoping for a deal.

I've told you before and I'll tell you again—if you don't set a cap on your advertisement spend, you could wake up with no money in your bank account. If you tell Google, "Okay, I want to target 'sell house fast [insert city]'" and agree to $3 per click, then go to bed without setting a spending limit, 200 clicks overnight would result in $600 spent. Yes, the point is to advertise and get those clicks through to your site, but you still have to stay within whatever marketing budget you set. Make sure to reign in your ad campaigns. Set a certain amount to spend per day—or you might blow right past your budget.

Another reason is much more malicious; your nefarious competition might have it out for you and want to waste your money. They might go to Google and search "sell house fast [insert city]" and purposely click the links at the top to rack up the competitions' bills with no results. Google has enacted some deterrents to this practice since it was rampant for a while, and it's easier to get some of your money back if you report the clicks to AdWords. Either way, the competition is robbing you of your money and time.

When first setting up these ads, you can choose to have your ad show up in line with the search results at the top of the page or off to the right-hand side. Make sure you test which one gives you your desired results. Split test everything, and you should start seeing trends on what works and what doesn't.

What specifically should you put in your AdWords campaign to get results? Well, think about what a distressed seller would type into Google to find answers or more information on their situation. Take off your investor or agent hat for a minute, and think of being in foreclosure. Maybe your grandma just died and you need to sell fast. You don't want to use agents, and you want to close quickly. You can also use the software inside AdWords or BingAds to tell you how high certain phrases or word combinations rank and what they are worth. Here are some examples:

- Sell house fast [insert city]
- Sell home quick [insert city]
- Sell house with no agent
- How to sell house in probate?
- For sale by owner [insert city]

Social Media Marketing

Love it or hate it, social media isn't going away anytime soon. The people who hate it usually aren't running a business and don't see social media for what it is: a tool. Like a good website, a well-maintained assortment of social media accounts can be great trust platforms when sellers, buyers, or potential money lenders search for you or your company online. I will just get this out of the way here so I don't have to repeat it under every social media section below: It's imperative you be consistently informative, educational, and interactive. What you don't want to do is approach social media as if it's the 100-yard dash with a quick win. While a quick win goes a long way, think of social media as an ongoing relay race from one platform to another.

It helps with search engine optimization (SEO) when someone searches your company and they see in the results your website, your Facebook, Twitter, YouTube, Biggerpockets.com, and maybe a blog mention or two. They want to see you aren't some fly-by-night person who printed business cards yesterday and went into business the day before. Along with your website, your social media accounts form an interconnected web that I like to call a Trust Platform Network. Everything works together to boost your ranking and forms trust in the minds of those who search you out on the World Wide Web. Social media marketing for sellers and deal-finders is very new, so I'll leave it to you as to whether you want to explore this further for your business.

Not all social media platforms are created equal—some are great for spotting trends and searching out people by what they post, and others are better for advertising to prospects directly. Let's take an overview of the top five social networks and explore how to use them to find deals.

Facebook

We all know what Facebook is, so let's skip the intro. Remember one thing about your Internet life—if it's free, they are collecting your data to sell or make it easy to advertise to you. These companies aren't in business to collect selfies from your ex and political rants from your crazy aunt. Facebook does a great job of making advertisers' lives easy by specifically targeting ads to age, location, gender, interests, and even "most likely to move soon." Yes, Mark Zuckerberg knows when you want to move before you do. Think you could use this to your advantage?

To advertise, you first need a business page. This is wholly separate from your personal page, where you post pictures of your lattes and Shnookums, your cat. I'd recommend a Facebook business page even if you don't plan to advertise on the platform. It's just another piece in your Internet Trust Network. Spend a few minutes to make sure your landing page looks good, pictures are formatted, logos are present, etc.

Now let's discuss how to get ads out and leads in. If you post something on your business page, you can then "boost this post" to get it in front of more eyes. This is where you decide how much you want to spend; you can test it with $5 a day—or more, or less. Facebook will tell you how many people it will reach based on your daily budget. It will also let you choose what the goal is for the ad—do you want more page likes or do you want actual engagement? You may test out a few strategies, such as:

- Target those likely to move soon. Maybe these people are having troubles and need to sell fast.

- Seek out older folks. As people age, maintenance gets to be harder, and they may not have updated their house since 1983.

- Fish for referrals. Put up something like, "Do you know someone who needs to sell their house ASAP? Refer them to us and you can get paid $$$." You can also use this to form a global army of sorts to help you nail down driving-for-dollars leads. Ask for the address of the worst house in their neighborhood. If you close on it, they get paid.

- Re-target your videos. Post links to interesting blog articles you wrote—anything to get your message in front of people. You are a house-buying machine and a professional. Let people see that.

- Ask for reviews. Facebook business pages have a place where colleagues and clients can review your business, leave you a five-star review, and post a few sentences about your service. That can go a long way in building that legitimate business trust factor, and I'm sure it does not hurt any rankings.

There are hundreds of ways to use Facebook to get leads in your door. These are just a few that smart investors and agents are using, so get in there and get going!

Twitter

Oh, Twitter. I remember when you were young and nobody thought you would last more than a few years. Well, it's still here and still in the top five.

As a business owner and investor, you will use Twitter a bit differently than the rest. Sure, you should be consistent in your informative posts, but you should be concise, as you are only allowed 140 characters per tweet. Be a master of the short form—and the hashtag. What is a hashtag? It's this # and it's your best friend.

When people post on Twitter, they usually include a hashtag relating to a trend or topic. They might say, "Didn't that [celebrity of the moment] look great? #celeblife," or they might say something more like, "Cleaning up after a bad tenant SUCKS #landlording #realestate." Hashtags like these are searchable and can help you find people talking about certain topics. If you use the search tools in Twitter to find people, motivated sellers for instance, in your area talking about the things you are interested in, you can now start interacting with them. You'd be surprised what people will talk about on social media—things they would never tell their friends and family. This could include foreclosure, bankruptcy, divorce, a death in the family, being behind on payments, etc. When we hear what they have to say, we may find we're able to help them, but we have to be careful about how we approach the situation.

People are weary of the hard sell these days. Messaging that burned-out landlord directly and saying, "I can solve your problem—sell to me today!" doesn't work like it used to. Social media is a fickle thing. As we get bombarded by ads and spam, we become skeptical and on the defense. *Who is this guy? Is he a Nigerian prince who wants me to wire money to him?*

Instead of using the hard approach, try interacting and asking questions or relating to your audience with a story to get them talking. When you begin to interact, they might look at your profile. From there, they might see you are also an investor and might figure you may be interested in buying their place. If you are dealing with a homeowner and not a landlord, their skepticism may be even higher and you might have to work hard to add value and not jump in for the hard sale.

While Twitter's search tools are great, uniquely allowing you to find what people are talking about and jump in the conversation, their ads look a lot like Facebook's. Your promoted posts will be shown inside a user's feed, between the friend's post and Katy Perry's post. It shows up organically in the daily feed, which is the point. You can target the same things you can with the other ad platforms online—gender, age, location, interests, etc.

LinkedIn

LinkedIn is like Facebook but for professionals. It's usually free of politics, cat pictures, and your twelve-year-old cousin posting about middle school drama. It can facilitate high-level networking, all without requiring you to leave your house or put clothes on. Here, the strategy is content. Post articles, videos, and other resources that are interesting, keep you in front of the right people, and connect with your target audience. You likely won't be looking directly for sellers here. LinkedIn is more about identifying the professional gatekeepers to sellers (attorneys, real estate agents, friends, asset managers at a bank, etc.).

Remember when I talked about direct mailing to probate attorneys to get in front of them? This is another way to do that, only using the magic of the Internet. On LinkedIn, people put their professions right in their profiles; it's kind of the whole point. Reaching out and connecting with two dozen probate (or divorce, bankruptcy, etc.) attorneys can be done in ten minutes. What you then choose to send them as an introduction is up to you. You might message each one, telling them about another attorney's problem property you helped or just sending a quick hello. Or maybe you follow a soft sale strategy, keeping your content relevant and on point and letting them come to you. I can't think of a better way to get your foot in the door with professionals who may turn into longtime partners or sources of referrals.

Of course, there is also advertising opportunities here. Like with the other ad platforms, you can choose to have your ad in front of every attorney within fifteen miles of you, every mailman in your city ("find us the worst house on the block and we will pay a referral when we close"), or pretty much anyone else. This can be a great way to network with other professional real estate investors. Maybe you trade deals with them or become their wholesaler of choice.

LinkedIn does have a review system like Facebook, where professional colleagues can leave glowing recommendations on your profile. LinkedIn also has an endorsement system, where your connections and colleagues can officially endorse you in your areas of expertise—real estate, REOs, short sales, etc. These public words of praise look great when you finally hook a few attorneys or real estate agents, who immediately go to check out your profile.

YouTube

Since when is YouTube is a social network? Well, since people got smart enough to realize that having a website isn't good enough anymore; now you have to have video as well. Think of video as the glue that holds your entire online presence together. Want to make a video that touts your professionalism when working with distressed sellers? Make that, and then promote that video on your website, Facebook, Twitter, Google+, and LinkedIn. Your video is now in front of a few thousand people. When you crosslink and get the video on multiple web platforms, Google (which is the #1 search engine and owns YouTube) treats your website and social media platforms more seriously. You are more likely to show up in searches. Remember "sell house fast [insert city]"? Well, once you have a dozen videos that have that in the title or as targeted keywords, all linked throughout your website and social media platforms, Google has no choice but to rank you higher when someone searches for that term. Then, maybe the searcher sees your smiling face in a video search result. Once they click on the video, they are much more likely to reach out to you to sell their house. It all started on YouTube.

Google+

For the sake of not beating a dead horse, think of Google+ as a lot like Facebook. The main difference is when you set it up for your business, consistently post good content and smart videos, connect with other users, and link to your blog on your website, Google treats this like gold. Like YouTube, Google+ is a, wait for it, Google product! So, of course, they are going to treat this a bit better than other content from Facebook or LinkedIn. The only problem is that there currently aren't nearly as many users on Google+ as Twitter or Facebook, but that does not mean you should ignore it. When you have a business account, it lets you put up your address, phone number, and hours of operation. When your profile is complete and verified, you start ranking higher. People can now leave reviews on your business page, and this also helps with search engine ranking.

The only issue with direct advertising on Google+ is that to be really effective you really need to have a thousand followers, or "friends" in Facebook speak, before you can actually run ad campaigns. I don't personally know anyone with these kinds of numbers of friends on Google+ (remember, it has a much smaller regular user base than the other social media options

I mentioned in this section), so getting good info on advertising on this platform is hard to come by. I'll just leave it at that.

The Rest: Instagram, Periscope, Snapchat, Pinterest, etc.

I have each of these types of accounts. Have I closed any deals from them directly? No. Have I closed any indirectly by being active on these platforms and letting all the Google power seep down through the nooks and crannies of the Internet, making my services or me easier to find? That's hard to quantify, which is why many businesses are hesitant to go all in on any social platform, let alone the platforms outside of the top five. I can say that I do get a good amount of attention and deals from other wholesalers by being accessible. That being said, you have to decide for yourself where to focus your time and attention.

The Last One, the Big #1: BiggerPockets.com

Okay, now you just think I'm shilling for the publisher whose name is on the spine of this book. I'm not. I am simply a Pro user, just like you are (or should be). By remaining active on this platform, I've easily closed twenty deals or so and made six figures from networking connections. I've sold properties on the Marketplace, I've bought wholesale deals from those I've met at my BiggerPockets meetup, I've been an agent for other BiggerPockets members, and I've made great friends there, too. I've found multiple masterminds that I'm still a part of, I've learned more than I could ever give back, and I once even out-bowled Brandon Turner, beating him by one point!

I'm saying that I wouldn't be where I am today without this site—the podcast, the articles, the forums, and the members. I certainly wouldn't be writing this book, and you wouldn't be reading it. Be active on the forums, write your own member blog, listen to the podcast, interact, connect, network, and if there is a local meetup, go to it! If there isn't, start one. All of these strategies will help you hone your deal-finding skills and connect with the right investors in your market.

Search Engine Optimization

You know what is a losing proposition? Playing games with my six-year-old son. Not because I don't love him (I absolutely do), but because any time we play, he will eventually change the rules on me. His mom gave up a long time ago. Halfway through, his Sorry piece has a rocket launcher and can blast my guys off the board. That's now how this works!

Likewise, anything I write here will likely be outdated three months after you read this. That is the fickle nature of Google. Google holds all the cards; we just play along and pretend we aren't mad when they suddenly have a rocket launcher and blow our guys off the board. It's Google's world, and we just live in it.

What this does mean is that all the hard work to get your sites ranked might end up meaning nothing, and you may have to switch strategies. What this does not mean is that you shouldn't try to play with Google even though the rug gets pulled out from under you. There are some fundamentals that most experts agree always work. That Internet Trust Network also works to get you better ranked in the search engine:

- Interconnected social media

- Your YouTube videos on your website and social media

- Blogs and articles from your website cross-linked to your social media

- Facebook and Google+ business pages, with verified phone numbers and address of your business

These help to keep your Google juice flowing, ensuring you and your brand remain relevant for your business category, search words ("sell fast," "real estate," etc.) and location (city, state).

Search engine optimization is simply the term used to describe all the strategies you use to ensure the visibility of your site and brand on a search results page. Here's a good overview of what keeps your website at the top of the page.

- Relevance. Are your site, your keywords, and your content relevant to what people are searching? Are you positioned to be the #1 most relevant result when someone searches "sell house fast [insert city]"?

- Quality Content. Do you frequently publish helpful articles, videos, and other content to your website? Do you write truly useful articles, rather than fluff stuffed with keywords? Google can tell the difference.

- User Experience. Is your site clean and easy to navigate, with relevant information a searcher might look for? Google knows how long a searcher stays on your site before going back to find something that was easier to navigate or better laid out. The length of the page visit matters. Attract people to your site and entice them to stay with a good user experience.

- Mobile-Friendly. With more and more of us surfing the Internet on our phones, if your site looks amazing on a computer monitor but looks terrible on mobile, your page views and ranking will eventually suffer.

- Links on the Inside. Google also looks at how interconnected your site is on the inside. Do you provide relevant links to similar articles you've written in your blog posts? In your article about avoiding foreclosure, how about a link to a pertinent video you made about short sales? The search engine pays attention to things like this, and you will rank better overall for it.

If you want to dive deep into SEO, it will only benefit you in the long run. You don't exist online unless someone can easily find you. We are looking for deals, so why hide in the shadows when we can be on the front page?

Targeted Direct Marketing

Direct Mail: The Targets

We have talked a lot about distressed homeowners so far. Some live in the property, some are landlords, some are in foreclosure, and some have experienced a death or divorce in the family. It should go without saying that if you, me, or Mary were to spend money on marketing, we would all want to have the best chances for deal-finding success. You don't want to waste your time on sellers who aren't motivated and have no reason to sell to you at a discount. That's why this whole section is about how to find distressed sellers.

Driving for Dollars

You have now done your Internet research and talked to plenty of investors. Because of this, you have decided the rough areas that you want to focus on. Let's take all that top-down Internet research and networking and start hitting the streets.

Mary knows that Bob likes to buy in the Washington Park neighborhood of their town. Knowing this is great, but what if Mary could handpick the candidates most likely to sell in that area? Instead of casting a wide marketing net, she could pinpoint houses to target and market to. This knowledge could also be instrumental to her intimate knowledge of the neighborhood. That's where driving for dollars comes in. The benefits to driving each street in your target area are obvious. You learn the area and get to know which houses are selling and why. Do the ones on the east side sell for more than the ones on the west side? Is one pocket more desirable than the rest of the neighborhood?

Taking decent notes while driving for dollars can help build rapport with a seller when they call in. Instead of lying when you say, "I was driving through the area," you can truthfully say, "I was driving down your street, and I noticed the hail damage on your roof." This shows you take initiative and do your homework. Some sellers might think it's a little creepy, but most will recognize you are a professional and that it's your job to look for properties like this. So now that we know the benefits, let's explore what the driving for dollars process looks like:

1. Grab a camera, paper, and pen, or maybe a GPS app on your phone so you can track streets you have already been on.

2. Drive your target neighborhood—every street—slowly enough to notice things noted below in #3 but quickly enough to not look suspicious and get the cops called on you.

3. Look for signs of distress.

    a. Boarded up windows and doors

    b. Poor exterior condition: bad roof, falling shutters, broken windows, beat-up siding, etc.

    c. City code violation notices

    d. Signs of vacancy: long grass, overgrown landscaping, flyers/ door hangars left on the door, newspapers piled up on driveway, curtains open and no furniture inside, no shoveling or car tracks for days or weeks after a snowstorm, full mailbox, etc.

    e. "Red tags" from utility companies, shut off notices,

delinquent notices

4. Once you find a house described in #3:

    a. Snap a quick picture.

    b. Write down the address of the property and quick notes (I grade the house on a scale of 1 to 5, with 5 being a "so-so" candidate meeting some of the items in #3 and 1 being "this house is a pile of crap and this seller should pay me to take it off their hands").

5. Find your local tax assessor website, usually by county, also sometimes called "central appraisal district" in some areas. Look up each address you wrote down, putting the following information into a spreadsheet:

    a. Owner name

    b. Mailing address

    c. Year purchased

    d. Last sold price (if your county records this info)

Like a super sleuth, you track down the information on these eyesores. Now you can plug them into the marketing machine and start getting leads to keep your deal pipeline full. End of story, right? You market to these leads and end up with lots of deals in hand, correct? Well, sometimes. Other times, you get a big stack of returned mail that the post office has kicked back to you because the addressee has moved or otherwise cannot be located. Let's go through a few ways you can track these absent homeowners down!

Skip Trace

When somebody moves or skips town, it can be difficult to locate them if they didn't go through the proper channels and leave a forwarding address with the post office. A skip trace service might be your best bet to help track them down. This is when a company, usually a credit report company, lets you peek into their secret stash of documents that they keep on everyone.

If someone moves across the country overnight and doesn't tell anyone, usually there are some traces left when they arrive in their new area. Did they connect utilities in their name? Did they change their address on their car loan? Did they apply for a new credit card at the local Sears? Sounds scary, but we can use this information to our advantage. These skip trace services, for a fee, will tell you a lot about the person you are looking for, including their new possible address, their cell phone number, their social security number, and even their possible neighbors' phone numbers.

I've used these services to track down vacant home owners who moved across the country. I either locate their current address or the skip trace service gives me the phone numbers of their old neighbors, who can tell me where to find the homeowner. The downside to these services is that they can get expensive depending on how many searches you are doing per month. Also, the process to get approved into one of these services can be a little stringent. But if you are looking up vacant homeowners and this is a big part of your business, the hassle to get in and the expense to use it can be worth it. It can be an extremely useful tool to a real estate investor.

Google/Facebook/Whitepages.com

I call this "skip trace lite" because it's where I usually start in my search for an absentee homeowner. I'll plug their name into Google and do some research. I'll then look up their information on Whitepages.com. If I can get a new address or a phone number, great! I can then either mail to the new address or call the number and see if I can't get Waldo on the phone! Facebook has half of the planet right now as users, with each user spending a significant amount of time on the site each day. See if you can find your homeowner on Facebook, and if you can, send them a message about their property. They might have skipped town and moved two thousand miles away, but their Farmville farm still needs attending to daily on Facebook. The more unique the person's name, the easier it will be to find using these methods. A "John Brown" is going to be impossible, while a cooler name like "Anson Young" might be a bit easier to track down (thanks, Mom).

Forwarding Address Requested

When you write these magic words on your envelope, the postal service will try to forward your super important mail piece to the homeowner at their new address. There are some limitations, though. If it's one year after the homeowner filed a forwarding address, you might get the mail back, but it will actually include the new address. Go ahead and note this in your spreadsheet and re-mail the piece to them. After eighteen months, they may no longer give you the new address and just send your envelope right back to you. After that, even USPS no longer cares where they moved.

Sticky Note/Greeting Card Left on Door or Garage

Placing a note on the door, a notice on the garage, or something up on the front of the house can get noticed quickly. Some people like to post a big red "NOTICE" sign they create; others just leave a handwritten note or envelope. I like to do this when I find a house where someone simply isn't home. If you leave a note on their door to "please call—it's important," usually you'll get a curious call. The goal with all of this is to think a bit outside the box when it comes to getting response from homeowners with houses that they likely want to sell. Use your imagination.

Mailmen

Enlisting your mailman to help track down homeowners is probably the closest you'll get to having a henchman. It should come as no surprise that mailmen know pretty much everything about what is going on in their local route, from address changes to vacant properties to foreclosures and newly divorced households. The idea is to get to know the mailmen (and mailwomen) in your target areas and to start building rapport. Some investors have a business card they hand the mailman that states what they look for in these areas and that offers a referral fee for finding a property the investor closes on. Some mailmen are more than happy to give you the inside information on what he or she sees—and some have no interest in you, your money, or your business.

This is a people business. Some people don't understand what we do and are afraid to lose their jobs. All my mail minions know the deal by now and understand what information they can and can't give out to the public. The last thing I want is for these hardworking people to lose their jobs, so I am never pushy.

ListSource.com

If we lived in the Matrix, ListSource would be the part of the mainframe that keeps it all together. Not only is it a great market research tool (something it's not designed for), but it does even better at providing great direct mail targets in any area in the United States. I haven't tried searching for distressed homeowners in other countries yet, but I'm sure ListSource either has that information or soon will. The goal here is to pull a list with likely criteria for distress or motivation. We have to guess quite a bit at times and set the parameters to give ourselves a best guess scenario. We can only assume motivation in some cases, from absentee owners to homeowners with high equity who have lived in a property since the 1950s.

Sure, you could get your title company to pull some of these lists for you, but the more you get to know the ListSource web interface, the better you will be in this business. If you learn how parameters can mean the difference between a great list and a useless list and creative ways to look for information on the site, you will be a direct marketing master in no time. The more narrow and specific we make our list, the less competition (rifle approach), but busting out the twelve-gauge shotgun and hitting a wide area has its uses, too! Go play with it. The site won't charge you until you have all the parameters set and are ready to check out.

Like any piece of technology, ListSource might change how it operates in years to come. Regardless, the basics will likely remain the same, and understanding what parameters to input to find your desired deals will serve you across platforms. No matter how you use it, first go to ListSource.com, log in, then select "Build List."

You'll again notice blue tabs—Geography, Mortgage, Property, Demographics, Foreclosure, and Options.

In the top left corner of the "Build List" screen, you will see something very important: your list count. Each time you change a parameter—say, "Single Family Homes" to "Townhomes"—the orange number in this box will change. This represents to the number of prospects or houses in a given list. Since you are charged for each prospect in your count number, your budget will dictate whether you pull 21,000 names or 200. In each category, from "Geography" to "Mortgage," there are dozens of different sub-options to choose when building your list.

I'll start with the ListSource basics—how to tell ListSource where to look and what basic properties you will need to input. I'll then give very specific instructions on pulling a few main lists I love to use. It will be up to you to customize them for your area.

Pro Tip: When you are logged into ListSource, you can save your list. I like to build a "primer" list, something with all my geography, as well as bed/

bath/year built preferences, already entered. I save the list, and when I go to pull an updated list or try to tweak something, it's easier to start off halfway up the ladder rather than from scratch.

Before we get into the specifics of each list, let's start with a few basic tips for any list you build.

- Geography Tab—No matter the list, you must tell ListSource where you want to start. You can choose your state, county, city, zip code, and even subdivision. Using your data from the "Market Research" section of the book, enter in the area you want to search. I most often use zip codes, so after choosing the Geography tab, I select "Zip Code."

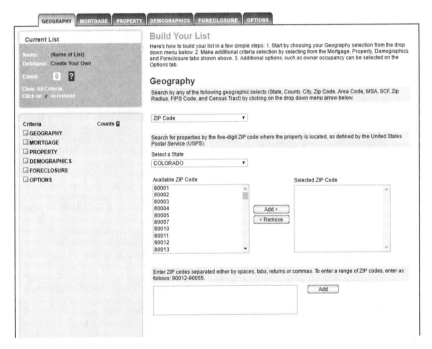

- From there, I select my state, and it automatically lists all the available zip codes. Now I can easily highlight as many zip codes as I want and push the "add" button to move the zip codes from "Available Zip Code" to "Selected Zip Code". Notice how when I add seven zip codes, my count goes from zero to 49,487? In those seven zip codes, there are 49,487 houses. I need to narrow it down a little from here.

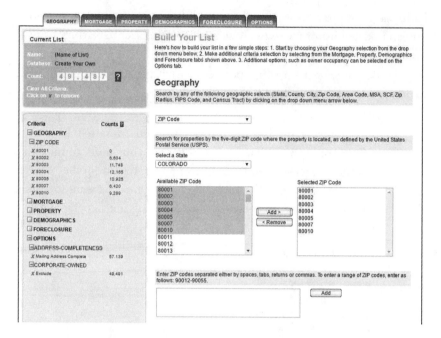

- Property Tab—We told ListSource to start in those seven zip codes, and now I want to tell it to search for "Single Family Residences" (SFR) only because I don't want to market to condos, townhomes, or multifamily properties. First, I select "Property Type" from the drop-down list. Then I select "Residential: SFR" and make sure to "add" it. My count goes down to 41,649 after including my SFR criteria.

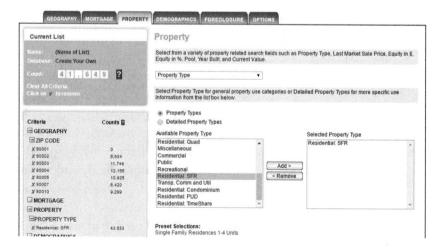

- Under the Property tab, you could tell ListSource you only want 1970-and-newer-built, three-bedroom, two-bathroom, two-story homes with full basements on two acres of land. You may not get many hits for going that specific, but it can be useful. For the following specific list examples, I will keep the seven zip codes and the SFR designation shown above.

List 1—Free and Clear

For a free and clear list, we will target properties that are most likely paid off over time. If the property has no mortgage, there will be more room for a deal. There are two main ways to pull this list, and I'll explore each one for the sake of covering all our bases.

1. Matured Mortgage

   - Go to the "Mortgage" tab.

   - Select "Matured Mortgage" in the drop-down menu.

   - Select "Only" below the drop-down menu.

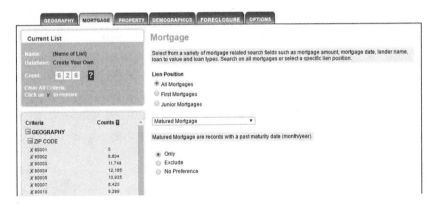

This estimates, based on when the deed was recorded, when the mortgage would have matured. For a thirty-year mortgage, this option would only pull those thirty years plus one day and beyond. Of course, this does not include any cash sales or investors or homeowners who never got a loan on the property. Selecting this takes us down to 626 properties with matured mortgages.

2. 100 Percent Equity

   - Go to the "Property" tab.

- Select "Equity (%)" in the drop-down menu.
- Ignore the preset "Select Equity" box and look below that where you can enter your own equity percentage. Enter "From: 100, To: 100" and then "add."

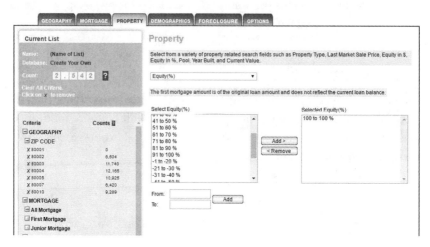

ListSource is estimating the equity percentage in the property here, the amount of mortgage debt remaining in the most recent tax assessor value. Our 100 Percent Equity list took us from 41,649 down to 2,542. You may wonder how this is different from the Matured Mortgage list above—2,542 is a lot more than 626! Our Matured Mortgage list only counts estimated paid-off mortgages, while 100 Percent Equity includes free and clear properties that were bought with cash from the start.

List 2—High Equity

We just covered free and clear properties, but what about those with mortgages that may simply have a large amount of equity? That's exactly what we will cover right now.

1. Purchased Long Ago

   - Go to the "Property" tab.
   - Select the "Last Market Recording Date" in the drop-down menu.
   - In the middle of the page, select your date range. Input "From: 01/01/1950, To: 01/01/1985."

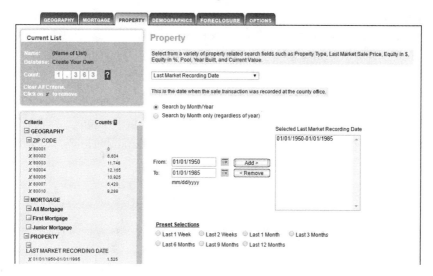

With this list, we are looking for properties that were purchased between 1950 and 1985. Our hope is to include properties purchased far back enough that they should be paid off by now or at least have plenty of equity. My count went down to 1,363, which is a good target list to start from.

2. Long Length of Residence

- Go to the "Property" tab.
- Select "Length of Residence" from the drop-down menu.
- Select "10+ Years" in the "Select Length of Residence" box and then "add."

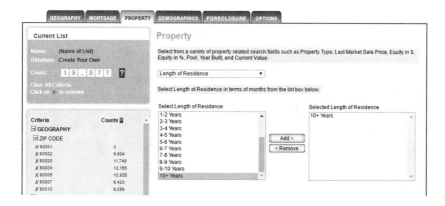

This is a good selection if you are looking up an equity list and want to make sure you are targeting homeowners or investors who have owned the property for ten years or more. As you can tell, this particular list didn't turn out very targeted since it only took us down to a count of 19,577.

3. High Equity Percentage

    - Go to the "Property" tab.

    - Select "Equity (%)" from the drop-down menu.

    - Ignore the box for "Select Equity (%)," and below that, enter "From: 50, To: 100," then "add."

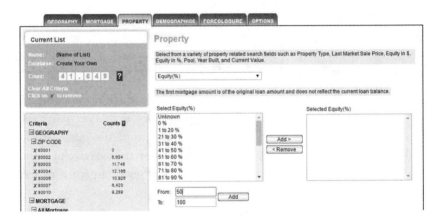

Like the Free and Clear equity lists, this tells ListSource that we only want to see properties that have 50% or more equity in them. This takes our count from 41,643 down to 12,940. That's still a large list, but we have now identified almost 13,000 properties with plenty of equity.

List 3—Absentee Owned

For a one-two punch in finding motivated sellers, try using the techniques above for locating high equity properties while adding other filters to zero in on absentee-owned deals. For this example, I kept the settings from the High Equity Percentage list, where I identified 12,940 properties with 50% or more equity. I now want to know how many of these are owned by absentee owners, most likely landlords.

- Go to the "Options" tab.

- Under the "Owner Occupied Status," select "Absentee Owned."

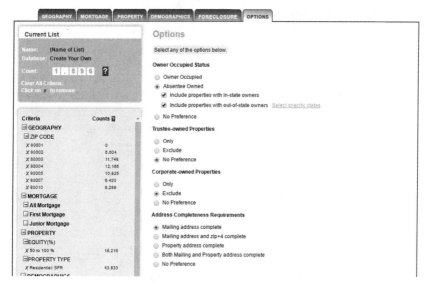

From here, you can either select "Include properties with in-state owners" or "Include properties with out-of-state owners." Some investors like to only target out-of-state owners, thinking there might be more distress or motivation when the owners aren't near the property. I would say that's usually correct, but I personally like to target both in-state and out-of-state owners. You never know what the motivation is, and I want to be in front of these owners when they need help. This took my list of 12,940 high equity properties down to 1,896 high equity, absentee owned properties! If I only wanted out-of-state owners, it would drop from 1,896 down to 238. That's a list of 238 highly niched property owners who may have the most motivation to sell.

List 4—Pre-foreclosure

- Go to the "Foreclosure" tab.

- Select "Pending Auction Sale."

- From the drop-down menu, select "Auction Date."

- Instead of running a pre-selected search of "Next 6 Months," I enter in my own dates in the "From:" and "To:" boxes. I go from 30 days from today to six months out. For this example, I put "From: 03/17/2017, To: 08/17/2017."

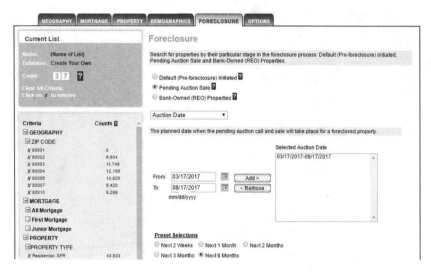

In my area, the notice of default includes an auction date. So, for me, this search makes the most sense. I'm not going to search for a list that includes an auction date in the next thirty days since we still must contact the owners and will have limited time to help them out of a pre-foreclosure situation. You absolutely *can* help, even up to a few days before auction, but most beginners don't know the hoops to jump through to stop a foreclosure sale or complete a deal in the space of a few days. This selection took my list down to only thirty-seven, so in these seven zip codes, there are thirty-seven homes with a pending foreclosure auction in the next six months.

List 5—No or Negative Equity

- Go to the "Property" tab.
- Select "Equity (%)" from the drop-down menu.
- Select any of the negative number selections, from -1% to -100%. I selected them all for this example and then clicked "add."

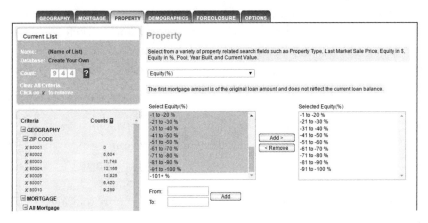

Why would we target homeowners with no equity? Coupled with the pre-foreclosure list, if we have a short sale process lined up, we can contact these homeowners and help them with a short sale. Even in this red-hot market, ListSource tells me there are 944 properties in my selected area that are underwater.

Pro Tip: You can pair up the pre-foreclosure search with the high equity search to find pre-foreclosure properties that also have equity. You would be surprised that some properties going to foreclosure auction have $100,000 in equity and the homeowner has no idea they could sell and make some money.

Delinquent Taxes Lists

Delinquent taxes, tax liens, and the entire tax sale process is very similar to the foreclosure process. Instead of defaulting on mortgage payments, however, these owners have stopped paying their property taxes. When owners don't pay their property taxes, the county goes after the owners much like in a foreclosure situation, first with fines and warnings, then liens, and finally, if nothing else works, they will auction off the property (tax foreclosure). We should all be masters of spotting potential distressed situations by now, and the signals in this niche are no different. If a homeowner owns their property free and clear or has high equity but can no longer afford their tax bill, it is a great opportunity to step in and help.

Having delinquent taxes are like being in pre-foreclosure; the owner is behind on the payment, but the county hasn't taken any drastic punitive actions yet. The property addresses and owner names are now public record—or at least accessible—in most places. Knowing the process in your area is key. How many years can an owner not pay before the lien or tax sale is pursued? This information can help gauge motivation. If the owner misses one tax bill, it's likely they can make it up and move on with their life. If they miss three and now have hefty liens on the property, they are likely more motivated to deal with the situation. If the property is being sent to tax sale next month, they will probably have a ton of motivation.

To get these lists, you should visit your local county offices and start asking around. It could be in the property assessor's department or a separate department that deals with property taxes. Many counties charge normal citizens for these lists, so be prepared. I've heard of a county wanting $1,500 for full county lists.

Pro Tip: Most mortgage companies will automatically escrow, or hold, the money for taxes and insurance for the homeowner. It's all included in your mortgage payment. The mortgage company does not want to leave the tax payment each year up to the homeowner because of possible delinquent situations. They do not want to risk losing their lien position because the homeowner can't or won't pay their own property taxes. Some mortgages, even today, do not escrow the money, which leaves these tax delinquent/lien/sale situations to happen even if the property has a mortgage. Most often you will see tax issues with free and clear, inherited, or probate properties.

Tax Lien Lists

After adding a few warnings and fines to the tax bill, the county will opt to put a lien on the property to recoup their lost revenue. Well, that's how most liens work—they record the lien with the county, and if or when the property sells, they get paid. Tax liens are a bit different—county government is a hungry, hungry hippo and wants their cash now. So, the county will auction off the liens to private investors for a return on the investor's money. The county gets paid now, and when the property sells, the investor receives their original investment plus interest. In many areas, if a tax lien investor holds the lien for two to three years in a row, they can foreclose on the homeowner and take control of the property. That's not what we are talking about here; I just want to make you aware of it so you can look up this strategy later.

When a homeowner has tax liens, you can find this information in the same place you found the tax delinquent lists. However, the motivation of the homeowner is usually higher now that they have recorded tax liens on their property. When you buy these types of properties, you should factor the tax lien into however much the seller owes on the entire property debt.

Mary contacts Joe about selling his home, and Joe just wants out. Joe has two mortgages, one for $40,000 and another for $10,000. But Mary found Joe from the tax lien list, and so she knows that Joe doesn't just owe $50,000 to his two mortgage companies. The total would be $50,000 plus however much the tax lien payoff is for.

Tax Sales Lists

You can get this list from the county or even the newspaper advertisement announcing the tax sale as public notice. Now these owners have a drop-dead date when their property will be foreclosed on and sold at a tax auction. This process is similar to mortgage foreclosure, but handled in a separate sale process. You should find out how your area handles these since knowledge is power in these situations. If you want to market to owners who are slated for tax sales, you should find out when the property is up for auction and start mailing or knocking.

Eviction Lists

When a tenant stops paying rent to their landlord, the landlord submits paperwork to the city or county and follows all the rules to legally evict the tenant. Many cities or counties keep these records, as they should, since in many places these are court records. Do you think that savvy investors like you, Mary, and me should get their hands on such a list and market to these possibly tired landlords? If you answered yes, you are reading the right book. Like many of these lists and strategies, this might not be available in your area, but do your homework because this could be a good list to get deals from.

Try these resources. Of course, be extra nice to the city/county/court employees because if you are in this business for long, you will want a great working relationship with the gatekeepers to this information.

- Clerk of the Court
- City offices or websites
- County offices or websites

Probate and Estate Lists

There is nothing more distressing than death—and dealing with the deceased's belongings and property. We have all seen the inheritance scene in the movies, where the old patriarch of the family has passed away and now the heirs gather in a room with a lawyer to hear the reading of the will. Like those handed a winning lottery ticket, the people in the room suddenly find out they now own a beach house in the Hamptons or half the company stock. These inheritances left by the dead are always priceless items and expensive properties worth millions of dollars. In real life, it's much more likely you are the last in line and you get handed your estranged Uncle Ralph's hoarder compound emporium that's eight states away. What the heck are you going to do with this property that you have zero interest in owning? Now you are responsible for the property tax and insurance. Well, would you call this person motivated or distressed? I think so. This person lost a family member and now has the burden of a property they likely can't afford to keep up and start paying taxes on.

Probate is the court-supervised process of gathering a deceased person's assets and then distributing them amongst inheritors and creditors. An executor must take responsibility for the estate, for better or worse. The named distributor is called an executor in most places, and this is most likely the person you will be dealing with the most when marketing to these leads. The newly named executor of the estate has the power to sell the items in the estate. Are you seeing an opportunity to get in front of these executors and people in charge of the property to help them? Good for you! Now, let's work out how to find these people.

Here is a breakdown of this section on where to find probate and estate leads:

- Obituaries
- Probate filings
- Probate notices
- Craigslist or newspaper ads
- Networking with attorneys
- MLS
- Obituaries

It's hard not to feel like you are exploiting someone's situation when you wait for distress or motivation. Let's be frank—there has to be a recently deceased person to trigger your next step. It seems crass, but that's the reality. One thing that a family does when a loved one dies is to contact the newspaper and publish an obituary. Sometimes it's the only way you have to find out someone you know died. If you have a morbid fascination with browsing the obituaries, you can use your weird hobby to further your business with these simple actions.

- Browse the obituaries and write down the deceased's name and any next of kin listed.

- Look up the deceased's name on the county tax records to see if they owned real estate.

- You wrote down the next of kin just in case the name is a very common one. There might be twenty John Smiths, but probably one John Smith who is married to Gertrude Smith.

- If they did own real estate, put the names and address of the property into a spreadsheet for future mailing.

- If you contact these people and want to help, it will show through your business, and you won't be lumped in with other investors only chasing after quick money at the expense of others.

Probate Filings

If the unlucky, newly deceased person did not have a will and needs the probate court to figure out the whole estate, those are conveniently, centrally filed with your county probate court. Even if they did have a will, the will gets registered with the court recorder, so that it's officially on file. Again, these things vary from state to state, so check out how it works in *your* area. Some counties have this information right on their website, and some require you to mine the depths of the courthouse records in person to find any useful information. In most places, you do have to show up in person, and the court recorder usually has restrictions in place and will charge you per record pulled. In my area, one county charges $1 per record and only allows twenty records pulled per day. Talk about a difficult process! But this can be to your advantage. Since the process is difficult, there will be fewer investors jumping through these hoops to compete with you.

Pro Tip: As with any method in this business, the harder it is to obtain the niche list of potential motivated sellers, and the less competition you are likely to have.

When you pull probate filings, you want some of the more recent ones. I usually pull the last two months' or so worth. In my area, you do get the name and address (and sometimes phone number) of the executor of the deceased's estate. What I don't find out is whether the estate includes any real estate in it. I know in other areas, the list of assets is declared in the file, including property address. Much like with the obituary lists, you want to gather the info and then crosscheck the county property tax records to see if they owned any real estate.

- Go to county probate court and pull records of recent probate filings.

- Get the names of the deceased, the names of the executors of the estates, the addresses, and any other information you think you will need.

- Look up the information on the county tax records to see if the deceased owned any real estate.

- If they did own real estate, put the information on a spreadsheet so you can be organized when you get ready to start marketing.

Like I said before, the methods for this section vary. In some areas, the county sells the list (like mine, for $5 a lead—ouch), or you can go manually pull the information. Some have it right on the website, and I'm sure there are other areas where the probate information is extremely difficult to find. There are services in most areas that sell lists of probates or even inherited properties. I haven't used any of these, so make sure that their information is good and current and that they aren't selling you an old list that they have sold over and over to a hundred investors.

Probate Notices

As part of the probate process, the court needs to see proof that the executor has filed a public notice of the estate, so that creditors, family members, and anyone who feels they have a rightful claim in the estate can come forward formally. Much like the foreclosure public notices, these are published in a newspaper and name the deceased individuals as part of the notice. Since the executor puts this information forth, it should be fairly accurate. Gather the names on a spreadsheet and cross-check each one with county property tax records to see if there is a possibility of real estate being left in the estate.

Pro Tip: In your area, there are likely one or two mainstream newspapers. The probate notices, notices of default (pre-foreclosures), bankruptcy notices, and other obscure public notices are often put in obscure newspapers in my area. These are the newspapers I have barely heard of, like the local Jewish newspaper or regional city-specific newspaper. Public notice, I guess, is public notice, but hunting down where these notices are published can be a hunt on its own. I suggest while in your networking journey, that if you talk to a probate lawyer, divorce lawyer, or other seasoned investors, you ask what the publication resources are in your area. Many are online only and require a yearly subscription; some you can find in small shops or other places.

Craigslist or Newspapers

Why would the family post an ad proclaiming the death of their loved one? Well, they wouldn't, but they would want to advertise the estate sale they are having this weekend to liquidate that obscure armor collection grandpa had. These are glorified garage sales, but can contain interesting items that the family does not know what to do with. It can be an opportunity to take note of the address and look up the information on tax records or show up and build some rapport with the family and ask what the plans are for the house.

Code Violation Lists

Do you have long grass? Trash in the yard? Is your siding falling off? Well, then, you just might have a city or county code violation on your property and not even know it. This is especially true if your property is vacant or you are a landlord who lives out of the area. These sound like minor issues, and when the city issues their first fines for the violation, it's not too big of a deal, maybe $100 and a warning. But if you let this go on for months or years, you might be looking at a lien on the property in the thousands or tens of thousands of dollars. Usually these are "green tag" items, indicating small to medium-sized infractions. If your property has a "red tag," you have some serious problems on your hands, as the authorities might have condemned the property due to the condition. It may even be slated for demolition. Either way, you will find some interesting things in your real estate travels, including many homeowners who don't realize they owe the city or county lots of money due to their property.

How can we investors use this to our advantage while helping the homeowner? Well, it all starts with getting a list of these properties that have been issued citations or violations by the local municipality, then contacting the owners to see if they are motivated to sell. Some violations (like the "red tags") cost so much to fix for the homeowner that it's not financially viable. Even some "green tag" items might have gone unchecked so long that the problem itself can be fixed, but the accumulated fine is now too big for the homeowner to pay.

This is a process that varies widely from city to city and county to county. Sometimes the city office handles code violations, and sometimes the county handles it. It makes a big difference who handles what when you go to procure this list. Sometimes there is a whole department that just handles code violations; sometimes the health department or the building department handles these. You might go from department to department, municipality to municipality, until you find what you are looking for. It's not every day that a citizen wants a list of these properties (good for the competition level, eh?), so be prepared to go on a hunt. It helps to be super friendly to the city/county workers. You might be in contact with them often if this is a niche you want to pursue. Sometimes you can't just get this list handed to you; you must submit a specific "open records request" to get the information. In other places, it's openly published on the county website. Understanding how the fining process works, what the deadlines are, and the increasing punitive damages can help you when you are talking to the homeowner about their property. If you know that on strike four they start issuing daily fines or begin to seek a demolition permit, you can let the owner know it's not going to get any better and they need to deal with this ASAP.

Check these resources in your area for code violations, health violations, condemned buildings, illegal additions, and meth lab busts:

- County offices and websites
- City offices and websites
- Police department
- Building department
- Health department
- Code violation department
- Permits and planning department

It's not very efficient, but you could drive for dollars looking for code violations. In my area, we don't really have any "war zone" areas or distressed pockets of properties. This makes getting a list from county more appealing. When you are canvassing your neighborhoods driving for dollars, finding a tagged property should shoot that address to the top of your list to market to.

Divorce Lists

Who says love doesn't last forever? Oh, I guess that would be multiple researchers who say the divorce rate is hovering around 40 percent. While very unfortunate, divorce can be a good motivation indicator. Many times, through the process of dividing assets and figuring out who gets what, the court may order the sale of a jointly-owned property. That's right—the court says, "You have to sell ASAP," and if either party hinders or slows the process, they can get in trouble with the court. Talk about motivation!

Like in short sale situations, this can be an extremely emotionally-charged time for all parties, and you can be thrown right in the deep end. My longest-fought deal was a short sale involving a divorced couple—and it was drama-filled, ridiculous, petty, and stressful. I questioned continuing in this business multiple times during those two years (yes, two years) it took to get the property through the short sale. But I persevered and made good money for my effort wholesaling that property. Where can you find divorced people? Well, there are generally three ways:

- Network with attorneys (see last section)
- Visit the county courthouse
- Purchase from a company

Since we covered networking, let's jump into the county courthouse. If you remember the different types of marketing target lists, you will notice a common theme. Motivation runs through the courthouse many times. Death, divorce, taxes, and foreclosure are all legally filed through a central location. In some areas, divorce records are open to the public in some capacity, and in other areas, it's difficult to find these lists. You might have to find a list provider to purchase a recently filed divorce list, and much like in the obituary process, you should start looking up the named individuals in the case to see if they own property.

Bankruptcy Lists

Are you sensing a common theme here? This is, of course, a situation of financial distress that can be a good source of motivation. When a person files bankruptcy, they are basically telling the court they can no longer pay their outstanding debts, and they need those debts restructured or wiped clean. When a house is involved, it can get complicated, so I suggest investing the time to learn about Chapter 7 and Chapter 13 bankruptcies and how bankruptcy affects the ability to sell a home. Some people who are behind on their mortgage payments wrap their home in the bankruptcy, aim to work out a re-payment plan, and have no intention to sell the home. They declared bankruptcy to stay in the home; most likely the bankruptcy stopped the foreclosure process and was done strategically.

Pro Tip: I have seen where bankruptcy delayed the foreclosure process for more than two years. The homeowner had no intention on keeping the house, but filed bankruptcy to push off foreclosure as long as possible. The owner stayed and did not make payments for a few years. These people aren't the most motivated, since if you buy the home, they'll have to move and start paying rent somewhere else.

Others do not include the house and need to get rid of it ASAP to move on with their lives. Some are ordered by the courts to sell. Understanding the process better than the average Joe will go far when dealing with people in this situation, as they often don't know the steps to drop their house out of the bankruptcy process if they do want to sell. Of course, you aren't a lawyer, so there is always a fine line between advice and "legal" advice. One can help you guide the process, and the other can land you in hot water or in court. I always tell people that this is how this same situation played out for a previous homeowner we worked with, but that I'm not a lawyer and they should consult one before proceeding. I never tell them exactly what to do because that would cross the line of offering legal advice.

You can find bankruptcy leads by using a few strategies:

- Finding public notices in newspapers

- Networking with attorneys

So, where can you find these folks? Section 107 of the U.S. Federal Bankruptcy Code makes all filings in a bankruptcy a matter of public record. However, the only public notice of a bankruptcy filing required by law is a notice sent to creditors that a debtor has filed for bankruptcy protection. Often, you will see public notices in the newspaper naming the person seeking bankruptcy protection. Otherwise, you need to head to the courthouse to manually search bankruptcy records.

Much like obituaries, public notices often run in very obscure newspapers. You should dig around your area to find these papers and most likely subscribe to *Duck Watchers Monthly* to get ahold of these leads.

Network with Attorneys

Many distressed sellers and situations, whether probate, divorce, or bankruptcy, have a common theme: attorneys. Think of the attorney as the gatekeeper to the bounty of leads you could be helping. Let's take the probate attorney. A probate attorney is obviously representing the family and the estate, so networking with a good one and convincing him or her that you can help their clients with problem properties is sometimes difficult. Like a guard at the gate, they have the power to keep you at bay with the tip of their spear. A good attorney will absolutely see the value of your services, and many investors get steady deals from probate attorneys. The same goes for divorce and bankruptcy attorneys. The ones who see your value are worth their weight in gold.

How do you reach out to these attorneys to network with them? Many law firms advertise exactly what they do and who they work with, so finding them isn't all that hard. The tough part is getting in front of them and convincing them that you will handle their client professionally.

- Marketing. Sending a professional, high quality marketing piece to their office is always step one. The advantage here is that not many lower-level investors are even doing this. The problem is that not many attorneys open their own mail, and the gatekeeper's gatekeeper (front office staff) might throw away your letter no matter how pretty it is.

- Networking. As usual, if you want to connect with someone, you should go where they go—meetups, events, charity auctions, golf tournaments, etc. A face-to-face conversation could lead to a beneficial partnership.

- Sphere of influence. Whether through LinkedIn, Facebook, or high school, we all know one or two attorneys. Start with who you know and ask around to find out who in your network knows any good attorneys. You may connect with someone who does not work with probates, but lawyers have lawyer friends and might refer you to someone they know. A warm introduction from a mutual friend goes much further than cold calling out of the phone book.

Direct Mail: The Method

While the world moves at blazing speeds and more and more communication is done online, don't underestimate the power of an old-fashioned letter in the mail. Today, people get so much spam in their email inboxes. Where it used to be very exciting to get an email, it's now shifted to where people are excited to get real mail. Direct mail is still one of the best deal-finding sources, even in 2017, and I don't see it going away anytime soon. Since more communication, marketing, and advertising is moving to an online platform, there is less noise in people's mailboxes, giving you an opportunity to stand out. Yes, we all still get a ton of junk mail, but ask yourself: Do you get more junk mail or junk email? We are bombarded every single minute on the Internet with advertisements and marketing. Open your email hoping to find a letter from dear old grandma and instead find ways to enlarge your sexual organs. It makes a trip to the mailbox almost refreshing. People still like getting physical mail, as long as you are doing it right. People sort their mail over the trashcan for a reason, but the right piece with the right message sent at the right time can be a goldmine.

There are dozens of methods to direct mail, many ways to reach out and touch someone and compel them to call you. An off-market deal-getter guy is mostly a marketer at his core. The goal here is to catch the attention of the owner via a piece of mail and give them a good reason to call you if they want to sell their property. What does that boil down to?

Every direct mail piece consists of the following:

- The target
- The message
- The medium

The Target

All through this chapter, we have discussed who we're trying to target, whether it's via a list provider or driving for dollars. Now we will be moving on to the message and the medium.

The Message

No matter who you are targeting or what type of medium you use, every message must contain the reason why you are contacting the seller. Your message should be tailored to who you are sending the mail piece to. Much of that skill is subjective and varies by area. Some homeowners hate yellow letters with simple messages because they look amateurish and unprofessional, and some hate super professional letters on company letterhead because they look too formal and stuffy. This is where we need to experiment a little and split-test letters to the same list to see what kind of response we get. Things that work for me in my market or another investor in his market won't work where you are. If you deal with $30,000 properties, your targets are much different than someone in San Francisco, where the lowest-priced house might be $600,000. Talk to other investors in your area, and if you can, find out what is working in your town.

The clear call to action will direct exactly what you want out of your target. You could say, "I buy houses—Anson xxx-xxx-xxxx," or you could say, "I buy houses just like yours—call me today and find out more! No obligations or pressure. Call me now xxx-xxx-xxxx." While your message can be short and sweet, staying simple and absolutely to the point, some investors have success with much longer letters as well. Some are informal, written by hand or kept casual in tone, and others are professional and branded with company logos.

The Medium

This is the actual mail piece itself, and while tightly correlated with the message, it deserves its own section. This is our opportunity to stand out from the crowd, to tell the recipient something that will compel them to call you first. Your entire medium and message will be secretly judged by the homeowner, from the envelope to the stamp to how it's addressed to what's inside. That's why testing is very important; figure out what works in your area for your targets.

While you carefully pick your target, then craft an attention-grabbing message and call to action, you also want to make sure the medium stands out from the rest of their mail. Your medium needs to be opened by the target, the message read and then acted upon. Don't fool yourself—there is some serious psychology going on here when it comes to direct mail.

Here is a typical yellow letter. This is a marketing piece in disguise. Its intent is to look like a quick, handwritten letter from a buyer, someone who just sat down at a yellow pad of lined paper and scrawled a quick message to a seller.

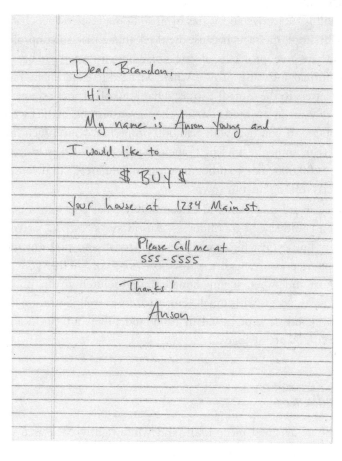

The message is very simple. It sums up why you are contacting the seller, it stands out because it seems to be private and handwritten, and it includes a clear call to action. Yellow letters have been around for a while now. Some swear by them, while others say too many investors use them and the market is saturated. I know for a fact they are still working. If you check out the Forums of BiggerPockets, you will see success stories from investors involving yellow letters and you may find a few companies who handle the yellow letter process recommended. Still, some investors struggle to make them work in their market since this medium is so popular right now.

Now, on to postcards. These aren't the ones you sent home from summer camp with a picture of Lake Tomahawk. These are cheap little marketing missiles shot to as many people as possible. Why so many? Typically, a postcard will get less response from a seller than a yellow or professional letter. Response rate from sellers is important when tracking your campaigns.

Hi, my name is Anson Young and I am going to buy a house in your neighborhood and if your property at 1234 Main St is for sale, call me now.

Hi Brandon,

I buy houses in any condition... Good, Bad, UGLY! I buy houses "AS-IS". I want to buy your house. Would you please give me a call to discuss? No obligation, hassle free, fair cash offer for your house!

I know you must have a ton of questions, so please call me today! I will answer any and all questions you have about our process. You have nothing to lose!

There are NO real estate agent commissions, no repair costs, and no fees!

So Please Call Me NOW – 303-555-5555

I BUY HOUSES!

Finally, let's talk about the professional letter. This is a branded piece of mail, and it should be paired with the medium of a company letterhead and business envelope of some type. This piece is there to verify to the homeowner that you are not some shady, fly-by-night investor, but an established business owner whose business it is to buy houses. This resonates with many people more than yellow letters. Imagine being an absentee owner who has a large amount of equity. I've met with these sellers, and they show me stacks of yellow letters they have received recently, and most wonder how so many different investors are sending the exact same mailing piece. A professional letter in a sea of yellow letters stands out in quality and will hit home with people who want to deal with a real estate professional. The verbiage is lengthier and professional, but conveys the same things I've been talking about—why you are contacting the seller and how you can help them.

Anson Property Group LLC
500 S Broadway Blvd
Denver CO 80205
303.555.5555
www.WebsiteHere.com

ANSON
PROPERTY GROUP

To: Mr. Brandon Turner
1234 Main St
Lakewood CO 80232

Dear Brandon,

I am sending you this letter of interest on your property at 1234 Main St.

My name is Anson Young with Anson Property Group, a Denver based company, and I am interested in purchasing your property. Have you thought about selling? If so, the benefits of selling your house to us include:

1. Fair price, all cash offer
2. No real estate commission
3. Will buy the house AS IS, no repairs needed
4. Close on the day you choose
5. No inspections, and no appraisals needed

Our offer process is easy, and no obligation. If you would like to discuss your options further, please call us at 303-555-5555. We can get you an all cash offer ASAP and selling to Anson Property Group is hassle-free.

Regards,

Anson Young

Okay, so when it comes to direct mail, how can we track our progress and build a system out of it? We need to evaluate and keep a reasonable record of our direct mail campaigns. We'll know how many people are calling and how many of those people who call have produced deals. One thing we won't ever have great numbers on is the open rate, or how many of our letters that got to the intended target were opened instead of just thrown in the trash.

Think of the process like this:

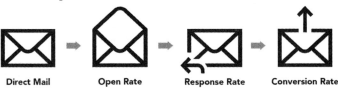

Direct Mail   Open Rate   Response Rate   Conversion Rate

Response Rates

Mary decides, like a smart investor, to split-test her marketing to see which one is going to net the most calls. She cuts her driving-for-dollars target list in half and sends one half a yellow letter campaign and the other half postcards. After four mailings to each half of the list, she can now effectively track how many sellers have called her from her marketing efforts and what is working best in her area or market. I'll give you the approximate average of response rates by medium/message. This is what other investors and I are seeing:

- Postcard—0.5 to 1 percent

- Yellow Letter—5 to 10 percent

- Professional Letter—2.5 percent

When I first looked at this from a top-down, 30,000-foot view, it looked bleak. Sending a thousand postcards will only get me five to ten phone calls? Yes. The good news is that this numbers game can be won, and you can build a steady business from direct mail. Consistency, tracking your numbers, and sharpening your marketing and conversion skills can be very lucrative indeed.

Conversion Rates

You've carefully curated your list of target properties and crafted a standout piece of marketing with a handcrafted message that you know will grab the homeowner's attention. Good work! Now you have to actually talk to this seller, build rapport with them, find out their situation, and gauge whether they will sell their property to you or not. You can generate a hundred calls a day, but if you can't convert those calls into actual sales, you are in big trouble. You've already spent good money on getting those calls in. Now it's time to close them! This is where conversion rate comes in. So-so investors might need sixty calls to get one sale, while rock-star investors can take twenty calls or less to get a sale.

Of course, you need to have people and phone skills to convert these warm leads into cold, hard cash—or hire someone who does. But a good chunk of the incoming leads you get will be garbage. Some will call just to get taken off your list, some will call to aggressively berate you for having the gall to contact them, and some will call you to sarcastically say you can have their pile-of-junk property for no less than $5 million. Some will call and have no real motivation, some will call on the fence, some will call with an unrealistic number at first, and some will call begging you to take their property. So, closing deals isn't all about skill. If you close one deal out of twenty calls, ten may have simply been terrible leads with no possibility of conversion. Maybe five were on the fence, allowing you to put them in your follow-up system. Maybe three called to be taken off the list, and you went on two appointments and closed one.

Setting Goals

Base your goal-setting on marketing, response rates, and conversion rates. This is a good way to work backwards. Let's say you are a wholesaler, and you want to make $100,000 this year. Now you need to find out how much marketing you need to send to make that hundred grand. Begin with the end in mind. Here are a few numbers we need to plug into our "let's make a crap-ton of money this year" equation. Your average wholesale deal nets you $5,000, your response rate is 5 percent, and your conversion rate is 2.5 percent out of those who called.

One hundred thousand grand for the year equals twenty deals at $5,000 each. For each deal, you needed to get forty incoming calls. To get forty calls, you need to have sent 800 letters. For the whole year, you will need to send 16,000 letters or more. Wait, why more? Because averages are just that, average. To ensure that $100,000, you should factor in some bad luck and below-average response rates. It's better to overshoot your goal by a bit rather than barely get there. Direct mail is a numbers game; you can't hope to send ten letters and get ten deals out of them. If you can hit those numbers, burn this book and write your own (and then send me a copy). Some investors send out 16,000 postcards a month to get four deals in the door (low response rate). You will, over time, get to know your numbers better and better and then track them. Then it gets exciting, because when you tweak something in the system, you can test and track it to see if it's improving your overall numbers or discover where a weakness in your system is.

Mailing Frequency and Sequence

What you send and what you say are important—but so is how often you send your marketing to the same list and change it up. You could send a postcard a day to a homeowner in hopes they will call you, or you could send one a year. Of course, those are both ridiculous, so let's agree that somewhere in the middle is the sweet spot. You also shouldn't just send the exact same marketing out each time and expect great results. A homeowner opening the same message they got from you last month has less impact than if you thoughtfully changed your message or medium. Different investors who market to multiple lists all do it a bit differently. I'm going to cover how I do it and some rules of thumb here.

Frequency

- Postcards—Every three to four weeks

- Yellow Letters—Every four to six weeks

- Professional Letters—Anywhere from four to six weeks to once a quarter

Who you are targeting also matters; a landlord with a happy tenant is less likely to respond than a landlord who just evicted a tenant. Some lists require one-time blasts, and for others, you want to "trickle" or "drip on" them consistently throughout the year.

- One-time blast and limited runs. These lists have a short window for the motivated homeowner to respond. It does not make sense to hit them month after month for years to come. A pre-foreclosure has a four-month window. After that, they've resolved the issue or have been foreclosed on. Similarly, a probate case has a relatively short window to get resolved.

- Every three to four weeks. These lists include people you want to "drip on" to make sure your company is in front of them throughout the year. That way, when the time comes, you have built up a consistent presence in their lives. These potentially motivated sellers may not want to sell today, but fourteen months from now, when they are ready, you have been there all along.

- Every quarter. The lists that require this frequency, four times a year, aren't as urgent as the previous. This is the tap on the shoulder reminding them that someone out there is still looking to help them. A tax lien list is perfect for this since taxes are paid once or twice every year. Hitting them before the next tax date can remind them, "Oh yeah, I'll owe the county another $1,200 before the end of next month. Maybe it's time to get rid of this house." This is also perfect for getting in front of professionals like attorneys or agents, whose tolerance for a monthly letter from you might be very low.

Every 3–4 Weeks	Every 6 Weeks	Every 3 Months	Every 6–12 Months
• Driving for Dollars • Probate • Pre-Foreclosure • Absentee Owned	• Absentee Owned • High Equity • Code Violation • Bankruptcy	• Bankruptcy Attorneys • Probate Attorneys	• Tax Delinquent • Tax Lien • Tax Sale

Sequence

The sequence of your mailings is also important so your targets don't think a robot is mailing them the same thing each month. Variety in your mailers will go a long way to extend the life of each list you mail. By switching up your medium and message, from yellow letter to postcard to professional letter, you have a good chance of hitting the right person with the right mailer at the right time. Even if you tweak your message but still use yellow letters, it shows a human is behind the scenes. Remember, people get mostly junk mail these days, with maybe one out of five pieces relevant or important (source: my mailbox).

Here is a sample sequence that I send out to a driving-for-dollars list:

Month 1	Month 2	Month 3	Month 4	Month 5	Month 6	Month 7–9
Yellow Letter	Professional Letter	Postcard	Handwritten Short Note	Yellow Letter	Professional Letter	Hold off for two months then re-start from month one

Door Knocking

Does the idea of passive, broad-market advertising annoy you? Does waiting for people to call you from one of your mailers bore you to death? Do you wish there was a more direct, in-your-face way to reach out and touch the prospective sellers on your lists? I have just the method for you—door knocking. Door knocking can't work in 2017, right? Wrong. If you have the time, the *guts*, and the right list of sellers to target, you can take advantage of this niche where none of your competition wants to play. Nobody wants to door knock these days; they would rather order a list online and blast out postcards from the safety and security of their couch. This is where you can stand out.

Picking your list is key. Who'll be the most receptive to a handsome, bearded guy standing on their doorstep ready to solve their real estate problems? I've personally had success with door knocking pre-foreclosure lists, driving-for-dollars lists, and code violation lists. But almost any of the targets I lay out in this chapter could be potential deals waiting to fall into your lap.

The most common question I get when it comes to this technique is, "What the heck do you say when they answer the door?" That depends on which list you are working from.

With pre-foreclosures, it's usually, "Hello, is Mr. Jones home? Oh, nice to meet you, Mr. Jones! My name is Anson, and I'm with a local business that helps homeowners. I don't know if my information is correct or current, but looking at county records, it says your house will go to sale on August 15th. Do you have any current plans for the home?"

The interaction can move one hundred ways from there, including the homeowners slamming the door in your face. You should be quick on your toes, know what you're talking about, and know the answer to common objections like "we are doing a loan modification" and "we just declared bankruptcy to delay the foreclosure." In these situations, I try to address the "issue" up front; you could insert dialogue about "tax sale" or "HOA lien" or "$15,750 in code violations." That way, it's all up front as to why I'm there. Direct honesty, more often than not, wins me points in the rapport department.

For more general lists of houses, like a driving-for-dollars list, my initial conversation might look a little different. I might not know the factors that would give the owner motivation to sell. It might go something like:

"Hello! My name is Anson, and I'm with a local business that helps homeowners. I was driving by this property, and it matches what we are looking for in this neighborhood. Would you ever be interested in selling your property?"

No matter who you target and what you say, here are some pros and cons to door knocking:

Pros:

- Direct interaction. This gets you right in the face of your potential seller, with no need to wait for them to call you on a mailer or your bandit sign down the road.

- Instant rapport. Most distressed sellers don't want to call someone for help. Help standing right on their doorstep can break down their walls and make them want to deal with their situation.

- Less competition. Most investors want to sit behind their desks and order a list of motivated sellers; meanwhile, door knocking is inconvenient and hard work. This is why most investors don't do it.

- Low cost for newbies. For the cost of your list and the gas in your car, you can get in front of real-world motivated sellers with an extremely direct approach.

Cons:

- Not scalable. If you are a solo business owner and split time between work, family, and your real estate business, finding time to go out and door knock can be difficult. The activity of door knocking can't be infinitely scaled like direct mail or Internet marketing. You will hit a quick cap on your time, the distance you want to drive every day, and the number of doors you want shut in your face.

- Instant knowledge. When standing in front of somebody in a tough situation asking you questions, you better believe you need to be quick on your feet and know the answers. If you don't, your instant rapport is gone, and you're probably wasting your time. Knowing how to overcome objections (which we will discuss later) and how to answer questions about foreclosure, bankruptcy, eviction, and everything in between will come in handy.

Craigslist

On the same site where you can buy anything from a crib to a vintage guitar, you can buy houses from motivated sellers. It's a one-stop shop, as long as you are willing to wade through the fake ads that come with it. I know when I want to quickly offload some item I don't want anymore, I list it on Craigslist. The same goes for motivated homeowners who don't want to hire an agent to sell their home or who just want to get rid of it fast.

Searching through the "real estate for sale" ads on Craigslist can be tedious, but if you develop a system and a method, you can probably find a half-dozen decent leads a month in your city. Like in the "remarks" section for the MLS, you would be looking for signs of distress like "divorce property" or "seller motivated." There might be no description, just a price and an area, and it's up to you to weed out the motivation from the sellers. A note on motivation—you're probably thinking you'd have to be desperate to list your house for sale on the same site where you can buy tickets to a Céline Dion concert or barter used shoes for landscaping services, and you're right. Motivation is what we are looking for in distressed sellers, right? I treat Craigslist ads like I would any direct mail call. I figure out their motivation, explain what I do and how I can help, and set an appointment to meet.

No matter how you choose to market—social media, bandit signs, direct mail, door knocking, etc.—the key is always consistency. You might get lucky and land a deal off one mailer, one round of bandit signs, or one search engine marketing campaign, but if you want to build a sustainable business around finding great deals, you have to consistently get in front of motivated sellers.

Case Study—Mail Out Land Deal

Type of Deal—Direct Mail
Investment Strategy—Wholesale

I got a call from a letter I mailed to a driving-for-dollars list, so I already knew the property was in bad shape. This was the seventh letter I had mailed them—which goes to show that you can't give up too easily on these lists. The owner had just died the week before, and the only immediate family this person had was a granddaughter in town for a week to wrap everything up. Letters one through six fell on deaf ears; there was no apparent need to sell at the time.

Direct mail is about hitting people consistently enough that, at some point, you will reach them at the right time. The granddaughter called me as soon as she found my letter in a mail pile. She'd been talking to agents, but knew the property was tiny and in bad shape. She also didn't have the money to empty out the place and get it ready to list. I gave her a fair cash offer on the spot, offering her to leave whatever she needed. The relief was immediate. I was solving a *huge* issue for her. I beat out two agents and two estate sale companies by providing the right solution to the heir of the property. I could only pay for the land value, and she understood that. I ended up finding a developer who had two projects in the neighborhood and wholesaled the deal to that developer. The granddaughter packed up everything important and valuable, and the rest we donated, sold, or trashed. It was a win-win deal, all based on consistent marketing.

CHAPTER 6:
Evaluating the Deal

"The code is more what you'd call guidelines than actual rules."
—Pirates of the Caribbean: The Curse of the Black Pearl, 2003

Now you know how to get your hands dirty and consistently market or network to bring leads in the door with the hopes of closing them and getting paid. You're on your way to becoming a professional deal-getting guy. Once you have a good, solid lead, you must evaluate what the house is worth, you must figure out the kinds of repairs it needs and the cost of said repairs, and you must negotiate with the seller to lock up the deal and get the best price.

It's like if you walked into a pawn shop and bought yourself a new camera. The guy tells you it's a deal, but if you don't know what the average person pays for a camera that old, in that condition, and with those specific features, how will you know it's a deal? The same goes for real estate—a seller could want $400,000 for their two-bed, one-bath house. Unless you know what it takes to fix up and what price it can sell for after being fixed, how will you know it's a deal? In certain cities, you might need to drop a zero—in Detroit, two zeros—off that $400,000 price to buy it. But in San Jose, that might be a steal. Maybe you could wholesale it to a developer who will knock down the little house and build a $2 million house on the lot. Or *you* could be the developer. The more you *know* about the market you are working in, the more tools you will have in your tool belt. You know that

$400,000 house is a waste of time to try to wholesale to a landlord, but you might easily sell it to a developer who would be happy to pay every penny of your fee. The more you know, the more money you can make.

A note on this for wholesalers: Some gurus say that knowing the after-repair value (ARV) and repairs of a property don't matter when you wholesale, but I vehemently disagree. Yes, your end buyer can do all the work and decide if the ARV and repairs meet his criteria, but why would you wallow in ignorance? If you are a wholesaler who wants to get into fix-and-flip properties or rentals, why not get experience now? Selling a property without knowing the ARV is lazy and willfully uninformed. There, I said it. After all, how do you know it's a deal if you don't know what it's worth?

Knowing your ARV inside and out will make you a top-notch investor:

- As a wholesaler, you will become known for accuracy and maintain a good reputation in the market. A wholesaler who does not underestimate repairs is worth their weight in gold.

- As a fix-and-flip investor, you will know with certainty what your project will sell for—and what kinds of repairs are needed to get there. A fix-and-flip investor who consistently nails their rehab budget can run a great business—and lenders love them.

- As a landlord, you will have a very good idea of what it would look like if you refinanced to cash out your equity to buy more projects. A landlord needs to know how much repair is needed to get the desired rents for the area. They will know going in what the loan-to-value ratio will be and the options therein.

- As an agent, your clients will love you when you consistently sell property for what you say you will. An agent who knows rehab budgets can be a great service to clients who want a fixer-upper or a seller who needs to fix a few things before selling.

Knowledge is power! Wield it responsibly, kids.

Evaluating Property

I talked a bit before about figuring out market conditions and trying to find your target market; you will use some of these same tools to find the ARV. The better the tools, the better (and quicker) you can nail these valuations. If you have no info and poor tools, your life is going to be rough. The good news is, most of us have the Internet—and the tools available there are pretty darn good.

Comparables

There is a very good reason why the phrase "comparing apples to apples" is extremely common. When comparing two things, you are usually going to want to compare similar attributes. First, let's start with the basics of a valuation—comparables, or "comps" for short. Comps are properties similar to the one you're evaluating, in the same general area. Obviously, you will have a hard time comparing a two-bed, one-bath, 900 square-foot home built in 1947 to a five-bed, four-bath, 3,500 square-foot home built in 1997 that is ten miles away. The closer you can mirror your subject property in the below criteria—especially in the proximity of location—the more credible your valuation will be. Here are different attributes you may want to match between your comps and subject property:

- Type. This refers to whether your property is a single-family home, townhome, condo, duplex, etc. This one is hard to get around—even though we'll talk later about how to adjust comps to better match your subject property, the type is what it is. Nobody will take you seriously if you are trying to compare your townhome deal to the five single-family houses in the neighborhood.

- Size. Square footage is obviously an enormous appeal to a buyer, and comparing your 900 square-foot property to other 700 to 1,000 square-foot properties around it is going to be the smart thing to do. There is a widely accepted variance here that I use. I'll start with 200 square feet below my subject property and a hundred square feet above. Going down, you know your property should be worth a little more than the comps since it's bigger. Going up in comparing square footage, I'm more conservative with the value. You could fudge it a little, but if you are trying to compete with a 1,300 square-foot house, you will have to start making comp adjustments.

- Bedrooms and bathrooms. Here again, I will start with my net a little wide. If the subject property is a three-bed, two-bath house, I will look for two to four-bedroom, one to two-bath houses. I might look in the three-bath range, but there is usually a decent price difference between a one-bath, two-bath, and a three-bath home. A two-bath house with one on the main floor and one in the basement feels a lot different than a three-bath house with one on the main floor, one in the master bedroom, and one in the basement. Ask most retail buyers—kitchens and bathrooms still sell houses.

• Age. Age is an extremely relevant factor in valuation—and not just because of outdated building materials that are no longer used (asbestos shingle or popcorn ceilings, lead-based paint before 1978, galvanized plumbing before the 1950s, aluminum wiring before the 1960s, and knob and tube wiring before the 1920s). Each of these will create issues for you, your renters, or your end buyers in the long run and must be factored in. If I'm looking at a house built in 1950 or before in Denver, I pretty much assume the clay sewer pipe that was installed when it was built has failed or cracked. It's just the way it is. Age also delineates neighborhoods; some were built in phases, where the older section might be more desirable, the newer section less so—or vice versa. Sticking within ten years on either side of your subject property's age is a good place to start.

• Condition. After doing close to 800 broker price opinions in my lifetime, I've adopted the bank's metric of rating a property based on condition, including: poor, fair, average, good, excellent. The hoarder house that should probably be bulldozed is obviously in poor condition. The five-year-old house in a great area that has been fabulously maintained is in excellent condition. Condition allows us to see what a pile of junk can sell for as-is—and what it can sell for if fixed up—if you can find good comps.

• Location, location, location. This is the mantra of your typical real estate agent. Here in valuation land, it is vital. I try to stay within a half-mile from the subject property. Of course, this could change if your house is in a rural area. I will start off with comps that are in the direct neighborhood—the same street is great, and same neighborhood is ideal. You know the areas and neighborhoods where if you cross one major street the entire feel and quality of homes goes way up or down? Having local knowledge is important. If you aren't finding what you need, you can expand your search, but depending on the area and property, the farther you go, the worse off you are. Other things to consider: Being close to schools/shopping/parks, on a corner lot or cul-de-sac, and close to transportation is often positive. Conversely, buyers will see properties as negative if they back to commercial buildings (gas stations, grocery, etc.), are on major streets, border power lines too closely, or edge train tracks.

- Lot size and zoning. The size of the land that a house sits on is very important when it comes to value. A typical lot in Denver is 6,250 square feet. There are much larger lots and even much smaller lots (3,100 square feet), often in the same neighborhood. Obviously, that 3,100 square-foot lot is worth less than the 6,250 square-foot lot. The closely related factor to lot size is how the city or county zones the property. Zoning dictates the usage of the land and is fun to pay attention to when you get into development or wholesaling to developers. The 6,250 square-foot lot a single-family home sits on that is actually zoned for a duplex may be worth more than the house itself. In many cases, the highest and best use of the land is to scrape the house and build something new (like an attached duplex). Paying attention to your local zoning can be a gold mine. Knowing when, where, and how lots can be split or developed will help you on valuation.

- Garage size. Common sense will say that a house with a two-car garage will be worth more than the same house without the garage. A one-car garage is worth less than a two-car garage, but more than the house with a carport or no garage. If all other things are equal, pay attention to the garage. I'm listing a property right now that has a 900 square-foot garage that's ultra-deep and can likely fit four cars. This house can easily sell for $10,000 more than others with two-car garages.

- Basement. Remember when I lived in Phoenix? A basement was about as common as a day you needed a coat. In other areas of the country, this space is very common. A house I'm working on right now has 1,200 square feet on the main floor, as well as a full basement with another 1,200 square feet. Do you think the value is different from a house next door that has 2,000 square feet above ground, with a 400 square-foot basement? They are both 2,400 total square feet, so they are 100 percent comparable, right? Wrong. Appraisers weigh above-ground square feet with much more worth than basement square footage, and so should you. My house, with 1,200 up and 1,200 down, needs a closer comparable to its above-ground square footage size. The one next door with 600 more can be used as a fourth or fifth comp, but it should be avoided in first, second, or third place. Next door is 50 percent bigger above ground, so we shouldn't use that as one of our comps. Other basement factors include full size vs. partial, finished vs. unfinished, conforming basement bedrooms vs. non-conforming (in my area conforming means it has a closet and egress window), and walk-out vs. enclosed.

- Building materials. Your house's building materials are important for valuation as well. In my area, an all-brick house is worth more than a frame-built house. Composite wood siding is worth more than asbestos shingle siding. An asphalt shingle roof is worth more than wood shake/shingle roofing. Other areas have block-built (cinder blocks for walls, stucco on the outside, frame and drywall on the inside) or manufactured (built offsite, trucked to the lot and placed on the foundation) houses. Know what is desirable in your area.

- Floor plan. Ever just walk into a house and feel like it was just wrong? Or walk into a place and instantly feel at home? Layout and floor plan speak to our brains on a certain level that science has yet to explain. You, of course, have the common ones—the ranch style and the two-story. From there, it gets a bit more complex, with the tri-level, bi-level, story and a half, etc. Each area has its own unique homes, and in every area, there is that smelly dog that nobody wants. Here it is the bi-level, where the front door is at ground level, and you are forced to take stairs up or down right when you walk in. That house will sell for $10,000-15,000 less because the floor plan is just the worst, and buyers will only buy at the right price.

- School district. It will benefit you to know which schools in your area are desirable and will fetch a premium. I went to the worst high school in one of the best school districts in town. My dad lived close to the dividing line, so if we had lived maybe four or five blocks over, I would have been in a much worse school district. His property value was easily $25,000 higher than if his house was moved over those five blocks. Now that I do this for a living, I know there is a very clear dividing line between these two districts. Even if one side of a street is Cherry Creek Schools (great!) and the other side of the street is Aurora Public Schools (not as good), you can see sold comps on either side of the road a good 10 to 20 percent higher or lower. Pay attention—this is obviously a big deal to a retail buyer and to potential renters, which makes it a big deal to investors like you and me.

- Status and date sold. We can all agree that having the most accurate information is important. When looking at comps in an area, I want to know what is on the market now, what is under contract, and of course, compare the sold properties as well. The solds are what truly count since the under contract and active properties haven't closed yet, and anything can happen to them before they do. You could have sold comps at $200,000 and two active comps at $275,000 in the neighborhood. Until they sell, I wouldn't feel comfortable competing with them at that high of a price when there is no track record in the area that high. Even sold comps from the last three months are absolute gold. I'll go back six months, nine months, or a year, even if the market is headed up, and still feel comfortable. If the market is declining, it's not recommended you valuate based on prices a year ago if this year the market is down 10 percent. I will sometimes call listing agents on the under-contract properties, find out what they say, and ask if they landed a contract close to list price. If I'm confident that the under contract is close to closing, I'll factor it into my comps as a sold. I always look at active comps to see who my competition is (or will be in the next month or so).

These are good guidelines to start your comping process. I'll usually try to cast a wide net in a radius around the subject property and then start eliminating properties until I have a good list of similar properties.

Here are some other factors to consider that negatively affect the price of a home. You may want to avoid proximity to the following:

- Hospital
- Shooting Range
- Power Plant/Landfill
- Funeral Home

- Cemetery

- Homeless Shelter

- High Renter/Rental Concentration

- Strip Club

- Bad School/School District

Of course, some of these things are very situational. Proximity to a hospital might be statistically bad overall, but in some areas, there are doctors, nurses, or students who desire to live close to work. Landlords might be looking for something close to work centers (hospitals, offices) or transportation (bus lines, light rail lines) because of higher rents due to those amenities. The grizzled old inspector I've used for years told me a story that embodies the fact that there's a property out there for everyone. He inspected a rural property that was close to a landfill and that shook when the train went by three times a day on the tracks fifty yards from the property. He met with the buyer and made a comment about the miniature earthquake they experienced when the 10:15 a.m. freight train went by. The buyer was giddy; he was extremely close to his job at the landfill, and he'd loved trains his whole life. He looked forward to the three times a day the train would barrel through a stone's throw from his house! This property would have repelled 99 percent of buyers, but for this buyer, it was perfect. No matter what, there is usually a buyer. I'm not always willing to take a risk on finding that needle in the haystack, but the property and its proximity to these negative factors are yours to consider if you want to roll the dice.

You might be asking, "Why do I need to know all of this when I can pay an appraiser to evaluate the property for me?" You certainly can pay $400+ for each property you need to evaluate, but you may run out of money fast. Plus, when you get good at this side of the game, you'll be looking at and crunching numbers for maybe ten properties a week. I don't want to spend $4,000 a week on appraisals that I'll get back in two weeks when I can do each one in fifteen minutes. The other option is getting a real estate agent to do a CMA (comparative market analysis) or BPO (broker price opinion) for you as an expert ARV opinion on the property. Again, make sure you are giving them enough value in exchange for their time. Some people pay agents a flat rate, and some provide value by giving them listings or referrals.

With MLS access or a good idea of how to use Redfin, you can quickly and easily inspect a neighborhood and find out what is going on. I talked earlier about "baselining" a neighborhood—finding out what investors are buying properties for and then finding out what the public is paying for those fixed-up properties. The lowest priced properties will most likely be investor-bought. The telltale signs are the condition, bad pictures, a cash sale, not being able to qualify for financing, estate/probate situations, and agent remarks in the MLS indicating "investor special," "needs TLC," or "fix-and-flip." Finding the nicest properties is easy. They'll be priced at the top of the market in the neighborhood, will be freshly renovated, will have glorious pictures, and their descriptions will include terms like "fully renovated," "new paint/carpet/kitchen/bathrooms/etc.," "perfect remodel," and the like. You can tell from the pictures alone that it's a flip. By evaluating these numbers, you can easily tell if you are getting a decent deal. If the property you are negotiating for is priced below the worst comps that have sold in the last three months, then as long as the property isn't in even worse condition than the comps, you can bet you are looking at a decent deal.

Let's take an example. The seller wants $150,000 for his property, which is in fair condition. Looking at the comps, he finds that the three lowest sold properties in the last three months in poor condition were for $160,000, $175,000, and $177,000. These were all-cash sales, had "fix-up special" in the verbiage of the listing, and had pictures that indicated they needed at least $50,000 in repairs. Yours needs $30,000 to fix and is priced lower than these three comps. When baselining the ARV comps, you see one with the exact same floorplan that was flipped and sold for $266,000 and two other good comps that were fully renovated and sold for $260,000 and $269,000, all within the last four months. It doesn't take a rocket scientist to see that at $150,000, you are sitting on a screaming deal based on those quick numbers. Remember this baselining information; it will come in handy not only for determining as-is value and after-repair value, but also for negotiating with the seller.

A good way to determine the ARV would be to average out the three highest comps to get a conservative estimate on value. Some guys just pick the highest sold comp and roll with it. I like to average them out and go from there. Same for the purchase price—knowing what the average investor paid for a similar property in the area is hugely beneficial. In the last example, the low-end as-is comps were $160,000, $175,000, and $177,000. Taking the average of those gives us $170,666. For the ARV, we can average the sale prices of the renovated houses at the prices of $260,000, $266,000, and $269,000 to get an average ARV of $265,000.

Now that we know how to find the averages of as-is value and ARV value for qualified comps, we can plug them into the purchase formula to determine what we can pay for the property.

Purchase Formulas

To determine what you can realistically pay for a property and still make money, you need a purchase formula. There are several options commonly used by investors, primarily the 70 percent rule and the fixed cost method. An investor running a good business will stick to their purchase formula, knowing that if they stay within their buying criteria, they won't take unnecessary risks and end up losing money on a deal. Don't get blinded by greed. If you hone your formulas and stick with them, you play a smart, conservative game. I've known investors who, when property was just a few thousand dollars off their formula, wouldn't budge. While I understand it now, it surprised me at the time. I mean, what is $5,000 when you could make $20,000? Well, when you compromise $5,000 on this deal then $7,500 on the next, soon you're doing deals for a pack of gummy bears and an energy drink.

The 70 Percent Rule

This rule is commonly used to determine an investor's maximum purchase price; however, every investor uses it a little differently, and the actual percentages might vary by market. In some markets, it may be more appropriate to use a 75 percent or even 80 percent rule. The 70 percent is simply a baseline.

Sample formula:

ARV x 70% – Repairs – Wholesale Fee (if applicable) =

Maximum Allowable Offer (MAO)

After Repair Value (ARV): This is easily the most important number we deal with. You *have* to know what the property is actually worth when it's fixed up! Otherwise, all the other numbers will make no sense. You'll never know what to offer on a property without this magical number; this is the foundation of our calculation.

Maximum Allowable Offer (MAO): This is the highest price you can pay for the subject property and still have a deal.

The 70 percent rule is usually used by fix-and-flip investors to evaluate a deal; wholesalers need to subtract out their fee from the formula to be sure it's still a deal. Keep in mind—wholesalers need to find deals and buy them *below* what another investor would pay for them.

Here is an example using the 70 percent rule:

ARV x 70% – Repairs = MAO

$150,000 x 70% – $25,000 = $80,000 MAO

The $150,000 is multiplied by .70 (or 70 percent), and then the repairs ($25,000) are subtracted to equal our MAO of $80,000. The reasoning behind the formula is that a flipper will want to account for desired profit, miscellaneous expenses, holding costs, closing costs, agent fees, etc. Investors use the 70 percent rule to make 30 percent of room to account for desired profit and expenses. The 70 percent rule does not work for every investor or every market. It fails in lower-priced markets—say, Detroit—where the ARV might be $40,000. When you start plugging everything into the formula, you might end up with a negative MAO!

$40,000 x 70% – $30,000 = -$2,000 MAO

"Mr. Seller, I'd like you to sell me your house, but you'll need to give it to me for free, plus $2,000 out of your own pocket. You may leave that cash on the counter when you move out." Sounds like an impossible scenario and a joke, but I've met investors who were paid by the seller to take their problem property.

This formula also shows its limitations when your ARVs start getting over $500,000. For example, a $750,000 ARV home might need $75,000 in repairs (bigger house, bigger repairs).

$750,000 x 70% – $75,000 = $450,000 MAO

There is a very apparent problem here. It is very unlikely you will get a $750,000 home for $450,000, with the end buyer investor expecting a $225,000 profit spread before expenses (MAO + repairs).

As I said, it's a good guideline. No two buyers will have the same numbers on fixed costs, and no two markets (even regionally) can fall into this neat little box called the 70 percent rule all the time.

Don't worry, there is more than one way to skin this cat!

Fixed-Cost Method

Where the 70 percent rule is broad and lumps a bunch of expenses into a big, the fixed-cost method is more accurate. This formula further breaks down the 70 percent rule, accounting for what goes into that arbitrary 30 percent. Just like with the 70 percent rule, we are working backwards from the ARV, but now we subtract the fixed costs, the investor's desired profit, the repair costs—and if you are a wholesaler, the wholesale fee—to get our MAO.

ARV – Fixed Costs – Investor's Profit – Repair Costs –

Wholesale Fee (if applicable) = MAO

These so-called "fixed" costs include all the costs involved in a fix-and-flip project, minus repairs and profit. The things that go in there include closing costs for both the buy side and sell side, agent fees, holding costs, utilities, permit costs, title fees, concessions, inspection fees, insurance, etc.

As you can probably already tell, this formula involves many more variables, and it's going to be much harder to know what each of these is, especially when you're just starting out. I'll give you a breakdown of what these fixed costs might be for the fix-and-flip investor:

- Financing Holding Costs (Points, Interest, Mortgage Payments, Fees, etc.): $7,500

- Buying Closing Costs: $2,000

- Property Taxes: $750

- Utilities: $500

- Insurance: $350

- Commissions: $8,000

- Selling Closing Costs: $3,000

- Home Warranty: $500

- Buyer Concessions: $2,000

These aren't universal rates, by any means; this is simply a possible guideline to work from if you are delving into this more complicated formula. When you add these up, you'll get a number to plug into the "fixed costs" in our formula. Every market is different, and so is every investor, so these costs might vary widely from market to market or investor to investor. Keep in mind, if you are selling these properties to a landlord so he can fix and rent it out, many of these costs (and the 70 percent rule) won't usually apply.

Landlords evaluate properties completely differently than fix-and-flip investors. They will not have as high a number for repair costs or closing costs since they aren't turning around and re-selling the property. Landlords do not fix up properties to the same standard as fix-and-flip investors. A fix-and-flip investor wants to get top dollar, so he fixes the property up with the comparative standard of the neighborhood, while a landlord may not put as nice of counters/flooring/tile/carpet, etc. into the property since it will only be rented out. My suggestion with determining fixed costs is to talk to fix-and-flip investors to see if they will share some of their typical costs with you. Plug those numbers into a spreadsheet with each item listed out, and you will be able to use this tool when evaluating deals. While networking with these investors, ask them what their typical desired profit amount is as well.

Using the previous example from the 70 percent rule, let's look at the same deal using the fixed-cost method:

ARV – Fixed Costs – Investor's Profit – Repair Costs = MAO

$150,000 – $17,100 – $20,000 – $25,000 = $87,900 MAO

Wait a minute—why is this different than the 70 percent rule for our MAO? When you have a fixed cost in the desired profit for the fix-and-flip investor, it messes with the equation. Now we have a hard number, and that amount is usually the *least* a fix-and-flip investor would want to make on the deal. In our real world example above, if you left the equation more open, solving for profit for the fix-and-flip investor, it would look more like this:

Fix-and-Flip Fixed Cost Method, Solving for Profit:

ARV – Fixed Costs – Repairs – Purchase Price = Profit

$150,000 – $17,100 – $25,000 – $80,000 = $27,900

While the fixed-cost method is great for nailing down the wide range of costs in the transaction for the fix-and-flip investor, and while it helps a wholesaler find the MAO, it does not calculate actual profit for the investor. Most fix-and-flip investors run their numbers more like the above, seeing what their potential profit will be.

Which One Should You Use?

While both serve similar functions in investing, these equations both have pros and cons in the real world. The 70 percent rule is more of a broad guideline—it lacks when you start evaluating lower-priced and higher-priced properties. In my market, it's more like the 84 percent rule. If you brought me a true 70 percent rule, I would run to your office with a check in hand, as well as a small case full of unmarked bills for you to take a decent vacation, because that would be a screaming deal.

In other markets, it might be common to find 50 to 60 percent rule deals, and maybe a 70 percent rule deal wouldn't be that great. The fixed-cost method brings its own set of issues—it's not beginner-friendly and requires knowledge of ten or so more variables than the 70 percent rule. Once you get more experience and more importantly start networking with fix-and-flip investors in your market, you should start to fill in the blanks. You can start with a 70 percent rule as a beginner, and as you get to know more fixed costs and desired profit amounts, you can start using the fixed-cost method more and more.

Purchase Formulas for Landlords

Landlords and aspiring landlords, you didn't think I forgot about you, did you? How could I? Some of my best friends are buy-and-hold investors. The problem with purchase formulas when it comes to rental properties is that every investor has different criteria, and there are a lot of factors that buy-and-hold investors factor into their decision to buy a property.

Two main formulas that the buy-and-hold types use are the 2 percent rule (or variations thereof) and cap rate. First, let's check out some of the factors that landlords consider when evaluating properties.

- Purchase Price. Obviously, the initial purchase price is a big factor;

that goes without saying.

- Rent. How much will the property rent for?

- Repairs Needed. How much work will the property need to rent out for the highest amount? Typically, a buy-and-hold investor will not tackle as many repairs as a fix-and-flip investor would. Take two houses in similar condition. One is going to be fixed up and rented, and the other will be fixed up to flip to a retail buyer. The fix and flip needs $30,000 in repairs to command the maximum purchase price for the investor, including good quality finishes, new windows, granite countertops, hardwood floors, etc. The rental might only need $10,000 to $15,000 to get the top end rental price in that area, so the landlord might install laminate instead of hardwood, fix and seal the windows instead of replacing them, and choose more durable choices instead of the nice stuff.

- Financing Type. Is the investor paying cash? Using a conventional loan? Employing a portfolio loan? This is a big factor when considering the long-term investment and how it affects cash flow.

- School District/Location. Just like a fix-and-flip investor, the landlord is concerned about what the neighborhood is like as far as proximity to transportation and the quality of the schools that their tenant's kids will go to. The things that are important to tenants should also be somewhat important to the landlord so they can maximize the amount of rent. A clean property in a safe area with good schools and access to transportation will command more rent than a property lacking those features.

- Vacancy Rate. This is a number that represents the amount of time per year a property will be empty and not generating any rent, whether due to being in between tenants or other factors. Search Google for "vacancy rate your city, year" to see what your city's accepted vacancy rate is.

- Other Expenses. While simple math of rent minus property loan might work for the amateur when calculating cash flow, veteran landlords never forget to factor in the following: maintenance, utilities, taxes, insurance, advertising, and management.

The 2 Percent Rule

Before we begin, let's get this out of the way: The 2 percent rule is a rough guideline. Some investors are happy with a 1 percent, a 1.5 percent, and some will only look at a 2 to 4 percent deals. What your purchase formula looks like depends on your business plan and what you can find in the area you invest. Disclaimer complete, let's get into this 2 percent business. The 2 percent rule states that the monthly rent for your property should be 2 percent of the initial purchase price and repairs needed.

For example, a house is listed for $40,000 and needs $10,000 in repairs to get the most rent possible. If that property rents for $1,000 a month, it is a 2 percent deal.

Rent Per Month/(Purchase Price + Repairs) = 2%

$1,000/$50,000 = 2%

As you can see, this is a pretty killer deal, and you can also see where a deal this good can be hard to find. In Denver, if you get a 1 percent deal, it's a property that most landlords would line up to buy and would look like this, with $1,000 rent and a $100,000 purchase plus repairs: $1,000/$100,000 = 1%

Like I said, some investors are happy with a 1 percent deal in their area, some won't touch anything but 2 percent, and some find 4 percent (no-brainer) deals. The percent rule isn't the only game in town, so let's check out the next one.

Capitalization Rate (Cap Rate)

Most smart investors I know look at the cap rate as a minimum standard with which to compare investments. Like the 70 percent rule for flips, the 2 percent rule leaves room for expenses without getting into detail. The cap rate is like the fixed-cost method and accounts for all the numbers in more detail. Cap rate is also a good way to compare a real estate investment to other types of investments like mutual funds or savings accounts.

Cap rate is the net income divided by the final price (purchase + rehab).

Net income means your total income (gross) minus all your expenses. This is where you get to plug in those fancy expenses that cut into your gross profit like a knife through hot butter. Expenses include loan payments, taxes, insurance, maintenance, utilities, advertising, and management. Let's take our 2 percent deal above and evaluate the cap rate on that deal.

Purchase price plus repairs: $40,000 + $10,000 = $50,000

Yearly rent (aka gross income): $12,000

Yearly expenses: $5000

Net income = (gross income − expenses): $7,000

$50,000/$7,000 = 7.14 cap rate

That might not mean much on its own, but the cap rate is a great way to compare an investment to another investment class, and it can be a great standard to hold deals to. A buy-and-hold investor might set a business standard to not buy any rentals under a 6 percent cap rate, and that may work for them. Of course, these aren't the only deal evaluation formulas or strategies, but they are the most common that real world investors use. No matter wholesaling, fix-and-flip, or buy-and-hold, there is one thing we have not talked about in detail yet that needs to get plugged into all these formulas. To know if you have a deal or not, you need an estimate on repairs.

Repairs

A big disclaimer: Each area of the country can wildly differ when it comes to material costs, labor costs, and what is repaired. This section is as in-depth of an overview as I'm comfortable giving. An entire book could be written about this, and indeed many have. You should perform local market research to find out what's going on specific to your area. A rehab in California might have 35 percent higher labor and materials costs than a similar rehab project in Oklahoma. Some cities will have insane permit fees (a $8,000 permit to cut down a tree), and some will seem non-existent. Materials like lumber and granite will vary widely from coast to coast. Obviously, there are large areas of the country where something like pools or basements are very common, and there are other areas where they just don't exist. Knowing what to fix in your area—and why—is important, as is figuring out your local costs.

I view the skill of estimating repairs much like evaluation. Yes, you could get someone else to do this for you and you might do just fine, but a good, well-rounded investor will know how to do this important task themselves. You could hire an appraiser or agent to run ARV for you, just like you could hire a general contractor to get repair estimates for you. I'm not knocking either method; I'm just not a fan of waiting for someone to do work for me or paying them for their work, especially when you're starting out. When you become a big-shot investor driving your Range Rover from closing to closing picking up checks, you may not have to ever evaluate repairs again. When you are starting out, driving from appointment to appointment in your Honda Civic, the knowledge and experience of estimating repairs is invaluable. This learned expertise will be a big help when you suspect a contractor is trying to overcharge after a few jobs or when selling properties to another investor and ensuring an accurate repair scope. When you know your stuff, you can control your costs better and spot any exaggerating contractor or material shop. Okay, so how do you go from not knowing which end of the hammer to use to repair estimating guru?

General Contractors

A good contractor is a great asset to have. The first hurdle will be to find a few good ones to build relationships with. Referrals are always preferred; ask for a good contractor from any other investors you know, BiggerPockets. com members, parents, family, friends, or co-workers. I'd rather work with someone who has done a great job for someone I know than open the Yellow Pages and start calling random companies. The next stop would be to go to your local hardware store like Lowe's or Home Depot. Like gazelles around the watering hole, contractors out in the wild gather around the pro desk at hardware stores.

Contractors usually check out through this special area known as the pro desk to order materials in bulk, get bids for larger orders, or set up deliveries. If you don't want to approach random contractors here, make sure you ask someone who works at the pro desk who they would recommend for your general contractor needs. In my experience, the fine folks who work all day with contractors are most likely going to refer you to ones they enjoy working with, who are professional and whom the store employees would like to see continue to be successful.

The question then becomes *how do you get them to help you estimate rehabs?* Like agents, they will not work for free forever, and some won't return your calls when they realize you are using them for repair estimates and never ordering work through them. How can you add value here? Some investors are up front with the contractors and offer them $50 to $150 for a full walkthrough with a good breakdown on pricing and unlimited questions asked during the tour of the property. This makes for a win-win with the busy contractor—they get paid for their time, and you get as much knowledge as you can cram into your skull. Referring these contractors out to friends/family/investors you know is also a way to stay on their good side. You might not be in a place to use them yet, but if you are handing them work, they will remain happy. Think outside the box—maybe grab two to four other new investors who are looking to get good at estimation, pool some money together, and take three contractors through a potential deal. For $100 each, you could have a group session, all learn plenty, and compare notes at the end of it.

Other Investors

This relationship is a bit difficult to get into without paying for a weekend boot camp from a guru or something similar. Getting another investor to take you under their wing and teach you the ropes on estimating rehabs will be difficult. As with the contractor, the investor's time is valuable, and unless you are providing value for them in some way, their time will usually be better spent focused on their business. I'm not saying it's impossible by any means; there are good-natured and big-hearted investors out there, who are willing to take a newbie out to some jobs and walk through each one in detail. Just remember to add value first before asking for something like this.

Online

Did you know I learned how to change a fuel pump on a 1996 Saturn from one ten-minute YouTube video? What a crazy world we live in! I'm sure there are plenty of things you learned from YouTube, forums, articles, and blogs. This area is no different. From BiggerPockets.com to YouTube, the sources of information are out there and waiting for you to go find them. The BiggerPockets Flipping Calculator gives you a place to input estimates on many repairs and can be a good way to keep important repairs at the top of your mind when evaluating properties. There are also some good spreadsheets out there—some paid and some free—that help with estimation. Like with most things, you will need to customize them to your area's prices, but it's better than starting from a blank page.

Different Ways to Estimate

As with the various purchase formulas, find out which of these works for you and your business. Some are simple, and some are much more involved and accurate.

Square Footage Method

This method bases the renovation cost on the square footage of the property. It's a pretty simple formula on its surface, but it hides quite a few traps if you're not experienced. An experienced rehabber can find their base numbers easily, then multiply them by the amount of square feet of the property to estimate the rehab. For this section's purpose, I'll give out a baseline.

- $5/sq. ft. for a light rehab
- $10 to $12/sq. ft. for a medium-level rehab
- $15 to $20/sq. ft. for a large-level rehab

A light rehab will include surface things—say, if a property needs carpet and paint. A medium rehab will include the light rehab items, plus counters/light fixtures/bathroom renovations/kitchen renovations and one to two of the major systems like a roof or windows. A heavy rehab will include most of the first two, plus most or all the major systems (roof/windows/furnace), floor plan changes, walls moved, etc. If you know your numbers, based on the neighborhood and area, and level of finish you want, this can be a good way to estimate rehabs. My latest project is a five-bed, three-bath, 2,400 square-foot property that needs a medium level rehab—carpet, paint, kitchen rehab (counter/appliances/tile/backsplash), bathroom rehabs (tile/toilet/vanity), roof, water heater, hardwood refinishing, light fixtures, and some light electrical.

$12 x 2,400 = $28,800

As I will break down in another example below, this is extremely accurate for my business. If you baseline and have enough experience, you can quickly estimate potential properties based on this method. Because I don't typically tackle heavy rehabs or light rehabs, it's extremely easy to plug in $12 a square foot on a usual house we evaluate.

Baseline Method

A full report of the breakdown in costs from a contractor can be great to baseline some costs in the future. As an example, maybe the house the contractor walked was 2,400 square feet, and he quoted $2,000 to refinish the hardwood floors; then maybe the new house I'm walking is only 1,800 square feet, so I'd know the price should be below $2,000. Of course, the more information you have and the more bids you have from contractors, the more accurate you can be when determining this kind of estimate. If, say, you had three repair estimates for the same property, you could get a range or an average of what contractors charge for things like tiling, hardwood refinishing, electrical work, cabinets, counters, drywall, etc. Put this all together, and you could form a good master price sheet to keep you more accurate when estimating rehabs. It's much better than pulling repair budgets out of thin air with no research or backup. If you can get three or more estimates for tile, cabinets, roofing, doors, carpet, and as many common items as you can, you can baseline these items for analysis.

Per Room Method

This is something that I do in my head these days if I'm walking a property I've never seen before. Like the square footage method, this is a pretty generic way to estimate repairs. Walking through, you assign a dollar amount to each room in your head depending on what's needed to fix it up: "kitchen: $7,500, two bathrooms: $3,000 each, three bedrooms: $2,000 each, living room: $2,000, dining room: $2,000, etc." It's not accurate enough to properly estimate, but if you have no other methods, it can work in a pinch. A $3,000 bathroom includes tile, paint, toilet, vanity, shower, light fixture, and window. A $2,000 bedroom would include paint, flooring, door, window, and baseboard. A $7,500 kitchen includes cabinets, counter, sink, appliances, flooring, window, and lighting. The finishes here assume a full fix up to fix-and-flip standards, rather than a cheaper rental standard.

As you can see, there are flaws in this system—it might cover or incorporate a ton of items, but things like re-pouring a concrete driveway, replacing the furnace or roof, fixing structural repairs, and other big items are completely missing. There are certainly better ways to do this, which brings us to the last method.

Breakdown Method

You may not be currently rehabbing properties, but I think this skill is good for every investor. Let's break down the breakdown method. Take a detailed repair scope list or spreadsheet, and let's get into all the components of a rehab project that you will need to account for. Here is a good list you can take notes from as you walk a property.

- Exterior:
  - o Roof/Gutters
  - o Windows
  - o Siding/Soffit/Fascia/Garage Door
  - o Brick/Stucco
  - o Exterior Paint
  - o Deck/Porch
  - o Concrete/Asphalt
  - o Foundation
  - o Landscaping

- Interior:
  - o Paint/Texture
  - o Cabinets/Counters/Vanities
  - o Flooring (Tile, Carpet, Vinyl)
  - o Framing
  - o Sheetrock/Drywall/Plaster
  - o Carpentry/Baseboard/Casing
  - o Plumbing
  - o Electrical
  - o HVAC
  - o Sewer/Septic
  - o Termites
  - o Mold
  - o Radon

Many of those categories have subcategories, but this gives you a good start to a list that you may want to carry with you on walkthroughs. That way, as you go through a house, you can note the condition of each item you see. When working from a given list, the better your notes, the more detailed you can be when writing up your breakdown estimate. For example:

- Exterior:
    - o Roof/Gutters. Roof material is composite shingle, two layers. Gutters are metal and look terrible.
    - o Windows. Sixteen count, aluminum, seals failing (can see moisture trapped between panes).
    - o Siding/Soffit/Fascia/Garage Door. Wood siding was replaced ten years ago. Soffit/fascia in okay condition.
    - o Garage door is newer.
    - o Brick/Stucco. N/A, house has wood siding.
    - o Exterior Paint. Peeling in areas, needs full exterior paint and trim paint.
    - o Deck/Porch. Porch looks to be in good condition.
    - o Concrete/Asphalt. Driveway has major cracking and heaving, needs to be replaced.
    - o Foundation. Looks good from exterior inspection, no red flags.
    - o Landscaping. Four evergreen bushes overgrown in front of house, need trimming. Fir tree at corner of house has become a hazard, needs to be taken down.

Once you have a full, detailed list on your walkthrough sheet, you can then build a repair scope with the full breakdown of what needs to be fixed. You can get bids for these items or use a baseline repair method. Over time, like most experienced investors, you will have a master spreadsheet with a price for pretty much everything. Mine has Home Depot SKU numbers and quantity amounts or per square foot cells. That allows me to take my walkthrough sheet and input each item or job, and then it spits out a total by category (kitchen/bathroom) and the grand total at the bottom.

If you do renovations for your rentals or fix-and-flip properties, you will likely want to evaluate the property with the breakdown method. If you are just starting out, the baseline or square footage method could be good enough for your first dozen property evaluations. If you wholesale properties, square footage might be good enough for your end buyer fix-and-flip investor (who will look at your numbers and run his own breakdown anyway). Not all formulas are created equal, but I believe the more detailed your estimates are, the more accurate they will be—and the better you will be as an investor.

Case Study—Vindication

Type of Deal—Direct Mail
Investment Type—Wholesale, Fix-and-Flip

Don't believe the power of a highly accurate ARV estimate? I'll tell you two short stories of vindication, when the work put in to learn ARV and repairs paid off in huge ways for me.

1. ARV. This is a property that I'm working on right now. I found this deal via direct mail, mailing a mixed list of absentee and probates in a neighborhood. I'm also working with a new private money lender, and we are firmly in the dating period of the first few deals. I had just finished up a deal with him where my ARV, my repairs, and my time to fix and sell the property were spot-on. On this next deal, I submitted to him my deal analysis (80 percent rule in my area) with ARV and repairs, of course. He opted out of walking through the property to double-check my repairs, thanks to my track record on the previous house. His wife, who is licensed, pulled my ARV and said, "This is spot-on. I'm getting to the point where I don't even have to double-check your numbers."

2. Repairs. I'd landed this direct mail deal by marketing to an absentee homeowner list. I had mailed this house twice when they called, and we worked out a deal. I contacted one of my favorite buyers to wholesale the deal, walked him through, and waited for him to run his own numbers. He came up with a repair estimate that was $15,000 higher than mine. As a wholesaler, I don't like to argue other people's numbers, but I knew mine were solid. He wanted a lower price, which would have meant going back to the seller to get a reduction. I knew I could get it done for the prices I gave, so I picked through his rough estimate and gave him phone numbers for my cheaper sub-contractors for electrical, HVAC, and roofing.

We closed at my price, and I followed up three months later to see what the house sold for and how much his repairs were. He admitted I was right; his costs were within $1,000 of my given repair estimate.

CHAPTER 7:
Financing the Deal

"I love money more than the things it can buy ... but what I love more than money is other people's money."

—Other People's Money, 1991

No matter what your investment strategy is after you find, negotiate, and close the deal, you first need to actually *pay* for that deal. Remember the contracts signed for the purchase price of $100,000? Unless you plan on bringing a suitcase full of hundred-dollar bills to the closing table, you must figure out how to pay that $100,000 you offered the seller.

You could bring the aforementioned suitcase full of your own money to closing. Or if you don't have that kind of money lying around, you could borrow the money. And, of course, you could take the more creative third option, work out a lease/purchase or seller financing scenario with the seller or partner with someone who has money.

Even if I had a liquid $250,000 to spend on real estate, I'd likely leverage a combination of private money, partnerships, and transactional funding to do deals. With my own cash, I could do one deal in my market; with other people's money (OPM) I could do as many deals as I could line up the money for.

So, where do you find funding for your deals? There is a massive trade-off when it comes to financing. The easier-to-find options are harder to get; you could walk into any bank to get a loan, but you need to have the credit, job history, and down payment to get that loan—not to mention the appraisal, loan conditions, and thirty-day close! The harder-to-find options offer better rates and looser standards; you could find a handful of rich guys who want to earn 10 percent, could fund in two days, and never want to see your credit report or ask for a down payment.

Just like how using the MLS is easy—and therefore it's hard to find a great deal—anyone can walk into a bank, but you won't find the best deal there if your credit isn't great and you don't have a 20 percent down payment. It's hard to negotiate seller financing or find the handful of rich people who want an easy 10 percent, but those are much sweeter deals for the investor because of less money out-of-pocket, less scrutiny on credit/job history/down payments, etc. You can get into deals with no money down with more upfront work. Funding and financing affect your investment process. They may not interfere with your deal-getting process (marketing, networking), but they'll impact everything from your analysis and your offer to how quickly you can close and what kind of investment strategy you do with those deals.

In this chapter, I will break down many of the common financing types, so that no matter how you are finding deals and what kind of investing you are doing, you will be able to fund whatever you choose. We'll also look at what kind of investor uses each funding type, where you can go to find this funding, and the pros and cons of each.

First, let's talk about leverage. Instead of paying for deals with your own hard cash, you can make more money and do more deals using OPM. This is called leverage—using financing to buy more property and do more deals than you ever could on your own. Starting out, you will probably have to leverage your deals, so you will get firsthand experience with this tool. If you become an amazing deal-getter, you will have many more opportunities each month to close deals. If you only have $100,000 in the bank ("only") and refuse to leverage your funding options, the number of deals you can do each month goes way down. Like I said, with OPM, you can do as many deals as you can line up the funding for.

Now let's talk terms before we dive in. Some common terms I'll throw around this whole chapter are defined below.

- Points. A point is a fee equal to 1 percent of the loan amount. If your loan is $100,000 and the lender is charging one point, the fee would be $1,000 (or 1 percent of $100,000). Depending on the lender, points can be paid at the closing table when you buy or sell.

- Term. The term is the length of the loan. A term of thirty years means you will be paying that loan for thirty years unless you sell the property before then.

- Percentage Rate. This is the interest payment that is charged for your loan and is added to the principle payment each month.

- Down Payment. This refers to the money you put down on a loan—the initial payment made when borrowing. A hard money loan that requires a 20 percent down payment on a $100,000 property would be $20,000 out of your pocket (20 percent of $100,000).

- Loan to Value (LTV). This is the ratio of the loan amount to the value of the property. If your private money lender will only loan 70 percent LTV on a property that will be worth $200,000 when fixed up, it means she will only lend you $140,000 (70 percent of $200,000). If you are under contract with the seller for $120,000 and the property needs $30,000 in repairs, you will need to have that extra $10,000 on hand to put in the deal yourself.

  $120,000 (purchase) + $30,000 (repairs) − $140,000 (loan) = $10,000

- Collateral. Collateral is something that you pledge as security for the repayment of a loan. You might put up a few rental properties as collateral on your fix-and-flip projects. Those other properties are pledged to the lender if you cannot repay your current loan.

Types of Financing and Who Uses Them

Cash

Who Uses It: Fix-and-Flippers, Buy-and-Holders, Wholesalers, Developers, Owner-Occupants

This is not OPM; this is your money, your cash money (YCM)! Remember that suitcase full of hundred-dollar bills? I have bad news: Most title companies or closing attorneys don't accept cash at closing. Who would have thought? Instead, they accept cashier's checks or bank wires of your hard-earned cash. This is the most obvious way to pay for property, but certainly not the easiest. Some people have cash to do this, while others need to pull from a refinance of another property they own. Either way, cash is king!

Where to Find It: Look under your mattress, check your savings account, and break some piggy banks open. Once you have enough money saved up, you can start buying real estate with it!

Pros: Quick close, no appraisal, no banks/lenders, easy transaction, the best offer to many sellers

Cons: No leverage

Self-Directed Individual Retirement Account (SDIRA)

Who Uses It: Fix-and-Flippers, Buy-and-Holders, Developers, Private Money Lenders

So, you have an old 401k from a few jobs ago or a current 401k or IRA you pay into for retirement savings. What if you wanted to take that 401k account (or any other IRA account you have) and invest in real estate, tax-free? Well, there are rules in place to do exactly that! A self-directed IRA (SDIRA) or self-directed 401(k) is a retirement account you control as opposed to a regular IRA or 401(k) at your work that is in the stock market managed by someone else. The profits from the direct investment return to your SDIRA, tax-deferred, which means you only get taxed when you start withdrawing it once you are ready to retire. So, tax-deferred, with your SDIRA, you can fund all or part of your real estate purchases or even become a private money lender and lend other investors money (see "private money" below). There are quite a few rules that go along with this that delve heavily into tax and legal advice that is outside the scope of this book, but I'll give you an overview and then you can check with your lawyer or CPA for more information.

Your SDIRA must be set up with a company that can handle loans and real estate purchases from your SDIRA. Let's say Mountain Trust Company is the local company you found. You won't own the property; your IRA will, and the title will be in your IRA's name. Title will be something like "Mountain Trust Company custodian for benefit of Anson Young IRA." Catchy, right? Any expenses must come out of your account, and any profits must go back into your account. You cannot directly benefit from the investment. For example, if you buy an office building, you would not be allowed to rent a space to your own business.

It's on you to get with a reputable trust company and figure out how to roll your own 401k or IRA into a SDIRA. You'll need to understand all the rules and laws to follow to get your retirement money to start making tax-free or tax-deferred profits. Another way to take advantage of SDIRAs is to take loans from other people's SDIRAs, combining private money with the benefits of this great practice. I'm sure you can find someone with an underperforming 401k or IRA who would love to make a better return.

Where to Find It: This method takes some of the most planning and forethought, not to mention strict regulations on how to borrow your own money. Rolling over an old 401k to an SDIRA is the absolute easiest way to do this, but not everybody has one of these lying around. An alternative way would be to fund a new account from scratch or letting your investment business pay into one for you. Having experts set this up for you is recommended. One of the big SDIRA companies should be able to walk you through, whether you are starting new or doing a rollover. You can then start putting money into your SDIRA by contributing the maximum amount each year. Once you have enough in your SDIRA, you can start using it to buy notes and real estate or even to become a private money lender. This is a long game, so be aware that getting up and running within six months may not be possible if you're starting an SDIRA from scratch.

Pros: Tax-free or tax-deferred, better returns on your retirement savings, funded from your own SDIRA, ability to become a private lender, potential for 401ks and IRAs to be converted to SDIRA for awesome real estate returns

Cons: Lots of rules to follow, need to act carefully to ensure you get the full benefits, must already have a 401k or IRA or the funds to start a new IRA

Bank Financing

This is arguably the most standard funding vehicle for most property purchases. You go to a bank and get a loan. Most people do it this way, and they get along just fine. This mini-section will go through the many, many types of loans you could get through a bank, as well as their good points and, of course, drawbacks. I've gone ten years in this business without having to use bank money, but like most investors, I've been coming around to the thought of better interest rates, especially on long-term projects like rentals and development deals. A bank or mortgage broker is a good member to have on your team to bounce deals off and see where you stand in the eyes of the lender. Do you qualify for a standard bank loan? Finding out is quick and easy, and at least you will know!

Bank money is the easiest money to find, with a big branch bank on pretty much every street corner in America. Big banks such as Wells Fargo and Bank of America have a loan officer in each branch ready to meet with you and scrutinize your credit and financials to pre-approve you for a loan. Smaller local banks and credit unions also have this setup. In my opinion, they have an advantage since you can build long-term relationships with them and they are more likely to do some outside-the-box lending (like portfolio loans). The last line of bank lending comes in the form of mortgage brokers. There are likely a few hundred within twenty miles of you right now. While a bank loan officer can only offer products from his specific bank, a mortgage broker will have access to dozens of different bank products and will be far more creative than a conservative big bank. When networking with investors and agents in your area, get some names and phone numbers of lenders that they like to use instead of cold calling everyone. I personally like mortgage brokers for me and my clients the best. I love the long-term game of building relationships with local banks and credit unions next, and my last resort would be to go to a big national bank for my loans.

Conventional Loan

Who Uses It: Fix-and-Flippers, Buy-and-Holders, House Hackers, Developers, Owner-Occupants

A conventional loan is the most standard investor loan, good for long-term projects like rentals and development deals. The bank or mortgage broker will absolutely want to make sure you have good credit, a good debt-to-income ratio, tax returns filed for the last two years, income statements (pay stubs or profit/loss statements if you are self-employed), and bank statements. Oh, wait. They'll also want to see that 20 percent down payment sitting in your bank account. Sure, some conventional lenders will do 10 percent or even 5 percent down-payment loans; the point I'm trying to make is that unless you have great credit, solid financials, and a down payment, this loan might not be for you. Many lenders will not lend on a property that isn't move-in ready (which are basically most real deals we get), and a conventional loan does not include repairs in the loan.

Pros: Best interest rate of any loan you could get, great for long-term deals like rentals, could be used for personal residence or investment property

Cons: Requires high down payment, investor must be financially stable with good credit, necessitates an appraisal, thirty-plus day closing timeline, may require property condition to be livable or move-in ready

Renovation Loan/Construction Loan

Who Uses It: Fix-and-Flippers, Buy-and-Holders, House Hackers, Developers, Owner-Occupants

While you will likely be turned down for a conventional loan if the property is in terrible shape, the conventional loan's hotter cousin may be able to save the day. A renovation loan is a conventional loan with the repair funds included in the loan amount. So, your down payment with your longer term may cover the purchase price, as well as some or all the renovation or construction costs. These loans were built for beat-up houses and even scrapes or raw dirt you want to build on.

Pros: Great for a fix-and-rent, fix-and-flip, or fix-and-live scenario; same pros as conventional loan above

Cons: Harder to obtain than conventional loan, need construction plans/drawings with a detailed plan of what the repairs or new construction will cost; same cons as conventional loan

FHA (Federal Housing Administration) Loan

Who Uses It: House Hackers, Owner-Occupants

FHA loans are for owner-occupant buyers only. An FHA loan is great for a first-time home you will live in or a house hacking scenario where you buy a two to four-unit building, living in one unit and renting the others. Long considered a "first-time homebuyer loan," the FHA loan provides looser lending standards than a conventional loan, but trades that off with tighter property condition standards and other rules and regulations. For example, if you want an FHA loan on a condo or townhome, the condo building and HOA must be pre-approved and on the "yes" list.

If the HOA is in a current lawsuit or if there are too many rental units in the condo/townhome community, they immediately lose their FHA certification. An FHA appraiser will call out bad carpet, holes in the wall, and no current oven/range/stove in the property, and you will not be able to close until the carpet is repaired, the holes are fixed, and a place to cook mac and cheese is installed. Since the mortgage is federally insured, they want to make sure the property is in decent condition and can be lived in currently.

I have had FHA appraisers call a missing outlet cover. Yes, we could not close on a $100,000 property until a sixteen-cent outlet cover was installed. In return, you won't need as high of a credit score, and your down payment will only be 3.5 percent. Again, the bad trade-off is mortgage insurance—a forced payment the homeowner makes that insures the lender in case you foreclose on the property. Mortgage insurance can be removed if you have 20 percent equity in the property, usually a few years after buying the property. You cannot have more than one FHA loan at any given time. If you live in a property for one or two years and refinance into a conventional loan, you can use an FHA loan on the next property you intend to live in.

The FHA loan shines for investors when it comes to house hacking. If you find a building with up to four units, you can get an FHA loan on it, and your lender can credit 75 percent of your potential rental income to you when it comes to qualifying for the property. Let me say that again: The property could be totally vacant with no other current renters, but the lender will take 75 percent of the rent that you will get in the future and use that to help pre-qualify you as the buyer. If you earn $1,500 a month through a job, and 75 percent of the potential rent for the property would be $1,500, the lender can qualify you at $3,000 a month for your income. This helps house hackers buy a $300,000 fourplex, whereas they might only qualify for $150,000 if they bought a single-family residence.

Pros: Low down payment, easier qualification standards (credit score, etc.); ability to live in the property, refinance it, and then buy another property using an FHA loan with the intention of living in it; great for house hacking a multi-unit building

Cons: Mortgage insurance required, high standard for condition per FHA appraisal, necessity for HOA and condo certification through FHA

FHA 203k

Who Uses It: House Hackers, Owner-Occupants

FHA cares very much about the current condition of the house, not allowing you to close until things they flag are fixed. Don't you wish there was an FHA program that was more of a renovation loan, throwing out those appraisal conditions and lending you money for the repairs of the house? Well, 203k is here to save the day! The FHA 203k program has all the benefits of the FHA program, but also allows you to borrow money for the fix-up of the new house you will live in or house hack. It does come with a few drawbacks, though. One is a 50 percent longer closing timeline and the necessity of multiple bids for the repairs from licensed contractors. The underwriters for the loan (the people who look at everything and then decide if the bank should lend the money or not) want to see that licensed contractors are involved; they aren't lending you money so your Uncle Jerry can go in and do a horrible job. They will also withhold portions of the money after closing until you meet repair milestones, known in the construction and rehab community as "construction drawls." This keeps you from taking the entire rehab budget in a lump sum at closing and going on an amazing vacation to the Bahamas. The appraiser will appraise the project as if all of the repairs you have a bid for were complete—not as-is. That works well since the bank will want to ensure they are lending on a good deal that will be worth something after your contractor is all done.

Pros: Purchase price plus rehab funds all in an FHA wrapper, appraisal done based on future repairs, same pros as FHA loan

Cons: Longer closing timeline (forty-five to sixty days), construction drawls, need licensed contractor bids in hand; same cons as FHA loan

Veterans Affairs Loan (VA Loan)

Who Uses It: House Hackers, Owner-Occupants

This option is popular among veterans of the armed services branch because, well, they are the only ones who can qualify for this loan type. I always think of the VA loan as a close cousin to the FHA loan; you can buy one to four-unit buildings, and you'll face many similar appraisal stipulations when it comes to property condition. VA loans were created by the U.S. Department of Veterans Affairs to help Army, Navy, Marine, Air Force, and Coast Guard veterans attain home ownership. These options are also extended to current military members and surviving spouses! You want to talk about down payment advantages? Conventional loans typically require 20 percent down, FHA requires 3.5 percent down, and VA requires a whopping 0 percent down! While the FHA requires private mortgage insurance because the down payment is so low, VA loans do not require mortgage insurance at all. Another interesting factor is the "benefit amount." Let's say it's $250,000. If you buy a triplex for $200,000, you would use $200,000 of your full $250,000 benefit amount. In the future, you could keep your triplex and use another $50,000 in VA benefits toward another property. If you sold the triplex, you would get that $200,000 back into your benefit pool to use again.

Pros: Zero down payment, no mortgage insurance, availability of a certain "benefit amount" that you can use across multiple properties

Cons: Thirty-day close, VA appraisal standards similar to FHA appraisal standards

Portfolio Loan

Who Uses It: Fix-and-Flippers, Buy-and-Holders, Developers

Typically, when you get a conventional loan, it's either through a large bank or bundled and sold to a larger bank or fund that buys these types of loans. Therefore, the entire loan qualification process and the way that the underwriters scrutinize the property, the borrower, the appraisal, and everything in between is pretty standard. No big bank or big fund wants to buy loans or lend money that weren't done top to bottom "their" way.

There has to be a hero, the little guy who thinks outside the box, right? There is—and it's the smaller, local bank that does not sell your loan but keeps it in its own portfolio, hence the name "portfolio loan." These allow investors to buy more than the four or ten properties that many larger banks allow and are, all in all, a great option for funding. At the end of the day, the portfolio lender has the experience to lend to investors, and they care a bit more about the deal being sound rather than nitpicky financial details.

Pros: May provide rehab funds and have looser lending standards, qualifications center more around the deal than conventional loans, allow for faster closing

Cons: Can be short-term loans (six to twelve months), may require the investor to have a track record, typically have higher interest rate than conventional loans

Other Funding Methods

Hard Money

Who Uses It: Fix-and-Flippers, Buy and Holders, Developers

I'd like to meet the person who coined the term for this kind of lending. It's an interesting term. Hard money is just that—hard to swallow. Hard on the pocketbook. Hard on the bottom line of a deal. The interest rate is high, the points you pay are high, and they usually want you to qualify like you would for a regular mortgage. Of course, some care more about the deal than your credit score, but those are few and far between.

If you can't otherwise get a bank loan, hard money is likely your next stop. But be prepared to pay 12 percent APR and two to five points. That means on a $100,000 loan held for six months at four points and 12 percent APR, your loan fees would be $10,000 between the APR and points! But if you are making $40,000 profit and paying $10,000 of that to a lender, it's better than making $0 and not doing the deal at all. This was a huge lesson from a big investor I met who was still doing 14 percent and four-point financing on dozens of projects. It's all OPM at the end of the day—and it allowed him to fix and flip as many deals as he could find.

Where to Find It: Like the big banks, hard money lenders are actively advertising in your area for borrowers to do deals with them. You might find them through referrals from other investors or manning a booth at your local REIA club. Regardless, the good ones are usually preceded by their reputation and are out there networking to get more loans closed. Finding these guys is usually easy; picking one that works for you is a matter of talking to enough of them about their loan structures, what interest rate and points they charge, the application process, and how much of a down payment they are looking for. Even a quick Google search for "hard money lenders [insert city]" would yield a good starting place. Make sure you are working with reputable organizations, ask for referrals and testimonials, and keep an ear to the ground for any investors' recommendations.

Pros: Easier lending standards than a bank, a fast close, ability to bring down points/APR over time by building relationships

Cons: Expensive, high APR, and high points

Private Money

Who Uses It: Fix-and-Flippers, Buy and Holders, Developers

So, what do you do when you're sitting on a few million dollars (besides seeing how many Twinkies you can fit into a swimming pool, of course)? You might put a bunch into mutual funds or the stock market, but savvy millionaires actually lend it out. A private money lender is an individual who acts like the bank. They do the work to qualify the investor, draft the paperwork, and wire the money to closing.

What do they get in return? A lot better return than the stock market, typically 8 to 12 percent APR. Finding these guys can be easy; they're often listed in public records as the lender depending on the state you live in, but getting them to work with you can be the hard part. If you had a few million to lend on real estate projects (usually fix-and-flip or wholesales—see transactional funding below), wouldn't you want to make sure the investor has a verifiable track record and that the deal is a no-brainer?

Your number one asset when it comes to private money is your track record. Seasoned lenders are looking for people they can trust with their hundreds of thousands of dollars, and that trust comes with experience. So brand new investors usually must start with hard money until they have an impressive enough track record to woo the private money investors. Do a good job for long enough, and your private money guy will find more money for you to borrow. Once he thinks you are a sure thing, he will tell his other rich friends at the rich-guy club as well.

Typically, there are two kinds of private money lenders—those who want an APR like a hard money lender or bank and those who want a percentage split of the profit. APR guys are easy; they act just like the bank and want a certain APR percentage either paid monthly or rolled into the end of the loan (instead of monthly mortgage payments, it's all due when you sell). The equity-percentage-split investors are usually looking for more money out of the deal and want anywhere from 20 to 50 percent of your profit at the end of a flip. That's not a bad deal if you are starting out; the lender is putting up his own cash on a risky prospect. Fifty percent of something is better than 100 percent of nothing!

Where to Find It: The amazing thing about structuring financing in this business is how creative you can get with it. You can potentially borrow from anyone you know or meet who has extra money lying around, including those who have an SDIRA themselves and want to invest with you using that retirement account. Whether it's twenty people with $10,000 each or one guy with $200,000, you can structure a relationship to borrow their money for a set return. Let's talk about people you know who may lend you money, then we'll get into borrowing from those you don't know.

Who You Know: Tapping into the sphere of people you know can be powerful, whether a direct acquaintance or friend of a friend. Getting the word out to friends, family, co-workers, and neighbors about what you are doing and what you are looking for is step one. You might tell your Uncle Bob that you're analyzing properties to buy and sell for a profit and looking at funding options at 8 percent or perhaps offering equity share. You may have to start out with Uncle Bob as a fifty-fifty equity partner, but soon transition to typical 8 percent loans after you get a few under your belt.

Who You Don't Know: In this scenario, you will be soliciting people you don't know to lend their money to you in real estate deals. Sounds sketchy, but the people I solicit have already lent money for similar projects. In Colorado, the lender on a property is public record, so finding lenders is as easy as looking up these records. Going to ListSource.com can be like going to "Private-Lenders-R-Us"; pulling their information under "private party loans" is as easy as clicking a box. I might buy a list of the lenders who have lent in my areas in the last six months. I could then track them down and cold call them or send them marketing via direct mail. Both methods have yielded enough funds for my projects for the last few years. When cold calling, I open with a simple dialogue: "Hi, Bob! My name is Anson, and I see that you were the lender for a project on 123 Main Street. My company does similar projects, fix-and-flip investments, in this area, and I was wondering if you were looking for more investors to lend to."

I then talk about our track record and ask if I can email them our company investment package that has examples of projects we have done, lenders we have worked with, and a bio of me and my team.

When sending direct mail, I always use a professional letter stating something similar to the cold call script. I've put an example of my track record in this mailing piece before, and sometimes I'll simply ask them to call me so we can discuss it further.

Good places to find lists of private money lenders in your area include:
1. ListSource.com
2. Melissa Data
3. Click2Mail

No matter the approach you use to find them, these lenders will want to keep a relationship with those who are getting good deals on a regular basis. Why is that? If you had $1 million to lend, wouldn't you want to keep as much of that money lent out to get the best return possible throughout the year? The true deal-finders (all of us after reading this book) will keep private lenders extremely happy by putting their money into good deals all year long.

Pros: Much easier lending standards than bank or hard money, emphasis on good deals and track record rather than the credit of the borrower, ability to close quickly, based on relationship-building, more wiggle room to negotiate for no monthly payments or lower or no points

Cons: Track record needed, can be hard to find one to work with

Seller Financing

Who Uses It: Fix-and-Flippers, Buy-and-Holders, House Hackers, Developers, Wholesalers

What if the seller herself was the bank? If the seller has the equity and is comfortable with it, they can easily accept a down payment (or not in some cases) from you, followed by monthly payments. This is known as "seller financing" (aka "carrying the note), and let me tell you, it's real! Let's say a seller agrees to sell for $100,000, with a $7,500 down payment and an interest rate of 7.5 percent for twenty-five years. That would be a monthly payment of $720.52, and you wouldn't have to qualify through a bank or go raise private money. A typical investor might then rent out the property for $1,250 a month and cash flow quite well.

This type of loan is great for buy-and-hold investors who might later refinance the property into a conventional loan or a fix-and-flip investor who wants low monthly payments while they are fixing and selling the property. Instead of selling the property, making $200,000 and being taxed on it, he is getting monthly payments and turning his equity into a loan that's taxed much differently than a big lump sum all at once. This isn't assuming the loan or taking over the payments; this is used when the property is free and clear, and the seller is acting like the bank.

Where to Find It: Ask and you shall receive—or get outright rejected. Most seller-financed deals are negotiated for and structured with the owner of the property. Basically, it's on you, the investor, to propose and structure the deal directly with the homeowner. Sure, there are a few deals out there, even on the MLS, where the homeowner is advertising "seller will carry" or "seller-financed" terms, but that is the exception rather than the rule. Many investors who are actively looking for seller financing will present the homeowner with a few offers, say:

- $85,000 purchase price, investor is getting a hard or private money loan, thirty-day close, etc.

- $100,000 purchase price, down payment of $7,500, and monthly payments of $720.52 per month to the homeowner

Depending on the homeowner's situation, the second offer might look light-years better than the first, but you would never get a yes if you never asked for the seller financing option. As an added bonus, seller financing is oftentimes a great way for sellers to defer taxes on any gains they may have from selling you an appreciated property so it can be a good negotiation point.

Pros: Negotiable interest rate/down payment/term, no credit check or qualifying through a bank

Cons: Doesn't work for REOs or short sales, getting an uneducated seller on board with an out-of-the-box financing method can be difficult, seller usually wants a long-term loan since they are trying to avoid lump sum taxes

Subject To

Who Uses It: Fix-and-Flippers, Buy-and-Holders, House Hackers, Developers

Subject to is when you take over a seller's mortgage payment; you literally buy the property subject to the existing mortgage staying in place. Your name gets put on title as the rightful owner, but the seller's name is still on the loan and they are trusting you to pay it each month. This can be great if the seller has a great interest rate and you inherit the low payment.

Many times, a seller will agree to this scenario if they are upside-down on equity in the home. This allows them to walk away from the property without having to sell it at a loss. Most investors who use this will rent out the property; if you have a payment of $750 a month and can rent the property for $1,250 or so, you pay the mortgage each month and pocket the difference. It can be even harder to achieve than a seller financing situation, but if you listen to the BiggerPockets Podcast or network in your area, you will find people are using this strategy every single day.

Where to Find It: This is very similar to seller financing above, but much trickier. Not only do you have to negotiate this with the homeowner and structure it like the above, but you have to be prepared for objections and an uphill battle convincing the seller. Be ready for objections like, "What happens if you get hit by a bus and can't pay my loan anymore?" and thirty more. Get a homeowner to agree to subject to by negotiating masterfully and framing your offer as a win-win scenario. You'll want to continue learning how to ask, how to structure, and most importantly, how to overcome the seller's objections.

Pros: Ability to get locked into a good interest rate, allows a seller to walk away, no credit check or qualifying through a bank, usually no down payment

Cons: "Due on sale" clause gives the bank the right to demand the entire loan paid off if the property changes hands without loan paid off (however, the bank rarely executes the due on sale clause; still, it can be difficult to sell this concept to a seller)

Lease Options

Who Uses It: Buy-and-Holders

I'm stepping into something whose scope that could be its own entire book. Lease options can get complicated, and there are a hundred ways to do a lease option, but I'll keep it simple. A lease option is where you work out a deal with a seller to lease their home (rent), with an exclusive option to buy the property at any time during the term. Most of the time, you work out the term and the future purchase price with the seller. Maybe it's $750 a month rent payment, with the option to buy it for $100,000 in two years—or anytime in that two years, whenever you are ready. They cannot sell the property to anyone else during this time, and they are required to give you first rights to buy it. Another way to say this—and another way to structure a lease option—is "rent-to-own," which might sound more familiar to the average seller than "lease option."

An investor might take on a lease option from a seller because the seller might be more comfortable with this scenario or maybe the investor is having a hard time getting financing. You might lease option a property from Bob, then put a tenant, John, in it. Maybe as the investor, you do another lease option with John (who might have a hard time getting bank financing for now, but is working on his credit), which would make the agreement called a double lease option or wrap deal. I told you, it gets complicated. Your lease payment from Bob is $750, and the purchase price is $100,000 in two years. You rent it to John for $1,000 a month with a down payment of $5,000 and a purchase price of $130,000 in two years. If John pays you the down payment, then the rent for two years and then buys at $130,000, you will have made $5,000 today, $300 a month in rent payments (for twenty-four months, or $7,200), and then $30,000 when he buys it!

When John is ready, you can close with Bob, then with John—and everyone gets what they want out of the situation. If John decides to not execute this option and wants to move across the country, you keep his down payment and then find another tenant to lease or lease option the property. Like I said, it's complex, and this is just one way you can do a lease option. Also note that you will want to know all your state's laws regarding lease options before pursuing this option.

Where to Find It: This is yet another strategy where you'll need to convince the owner to do it. You will also need to negotiate and structure this with the seller directly.

Pros: No qualifying and no loan necessary, ability to have negotiable payment/down payment and terms

Cons: A hard sell to sellers, advanced strategy, requires expert knowledge

Transactional Funding

Who Uses It: Wholesalers

Need money, but only for a day? You could either be a serial gambler down at the horse track or maybe a double-closing wholesaler. The solution is called transactional funding, or "flash" cash. A transactional funder is a rich guy, a fund, or a wealthy aunt who is willing to fund your wholesale at the closing table, while your new buyer wires in the funds for his side of the closing.

You close with the seller, and your buyer closes with you. When you absolutely have to bring your own funding to the table, flash cash transactional funding guys can help you out. You typically sign a deed and promissory note to pay back the money at the next closing, within twenty-four to forty-eight hours. They want to see all the contracts in the transaction (one between you and the seller and the contract between you and the new buyer). They wire in the money and are paid when you walk into the next room to close with your investor-buyer. Typically, they charge 1 to 3 percent of the deal, or one to three points. On a $100,000 loan, that would be $1,000 to 3,000 in lender fees. If you are making $10,000 on a wholesale deal, it's well worth it.

Where to Find It: Many hard money lenders also do transactional funding, so asking them is a good start. From there, get referrals from other investors. This is a relatively low-risk lending scenario. If you have the property under contract and are also under contract with your investor-buyer, many investors will likely step up and lend you the money for a day. Once, when looking for a good transactional lender, the investor I asked for a referral ended up simply letting me use his money. You never know unless you ask.

Pros: Lender cares about the contracts and the deal but not about your credit, easy to obtain, easy to execute, has a quick close, keeps deals separate with two closings

Cons: Three percent is high, two closings means twice as expensive

Partnerships

Who Uses It: Fix-and-Flippers, Buy-and-Holders, House Hackers, Developers, Owner-Occupants, Wholesalers

Why are we talking about partnerships in a chapter about financing? Well, sometimes you have the deal but no money, and you meet someone with money and no deals. You're like a Disney match made in heaven, ready to live happily ever after. I found it a good way to line up funding for my first flip deal. At a Starbucks on 32nd and Lowell in Denver, we struck a deal: He would fund it and do the work, while I would bring the deal all locked up and ready to go, evaluate the ARV, and sell it when completed (more on this deal at the end of this chapter). Thirty-three percent of a $44,000 profit is better than nothing, right? Partnerships are complementary; each has something the other party lacks. Leveraging partnerships can be a great way to finance deals; a quick Starbucks meeting might be all it takes to lock up funding for your next deal.

Where to Find It: A partnership is born out of luck and opportunity. Most partnerships I've experienced and witnessed have formed due to being in the right place at the right time, networking, and getting to know the right people in the right circumstances.

You might be an expert deal-getter but have bad credit. Could you find a bankable partner who has no time to find deals but still wants to invest? Directly soliciting partners online or otherwise is a low-return endeavor, like meeting your perfect spouse. Think of it as more of a courtship with people you know already who could become your partner. Until they release a Tinder-style app for partnerships, you'll need to form relationships with people you meet and network with. What do you bring to the table? What do you need to get to the next level? Do they provide that? Do they need what you are offering?

Pros: Ability to leverage relationships is limitless, partners don't often care about credit and down payments.

Cons: Can sour over time, possibility of giving up equity in or percentage of deals.

Crowdfunding

Who Uses It: Fix-and-Flippers, Developers, Some Buy-and-Holders

Is borrowing a large sum of money from a bunch of strangers your preferred strategy? Thanks to the power of the Internet, you can now do just that. Crowdfunding is the practice of pooling funds from a large group of people who donate various amounts of money. General crowdfunding online platforms have been around for a little while, funding small loans to people who might need them for a car repair or to get to the next pay period. Now there are many more options to borrow money for real estate investments. Within the last few years, 125 (or more) real estate crowdfunding sites popped up. With rates ranging from 4 percent to 36 percent, crowdfunding varies from fantastic to not so great. It's up to you to find the one that meets your property funding needs. For now at least, the backend lenders of these crowdfunding sites need to be accredited investors, which means they are verified to make $200,000 a year plus reserves. This group is more or less millionaires. The Securities and Exchange Commission governs who can lend to these types of funding sites and who cannot. I expect in the next year or two, the average Joe could lend to these sites just like only accredited investors can today.

Where to Find It: An online search should bring up many of these. Every company and service is different—some only do commercial real estate loans—so it's up to you to do your homework and figure out what will work best for your company. A list of operating crowdfunding sites is available at www.biggerpockets.com/rei/crowdfunding-real-estate/.

Pros: Loans secured by the property, quick funding on some sites, underwriting process for the loan/property not as strict as conventional financing

Cons: Long verification process to get signed up and projects submitted; can take thirty days to get commitment to fund; monthly payments, track record, and credit checks required

Summing It Up

As you can tell, there are many different ways to fund your real estate deals. Why do I spend so much time talking about funding in a book about finding deals? The type and quality of funding that you have will directly impact deal analysis, figuring out your MAO, and negotiating with the seller. The better your funding terms are, the more deals you will get.

Take, for instance, Mary, whose private money lender will loan her money at 12 percent, no points and no payments, and will fund 100 percent of the purchase and repairs on her deals. Oh, and her funding can close in three to five days. Then take Jim, who walks into his local mega-bank and gets a conventional loan lined up. The interest rate is good at 5 percent, but he has to put 20 percent down on the loan and come out-of-pocket for the repair money. Conventional loans need an appraisal and have to go through the bank's underwriting, which makes closing at thirty days.

Mary and Jim are both marketing for distressed homeowners, and they both get a call from Bob, who got their letters and wants to make a deal. Bob is in a pickle and needs to sell his house fast; he has a foreclosure date in two weeks. Jim offers $100,000, with a contingency for the appraisal and loan conditions. He can close in thirty days. Mary offers $100,000, with no contingencies—and she can close in a week. Because of funding restrictions, Jim will lose out on deals like this. The terms necessitated by Jim's money do not work well for Bob. Mary would easily get this deal over Jim since she can solve Bob's issues. With the foreclosure coming up, Bob needs cash sooner than later, and he wants this property sold before it goes to auction.

Mary could easily do five deals more than Jim at any given time since her funding allows for close to no money out-of-pocket. Jim demands 20 percent down and the entire repair budget out-of-pocket. If Mary lined up the funding, she could do a hundred deals to Jim's one. That's the power of OPM and leverage.

Let's say that Bob doesn't have a foreclosure date coming and is an absentee landlord—or maybe he inherited the house. Many sellers want ease of transaction. Appraisals, loan conditions, and long closing timelines are anathema to solving the seller's problems quickly and easily. If Bob called Jim alone to check out his house, Jim's conditions and thirty-day close wouldn't be a big deal because that's how real estate normally works. It's when Bob looks at Mary's and Jim's offers together that it's obvious which is better.

That doesn't mean there is no place for conventional financing in real estate investing. Many investors use it and do just fine. For some investors, the thought of paying 12 percent is insane, so maybe they would rather go with bank financing.

Funding goes hand in hand with evaluating your deal, turning slim deals into great deals and home runs into duds. Unless you are paying cash for everything, the numbers you plug into your MAO equation will always have financing costs and will absolutely affect your deal. Having multiple funding sources lined up never hurts and gives you more options when you go to evaluate deals.

Here are a few examples using the fixed cost method as opposed to the 70 percent rule. In this example, you are a fix-and-flip investor.

The house you're evaluating has an ARV of $250,000 and repairs estimated at $40,000. Your financing holding costs will accrue for three months—two for repairs and one to sell the property. Your exit closing costs (fixed) are the same for each property:

$12,500—Agent fees

$2,000—Closing costs

$1,250—Miscellaneous holding costs like insurance/utilities

= $15,750 Total exit costs, no matter the financing

The seller throws out a price of $160,000. Your financing costs are based on his initial price of $160,000; if you are borrowing the repair money as well, add purchase plus repairs. Let's see if we are in the ballpark!

Private money lender: 15% APR, no points, 100% funding of purchase price and repairs

$250,000 (ARV) – $40,000 (repairs) – $15,750 (exit costs) – $25,000 (desired profit) – $7,125 (financing costs) = MAO $162,125

You have some room between the seller's initial ballpark price and your MAO. Every dollar you negotiate below your MAO goes right into your profit.

Conventional financing: megabank, 5% APR, 2.5% closing cost points, 20% down payment, repair costs out-of-pocket

$250,000 – $40,000 – $15,750 – $25,000 – $1,500 (financing costs) – $3,000 (2.5% closing cost points) = MAO $164,750

Again, you have room between your seller's ballpark price and your MAO. The difference here is the amount of money you have to pay out-of-pocket is $73,000 because of a $30,000 down payment, $40,000 for repairs, and $3,000 for those 2.5 percent closing cost points.

Hard money: 13% APR, 4 points, 10% down payment for purchase plus repairs

$250,000 – $40,000 – $15,750 – $25,000 – $5557.50 (financing costs) – 6,840 (points) = MAO $156,852.50

Ouch. Your money is so hard that your MAO is below your seller's ballpark price. You could, of course, negotiate your way into a deal at this point if you get him down to $155,000 or so. And remember, you have to bring $19,000 out-of-pocket for the lender's 10 percent down payment.

Subject to: $750 monthly payments, repairs out-of-pocket

$250,000 – $40,000 – $15,750 – $25,000 – $2,250 (financing costs) = MAO $167,000

You convince them to let you take over their loan payments; maybe they were at a breakeven price between their loan and the value of the property at $150,000 or so. Here, you do have to come out-of-pocket for the repairs of $40,000, but your financing costs are extremely low because you only have to make the existing loan payment for three months.

Partnership: you find the deal, the partner puts up the money, you split profit 50/50

$250,000 – $40,000 – $15,750 – $40,000 (desired profit) = MAO $154,250

Because you are splitting the profit, your minimum profit needs to be $40,000 instead of $25,000 like in the other examples. Like in the hard money example, you aren't too far from the seller's ballpark number. To get him under $160,000, you negotiate a bit. Your split is only $20,000 in this example, whereas the minimum desired profit was $25,000 in the other examples. But that's okay. You don't have to factor in the financing; that's your partner's contribution.

SDIRA: company charges $295 for the transaction paperwork, interest-free loan

$250,000 – $40,000 – $15,750 – $25,000 – $295 (SDIRA transaction fee) = MAO $168,955.

There's lots of room to breathe here—and $25,000 to put back in your tax-deferred SDIRA.

Transactional funding: you decide to wholesale this property to a fix-and-flip investor instead of fixing it up yourself

$250,000 – $40,000 – $15,750 – $5,000 (estimated loan costs for your buyer) – $25,000 (estimated profit for your buyer) – $10,000 (wholesale profit) – $3,000 (transactional funding costs) = MAO $151,250

Transactional funding is 2%. Wholesalers must find deals at better prices than the average investor, as shown by this example. To try to sell this property to another investor for $161,250, you will have to negotiate from the seller's ballpark price of $160,000 in order to make your desired $10,000 profit.

Cash: cold, hard cash

$250,000 – $40,000 – $15,750 – $25,000 = MAO $169,250

Now you know why a cash buyer can sometimes beat you out even if you are working from the same ARV, repairs, and closing cost numbers. Without any financing costs, the cash buyer can pay a little more and still make the same $25,000.

These rough numbers show you how different financing types can affect the deal with the same seller. Bob doesn't care about your numbers; he cares about your offer price and terms. It's up to you to go out and find funding sources appropriate for the type of real estate investing you are doing and to know the deal analysis math backwards and forwards.

Case Study—Partnering as a funding method

Type of Deal—REO
Investment Type—Fix-and-Flip

I see partnerships as a great way to find money and do deals, especially for newer investors. When I started out, I was stuck since I couldn't get a bank loan, and I didn't even know what hard money was. I was getting good at finding and evaluating deals, but never jumped into the pool, afraid that I had no way to fund them. I complained about this to an agent friend of mine over coffee, specifically about an REO deal that I just found.

I had a deal but no money. It turned out he had some money after selling his house, but no deals. He also had the contracting and fix-up experience to go along with it. Right there, we formed a partnership that would allow me to fund this deal, gain fix-and-flip experience, and get paid. We closed on the property I'd found, he funded it and did most of the repairs, and I sold it. This was perfect for my very first fix-and-flip since I didn't have cash and was not bankable. I didn't have to take on all the risk, and two heads are better than one when it comes to evaluating ARV, repairs, and everything in between. Since then, he and I have become good friends. We've worked together on a half dozen deals and still find excuses to keep working together.

CHAPTER 8:
Negotiation

"Two little mice fell in a bucket of cream. The first mouse quickly gave up and drowned. The second mouse, wouldn't quit. He struggled so hard that eventually he churned that cream into butter and crawled out."

—*Catch Me If You Can*, 2002

So far, my investor friend, you've created a deal-getting plan and perhaps even come up with a direct mail marketing plan targeting motivated sellers. Finding your initial target neighborhoods, baselining subdivisions, and evaluating your market has left you tired from staying up late. You put 1,000 miles on your car, driving your new target areas, and you found a good list of driving-for-dollars properties. Now your hand is cramped from writing letters and you have nightmares where you cannot get the taste of stamp glue out of your mouth. You've started to get an idea on typical repairs, paying a contractor to walk through some sample properties and taking notes furiously. To sharpen your skills, you have scoured through a hundred properties in the area and found good high and low comps for properties you are targeting.

Then the phone rings. It's a seller. A real, live human being who is motivated to sell, right on the other end of the telephone. Now what? Your palms are sweating and your tongue weighs a hundred pounds in your dry mouth.

You aren't alone. Many investors I talk to laugh about their first dozen or so calls. The phone rings and you freeze. *Now what?* One investor told me she even threw her cell phone across the room the first time a potential seller called in. Fear of the unknown, of rejection, and maybe even of landing a first deal is powerful. Now the real work begins. While you may not realize it, negotiation started before you even picked up the phone. Now that you have them on the line, everything you say will dictate your future relationship and your potential to get the deal. No wonder you're nervous!

You might be a natural negotiator—a phone expert, a people master who loves the subtle art of building rapport. Then again, you might be an introvert who dreads the back and forth interaction that comes with haggling, negotiating a car or—gasp—buying a house. While the natural negotiator will initially have an easier time, I think with some experience and motivation, both personalities can do well in this business. The same principles work when negotiating bigger items as when haggling for small things. You are either selling them on yes, or they are selling you on no. Most of the same basic pillars of negotiation apply.

This chapter covers the process from the first contact with a seller, agent, or bank to negotiating the price you need on a property (and renegotiating if issues arise) to getting the deal to the closing table. All that planning, market research, marketing, networking, repair estimating and valuation don't matter if you can't negotiate the price you need for the property and close it. Let me say that again. Everything in this book so far does not matter one bit if you can't get across the finish line and get paid. Each strategy, from MLS properties listed with agents to bank-owned foreclosures, needs a unique approach, and that is what you will find here.

Let's go through some of the basic foundations of negotiating that apply to all situations we find ourselves in—real estate and beyond.

Getting Over Fear of Rejection

"No." Nobody likes to hear this little two-letter word. It might be the most powerful word in the English language. "No, you cannot have that raise." "No, I will not partner with you on this deal." No has an entire negative psychology attached to it, and we are always finding ways to soften its delivery so as not to offend. Hearing no may affect the way you approach similar situations in the future. To learn resilience in the face of rejection, there are two basic strategies—getting to no and getting to yes.

Getting to No

Go out in the world and get to ten nos as fast as possible. The more you hear no, the more you get used to hearing it. When I started out in real estate, I was knocking on doors of pre-foreclosure properties. My first day involved forty-five nos—and not all nos are created equal. There was the no followed by the door slam, the no followed by a threat to beat me up, and, of course, the no followed by a threat to call the cops. The more you get used to rejection, the less emotionally attached you get to the word. It's just business; you aren't being held over a cliff by your toenails, your family is not in jeopardy, and your life is not on the line. If someone says no to you in real estate, you move on to the next deal.

Getting to Yes

Honing your skills and getting yesses builds up momentum. The more you win, the better you get. The better you get, the more you win. As they say, success begets success. Getting over your fear of rejection is key, and that means hearing no enough times to where its impact no longer affects you—and hearing yes enough to build confidence in your abilities and start making money in this business. The more you get yes out of a seller, the more you internalize what worked in this or that situation, and your brain figures out how to apply that to the next situation. The experience of enough nos leads to an eventual yes, and the more yesses you hear, the more you will begin to get.

Win-win

The end goal of a negotiation isn't for you to win, but for everyone involved to win. You might think, "I'm here to learn how to get great deals, close them, and get paid. That's what it means to win." Everyone I know in this business eventually recognizes that to have success with longevity, everyone needs to win. You aren't trying to swindle or pull one over on the seller; you are trying to help them. A perfect real estate deal is a win-win deal, where the seller gets the help they need, and you walk away with a deal. When you get to yes, you should feel confident that everyone is walking away satisfied. If you do right by people, it always comes back to repay you.

There is a saying in real estate: The goal isn't to make money; it's to solve problems. If you can solve problems, money will never be an issue for you again. Win-win scenarios will get you paid, both monetarily and in less tangible ways. You might be able to pull one over on a seller a few times, but it always will come back to bite you. Online reviews, BBB reviews—and even worse, lawyers—will eventually haunt you. You might be able to obfuscate numbers on a deal, but your reputation will get thrashed in the process. Creating win-win situations is a long-term investment in your future, your business, and your reputation.

Listen More Than You Speak

When you think of an expert negotiator, you might envision a slick guy in a nice suit jabber-jawing incessantly with overpowering speech at a mile a minute. You would be wrong. The best negotiators listen more than they talk. Sure, their speech might be persuasive and carefully worded, but it's strategically placed in the flow of conversation. Think of the 80/20 rule, where 20 percent of your efforts account for 80 percent of your successes. When talking to a seller, this rings true. Aim for that 20 percent, and let the other party do 80 percent of the talking. There is an old saying that states, "He who names the price first loses." In most negotiations, there is a "meet in the middle" or "split the difference" mentality. It's a compromise between two given prices, and your job is to define where that middle line should be. People don't usually want to give away more than they have to or give less than they get, so they try to meet somewhere in the middle.

Two quick examples:

1. Mary is negotiating with Bob for the purchase of his house, which is off market. Her MAO is $180,000 based on comps and the current condition. Bob needs to get $150,000 for his house to pay off his ex-wife as part of a divorce. If Mary goes ahead and says, "I can pay $180,000 for your house," Bob will absolutely be elated. He might even try to get her up more by saying, "Well, I was hoping for $200,000. Would you meet me in the middle at $190,000?" Mary just lost by naming a price first. If she lets Bob speak first or asks Bob, "What would you take for the house, as-is?" or the bold "What is the lowest price you will take for the house as-is?" it puts Bob on the hook to talk first. His mind will race, knowing he needs the $150,000. He might say, "Well, to pay

off my ex-wife and move on with my life, I need $165,000." Bob thinks the extra $15,000 bonus is nice; he could go to Reno for a week and have a bunch of money left over. Now Mary is the elated one and has the power to meet in the middle or compromise a little with the seller, saying, "That might work. Would you take $160,000 if we close in two weeks?" Bob agrees, and he gets $10,000 more than he thought, and Mary gets a property below her MAO. Win-win. When Mary speaks first, it gives away her negotiation position, and the price she states will now define the rest of the negotiation. She might think that shooting straight with the seller and starting off with her MAO price is a good idea, but it's not. After that, Bob has zero incentive to go lower than the price Mary just offered him, even if he would have taken $150,001 for the property.

2. Mary is negotiating with Joe for the purchase of his house, which is already listed on the MLS. "Already listed" is a different beast since the seller has already raised their hand to sell and has a price in mind. It is listed for $200,000, and Mary's MAO is $180,000. If Mary comes in with an offer at $180,000, which is where she wants to be, Joe might want to meet in the middle, at $190,000. If Mary comes in with an offer of $150,000, however, then as long as the low number does not offend Joe, he will naturally counter at $175,000 to split the difference. That's a decent compromise for Joe; he just raised her offer by $25,000. Mary can now take the $175,000, which is below her MAO. Everyone is happy, all from simply re-defining the middle line and Mary appearing to give away $25,000 and compromising by meeting Joe halfway. Mary could then re-define the middle by countering, "Well, $175,000 is a bit more than I'd like to pay for the property in its current condition. Could you do $165,000?" Now Joe will likely want to meet in the middle again and agree to $170,000.

This works on so many levels. It's human nature to seek out a give-and-take, meet-in-the-middle compromise. If Mary was to offer Joe $180,000 and he were to say, "Yep, let's sign that right now," she would immediately feel like she was leaving money on the table. It might feel wrong if the negotiation was too easy—but remember, if the price works within your MAO and your business plan, you don't need to feel bad. With more experience, you can work at not leaving money on the table. Let the other party speak more than you do and name a price first.

Two more reasons to let the other party speak more than you do:

1. You will find out much more information. I learned from a bartending job years ago that I love hearing people's stories—and people love an attentive listener. I always ask about family, point out pictures on the walls, and let people ramble on with stories about this or that. Not only does this go a long way in building rapport and trust, but people let vital information slip all the time. Bob might be talking to Mary and say something like, "The judge is making me sell for $150,000 to pay off my ex-wife. Can you believe that? I just want to move on as quickly as possible and get out of town." By listening intently, Mary learns two very vital facts about Bob: first, $150,000 is his lowest price, and second, he needs to sell quickly. Bob might not even realize how much he gave away in that conversation. Now Mary could come in at $150,000 or $160,000 with a quick close and know with good certainty that Bob would take that deal. I've heard sellers give away the farm from normal conversation. If you have built up rapport and trust with the seller, they may feel they can tell you nearly anything. You will hear the dirt on the family, who the holdout in a probate situation is, how much the estate needs to get, the payoff of the mortgage, how much the bank needs to clear before foreclosure, etc. Be a good listener; it literally pays off in the end.

2. Don't be afraid to use silence. Get comfortable with the uncomfortable. Most people inherently despise silence and will scramble to fill in any gaps of perceived awkwardness. They will start telling more stories or giving away more information just to keep the flow going. A good negotiator uses silence like a sharp sword, letting the other party fall on it. If Mary is smart, she lets Bob name a price first by staying nearly silent. Her slight disappointed look wreaks havoc on Bob's mind, which expects a socially acceptable back and forth. To appease Mary, compromise, or just fill the silent gap, he might say, "Well, I'd like to get $165,000, but I could probably take $160,000 or $155,000 at the lowest." Without saying a word, Mary gets Bob to negotiate against himself. Don't just stand there like some weirdo creeper; learn to use silence, along with body language and facial expression, to

your advantage.

Being an active listener will help you negotiate better and understand what is truly needed in the situation.

No Is Not the End

It's easy to tell yourself that it doesn't matter if a seller rejects you outright, but it's harder to get your feelings on board. The more you hear no, the easier it gets—but only if you use it to better your negotiation skills in the long-term. What could you have done differently? Was it something you said? Something you didn't say? In all honesty, you could do everything right and still get a big, fat no. When you spend time, effort, energy, and money to get leads in the door, each no might represent $150 expended just to get to that point. Some things you can't control, no matter how hard you try. Just remember: Next week, it will not matter that Bob the seller said no to you. If you are consistently marketing, by then, you'll be talking to Jim, then Sally, then Suzi, and on it goes. Maybe you get told no eight times—but you still get up and learn from those eight times when you go on the ninth appointment. You simply have to leave emotions out of the process.

Two keys here: Be detached from the outcome, and always be willing to walk away. You should separate yourself from the situation and imagine you are seeing this back and forth negotiation as a third-party observer, someone detached from the outcome. There are no hurt feelings, embarrassment, or awkward endings in this view. If a seller gets angry, threatens to call the FBI on you, slams the door in your face, or calls you a lowlife scum who preys on the weak, do not take it personally. This is a life lesson: Don't take anything personally. You never know what someone has on his or her plate.

- Be detached from the outcome. You don't need this seller since your marketing or networking is bringing in ten more this month. It's empowering to know this and use it to your advantage. The cool, collected negotiator who is detached from the outcome will win more than the emotional, heated negotiator who *needs* this deal to pay the bills next month. The desperate negotiator nearly always loses. People can sense desperation a mile away. You might *actually* need this deal to go through or your car payment will be late, but the seller can't know this on any level. Fake it until you make it, stay detached, and keep knee-jerk reactions out of it.

- Always be willing to walk away. If you can walk away at any time, you hold the power. The seller who is truly motivated and needs a solution to their problem is the desperate negotiator in this scenario. If you need to walk away in the middle of a negotiation because a stubborn seller can't get down to your price, then just walk! If you have tried everything in the book, every solution you can come up with, and they are still unrealistic, you can't help them, and it's time to spend your time on leads that will turn into deals. Walk away politely by saying, "Sounds like we are just too far apart for this to work for my company. I'd love to help, but it looks like we should remain friends and part ways for now." They will likely call you the next day, motivated with the price or concessions you need. Try this next time you are haggling for a bargain on a car. The price does not work and the other party is dug in? Just say, "Thanks for your time. I'd love to make this work, but it seems like we are too far apart on price (or terms)." Turn around and whistle as you calmly go on with your day. Watch as the sales manager runs out to the parking lot before you get into your car. They are now operating out of desperation, watching the sale they thought they had slip through their fingers. The car salesman already mentally bought something with the commission provided by the sale, just like the seller has already thought of all the things they could do with the proceeds from the sale of the house. The effect is powerful.

Build Rapport

I saved the best for last. This is Social Skills 101, and it boils down to getting to know people. While you do want to remain emotionally detached from the deal itself, building rapport does mean genuinely getting to know the seller, which involves getting personal. A seller whom you have built genuine rapport with will sell to you over a higher offer placed by someone they don't know.

There is no checklist or series of questions to cover when building rapport; it involves a natural flow of conversation. People sense disingenuous people. I could title this section "be a good person and listen to others," but that might be above my pay grade. Break the ice, ask questions about family, and find common interests and hobbies. Maybe you grew up in the same town, perhaps their grandson is the same age as your daughter, and they may follow the same football team that you do, I usually don't start off with anything about the property. I ask them how their week was, comment about pictures on the wall, ask about their kids and what they are into, etc. A sincere, genuinely interested person, ready to solve the problem at hand will get the deal. I've met insincere, smarmy, slick, disconnected buyers before, and they are just not pleasant to work with. A seller can tell who is there just for the house and who is there to genuinely help.

This strategy, of course, works with others that you network with, including agents, probate attorneys, the lady at the pro desk at Home Depot, title company reps, and pretty much everyone else. You are the ambassador for your brand, and everyone wants to work with a genuine professional. The guy who asks you about your kids and remembers details from the last conversation will stand out. I remember when someone texted me a week after I mentioned my son's surgery to see how recovery was. "What a nice gesture," I thought to myself. That guy will get my business every time.

While a lot of this comes naturally, if you consciously work to build rapport, your business will be much better off. You can systematize some of this—put birthdays in your calendar, make notes next to your seller's name about kids/hobbies/interests/favorite team, and jot in your to-do list to follow up with Jim about his wife's knee replacement surgery. Go the extra mile in these interactions, and it will repay you a thousand-fold.

The conversation should be 80 percent about them—and very little about you. If you go on and on about how good you are at this business, the seller won't feel a connection. Instead, get them to open up, answer their questions, and let them know you are there to solve their problems.

- What are *their* concerns?
- What are *their* fears?
- What do *they* need?
- What do *they* want?

Playing Telephone

No, this isn't the game you played in kindergarten where your class sat in a circle and whispered a phrase from person to person until it distorted into "the Iguana should be named Zoltar." Instead, let's talk about the first time you talk to a seller on the phone, including what to ask and how to set expectations. Instead of throwing your cell phone across the room in fear, pick it up and do these things:

- Introduce yourself and begin to build rapport
- Ask why they are thinking about selling/coax out motivation
- Ask about the property using a checklist
- Explain your company and your process
- Broach price expectations

Introduce and Build Rapport

Introduce yourself, thank them for calling you, and ask them how they are doing. I ask their full name (and look it up on tax records or my mailing list to make sure I'm talking to the owner/decision maker) and write it down on my property information sheet. I usually ask for the best number to reach them in case we get disconnected.

Learn Their Motivation for Selling

I usually start off with, "What can I help you with today?" and let them talk. Let them tell you the situation—what is going on, who died, etc.

- How long have they owned the house?
- Are they living in it now (owner-occupant vs. absentee owner)?
- Are they currently listed with an agent? If so, for how long?
- How much is owed or is they property owned free and clear?
- How quickly would they like to sell?
- Do you have any other properties you are trying to sell?

Ask about the property with a checklist. It sounds robotic to work off a list, but you'll learn to intersperse the points organically during the conversation. Best of all, it keeps you on track to get all the information needed.

- Number of bedrooms and bathrooms
- Style of home and construction

- Age of home

- Square footage

- Presence of garage or carport

- Basement/crawl space/slab

- Date when kitchen and bathrooms were last updated

- Flooring types

- Ages and type of roof

- Ages and type of furnace/HVAC

- Ages and type of windows

- Repairs needed

After you have gone through your checklist, you will have a much better idea of what is going on at the property, assuming the seller is being honest with you. I don't ask simple questions that can be quickly looked up on tax records, like bed/bath/square footage/year built. I will usually confirm these numbers with the seller, since sometimes tax records can be a little out of date and won't list additional bedrooms added in the basement ten years ago, for example. I try to stick with the situation and condition of the property; the rest can be quickly looked up or confirmed without bogging down the conversation. Then, with a price per square foot or baseline repair method, you should be able to estimate repairs, which will help when determining a ballpark price expectation.

Explain Your Company and Process

You build trust with the seller when you communicate that you know what you're doing and can answer their questions or overcome their objections. Before I ask about price expectations, I aim to put the seller at ease and ask them if I can tell them a little about me, my company, and how the process works. "I've lived in Denver all my life and have been in real estate for ten years now. I work with sellers like you to help sell houses quickly, as-is." If I feel like I need to support this with numbers, I'll add, "I have helped over 100 sellers in the Denver area with their real estate issues."

Then, explain more about the process: "We start off by talking to the seller over the phone, like we are doing now, to get an idea of the seller's situation. I like to ask about the property to get a better notion of what is going on. That way, I can learn if you have remodeled the house, if an addition was built, or anything else you wouldn't know by looking at the property from the street. I then run numbers and get a better idea of value based on what other properties are selling for in your neighborhood. If we are in the same ballpark on value, I'd like to set an appointment with you to come visit and walk through the property so I can see the inside and estimate what it will cost to repair. After I have done the homework and been inside the property, I can tell you what my offer would be for the home. This will simply involve a phone call and a quick visit; I want to respect your time."

Broach Price Expectations

As a bright-eyed newbie, I would set an appointment with every person who called. Now I try to get an expectation of price from the caller to see if we are in the same ballpark. If we are, I will immediately set the appointment. If the seller's price is on Jupiter while mine is here on Earth, I will put them in my follow-up pipeline to keep mailing letters. If we aren't even in the ballpark, setting the appointment would be a waste of everyone's time. Still, their first number isn't always their true number, so it makes sense to try to flush out their actual price expectation. This is a skill to craft: Which sellers are just blowing smoke and giving you the Jupiter price to see if you will bite and which ones make sense to pursue harder? Here are some examples of questions you could ask to gauge price expectation:

- What are you looking to get for the house?
- How did you arrive at that number?
- Do you know what similar houses are selling for in the area?
- If I can pay cash and close quickly, what is the least you would be willing to take?
- What will you take for the property?
- What is the lowest you will go?
- What price will work for you?

Beware the seller who will not give you a price no matter how much you ask. Some sellers might say, "Just make me an offer," or "I'm just seeing what you will pay for it." Remember the quote, "He who names the price first loses"? This is a tiger trap laid out for you. Throwing a price out without seeing the property, finding out motivation, or having any hint on expectation of price will almost always work against you in negotiations. As an investor, you will likely err on the conservative side and give the seller a low price that might offend them and turn the negotiation against you. It's a lose/lose scenario.

Can't get a price out of the seller?

Seller: "Just make me an offer."

Investor: "I understand what you are saying, but without knowing what you are looking to get out of the house, I'm just shooting blind. I'm always extremely conservative without any baseline of what you are looking for, and I don't want to offend you by coming in very low trying to be conservative. When you go to the grocery store, everything has a price on it. When you go to the car dealership, the cars have prices on them. I'm sure you have a price in mind, so perhaps we can start with that."

Many sellers who call in due to direct marketing are very skeptical about a person or company that wants to buy their house. Is it a scam? Is this person for real? Breaking the ice by being personable goes a long way to set the initial tone of the entire conversation. They might call in irate about "these stupid letters you are sending me," but may calm down after a minute or two of pleasant conversation. For those who just won't back off, simply be polite and end the conversation.

Maybe you ask them, "What are you looking to get for the house?" over the phone and they come back with a ballpark of $175,000. Now what? If you're quick and in front of your computer, you might pull comps and tax records on the property in between asking questions and gathering information (make sure to not be too distracted). With experience, you'll be able to immediately tell if you and the seller are in the same ballpark and whether to set a face-to-face appointment to talk and see the property. If you are not experienced, ask them to let you run the numbers to see if it's a good fit. Then simply get back to them in a reasonable amount of time.

If the seller's ballpark of $175,000 makes sense to you based on comps and repairs needed, schedule a time and meet with the seller. The seller got an initial impression of you from your marketing, and you then solidified that view with your phone conversation. You have built some rapport and run your numbers—and now you are ready to lock up this deal, solve problems, and get paid!

Do:

- Meet with the decision-maker, the actual seller.

- Show up early.

- Dress nicely.

- Build more rapport.

- Bring contracts/paperwork/comparables.

- Tour the property, jotting down notable items on your repair checklist.

- Ask questions about the property. ("Looks like a drywall repair over there. Was there a leak?")

- Gather more information.

- Get down to business at the right time in the meeting.

Don't:

- Verbally bash the property. ("Oh, this roof is bad! This bathroom is pink? What were you thinking? This paint color is horrible! My blind grandma could have thrown a dart into the paint section of Lowe's and randomly hit a better color than you picked!")

- Be all business or eager to start talking numbers before the seller is ready.

- Be afraid that you may not know all the answers. Saying "let me find out and get back to you" is much better than giving the wrong answer.

Let's talk a little bit about attire before we move to face-to-face negotiation. Admittedly, I'm not the best with this. I run a business out of my house and love the freedom to wear shorts, a polo, some Adidas sneakers, and a baseball hat (usually with my company logo). I'm that guy who wears shorts in the dead of a Colorado winter. When I have time to change for a networking meetup, seller appointment, lender lunch, or something fancier, I make sure I throw on jeans and maybe an untucked dress shirt with the sleeves rolled up. Fancy, right? I make sure my jeans are clean, my shirt looks good, and my hat is neat and clean. I'll comb my beard before getting out of the car; I'm not a savage.

This works for me in my market. I don't wear slacks, formal dress shirts, ties, or suits, as I feel it throws people off more often than not. If you show up in a full slick suit driving a Mercedes in a working class neighborhood, you'll probably give the wrong impression to your Average Joe seller. I take this philosophy over to my real estate agent business as well; I find that many are tired of the flash of power suits and expensive cars. I have an older 4Runner, and it never intimidates anybody. Think about your area, the people in your target neighborhoods, and your target seller. What do they wear? In Hawaii, it's common to wear chino shorts and loud print, short-sleeve, button-up shirts. Wear that in Minnesota, and you're an outcast. Wear a Gucci suit while driving a Range Rover into an $80,000 neighborhood, and your seller may immediately resent you. The gist is to dress appropriately and look nice—but not too nice—in the eyes of your seller.

There is a neat social tool called mirroring that you can use to your advantage in these situations. Like a hawk, your subconscious is always scanning and analyzing people you interact with. You can tell by subtle clues that people are either comfortable or uncomfortable in a situation. If your normal selling style is making the seller uncomfortable, change it up. Try to match your seller's energy level, body language, words, and tone of voice. By mirroring your seller, you send the signal that you're to be trusted because you're just like them. When the seller folds their arms, mirror it. If they are an animated, loud talker, mirror those actions. Carefully watch to see how the seller likes to be sold—and cater to that innate desire.

Understand that it's not always about price alone. We may naturally assume that a seller only cares about the money they'll get from the property, but that isn't always the case. A great negotiator knows the motivating factors and how to solve the seller's problem. This means paying attention and crafting your offer in a way that meets their needs at the same time it meets yours.

The Price and the Terms

Price is, of course, the price you are willing to pay for the property. The terms are a much broader and more creative piece of an offer. Everything is negotiable in real estate. I've heard of investors throwing in an old car as part of the deal because the seller needed new transportation. Or the investor gives the seller an old cell phone because the seller needs one. You could even hire movers for the seller or buy a car the seller can't take with them. Most often, the seller's number one priority is not price alone; humans have a variety of needs based on the array of situations they find themselves in. As an investor, you may initially question why a seller would drop the house $5k in price in return for a $500 cell phone, but maybe that phone is the seller's immediate need.

Some common unexpected concessions that might solve the seller's problems and get you the deal include:

- Quick close. I can usually close in as soon as three days.

- Long close. The seller might need three months to move out.

- Rent back. The seller needs the money ASAP, but can't move out for a few months. We buy the property, and the seller rents it back from us for a few months. Make sure you have the right paperwork to protect you (lease agreement, etc.). This should be a short-term, month-or-two situation to avoid too much liability.

- Seller can leave anything they want. Some people dread giving away/throwing away big items like couches. We tell them they can leave whatever they want, and we will take care of it. We have bought entire hoarder houses with everything left inside. It might take seven dumpsters to clean it out, but we've solved their problem for them.

- Moving assistance. We provide a truck and a few guys to help them get to the next place. For the cost, it's a bargain for the buyer.

- Waive inspection. We use this more often with REO/bank owned foreclosures and hot listed properties. This means you cannot renegotiate or terminate based on your inspection findings. Sound risky? Often only pro investors can get away with this since they know what to look for during a walkthrough and can mitigate the risk through experience.

- Find a new place to live. I've helped sellers find a new, smaller place to live; sometimes they are tired of the maintenance on their current place and want to move into a condo across town. If you can solve this problem, they will sell for less with a win-win solution in front of them.

- Buying or getting rid of unwanted vehicles. The seller sometimes needs a car to move on with their life. I have a good friend who got the seller to come down $10,000 by throwing in his old Saturn four-door. The car was probably worth $2,500, but to the seller, it was gold.

- Ask the seller to carry the note. A common term in an investor's contract asks a seller with a lot of equity to seller finance the property, an agreement where the seller acts as the bank. They hold the debt on the deal, and you buy the property. You then pay them monthly instead of getting financing yourself.

Going above and beyond to help a seller will set you apart from your competition. Sellers may have unique problems that more cash won't solve, but those might be alleviated by an experienced investor. Leaving whatever they want behind is something I always offer; it might cost me $200 or so to get rid of those twenty items, but the peace of mind for the seller is worth $3,000 to $4,000 or so. Carefully listen for motivation and cues as to what's driving the seller to sell. If you have worked with another seller in a similar situation, try mentioning how you've helped in this type of situation in the past. It will drive home to the seller that you're a helper and will lend you more credibility.

Make Your Offer

After initial chitchat, a tour of the property, filling out your repair checklist, and building more rapport, you'll generally end up in conversation over the kitchen table or in the living room or driveway. Every deal I've done has occurred in one of those three places. The tour winds down, and the seller begins to look for the final say from the stranger they just took through their house. From here, it might make sense to re-iterate what was discussed over the phone—the general price expectations of the seller. The repairs might be more than initially thought, and you may have to negotiate the price down based on those repairs. It's time to present your offer to the seller, being crystal clear about its important pieces:

- Price
- Closing date
- Other concessions you're throwing in or need

I always bring contracts with me, just in case the seller is ready to move quickly. Your seller should never feel pressured into signing a contract; because of this; I keep my paperwork in the car or in a folder until it comes up. I also always bring comps—usually the three comps most like the property—as well as two or three of the lowest sold properties in the neighborhood from the last six months. Showing a seller exactly what other properties are selling for can get them on board with your price more easily.

"Jim, I like this house, and I want to help you. We talked on the phone about a ballpark price of $175,000, and I think we are close on price here. Walking through, I noticed a few more items than I initially thought that need to be fixed, but nothing we can't handle. Based on the comps for similar properties in this condition [show comps], I can offer you $165,000 for the house, as-is. Since I know you and your family took that new job in Washington and are moving next week, I'd like to offer to close in ten days. You can leave any items here for donation or disposal; we will take care of that so you can move on with your new adventure in Washington!"

By listening carefully, you can craft your offer to meet the needs of the seller. He will be much more willing to take $10,000 off the price if you are solving his pain points: wanting the money quickly, having a ton of junk to dispose of, and needing to move ten states away in a week. He is thinking about his new job and taking that drive to Washington next week in a U-Haul with his wife, two kids, and dogs. He is preoccupied by the thought of packing up this house, putting a deposit down on a house in Washington, turning utilities on at the new place, attending two weeks of training at the new job, etc. The house, at this point, is a huge burden, and by closing fast, you are absolutely solving his problems.

Break it down for them. I like to show sellers what the net price to them will be after concessions and closing costs. That way, there are no surprises. I also show them how much money they're saving in real estate commissions as compared to selling through an agent on the MLS. These savings usually stick in the seller's head; they would have had to pay *how* much to those agents?

- Make the offer about *them* and not *you*. Each important part of your offer should work to help solve their issue: "We can close in two weeks, which will help since you want to leave town," or "Take whatever you want and leave whatever you want thrown away or donated. We will take care of that so you don't have to move it all the way to Washington or scramble to figure it out before you leave." It shows you were listening the whole time and that you want to craft a win-win scenario.

- Receive your "yes" answer. You presented your offer, and it makes sense to the seller. Congratulations! It isn't always going to be this easy, but sometimes motivated sellers provide very smooth deals.

- Receive your "no" answer. Remember, no isn't the end. If they haven't told you to get off their property at gunpoint, assume there is room for countering. This includes figuring out what the seller wants and overcoming objections.

- Figure out what the seller wants. This might be as simple as learning something they haven't yet revealed about the situation. There might be a hidden motivation that your offer just did not touch. Figuring it out involves opening the can of worms even further with some questions: "Okay, it didn't sound like we were that far off on price or terms. Can you tell me what you were hoping to hear?" Or you might ask, "What didn't you like about the terms of the offer? Was the close date too soon? We can close when you are ready!"

- Overcome objections. Many times, common objections are based on a lack of understanding or need for clarification on the price, breakdown, or terms you are asking for.

A seller who comes up with objections to your offer is likely interested in your offer, and you likely aren't far off on price or terms. Maybe they simply have some fear, hesitation, or doubt to overcome.

When overcoming an objection, it helps to do the following:
- Acknowledge the objection. Always repeat it back to them or agree; this way, they know you are listening intently. Use phrases like, "I see what you are saying," "absolutely," and "I understand."

- Answer the objection. Have a good answer ready that explains exactly why the seller is mistaken. Make sure to do it very gently with some good counter-advice that makes sense to the average seller. They might have bought into a piece of advice from an agent or a know-it-all aunt. Remember that the average person buys a house every eight years. If I buy one to four houses a month, I have approximately 19,100 percent more experience. If they bought the house twenty to thirty years ago, they may have very little experience in this arena and may be ignorant on how things work.

When dealing with someone who is *not* the decision maker, consider stating the following:

Seller: "This sounds pretty good. I'd like to run it by my [dad/uncle/brother/sister/hamster] first, though."

Investor: "I totally understand. I want you to feel comfortable with the entire process! We would love to move forward quickly to help you as fast as possible, but understand the importance of running it by a trusted family member. I'm always here for any questions, and your [dad/uncle/brother/sister/hamster] can call me anytime."

Now let's look at some specific scenarios on overcoming objections in difficult situations.

Bankruptcy:

Seller: "I'm going to file bankruptcy instead."

Investor: "Bankruptcy can seem like the easiest way out, and I get that. Some people don't understand that bankruptcy can negatively impact your credit for years to come. This can prevent you from buying a car or house. Certain jobs will even withhold employment if you have a bankruptcy on your record."

Foreclosure:

Seller: "We are just going to let it go back to the bank."

Investor: "I understand why you'd be looking at that option; however, most people don't realize just how negatively that affects you for the next seven years. There might even be tax consequences. I've worked with homeowners for years in situations like yours, and I always advise to find a way to avoid foreclosure if at all possible. Thankfully, there are always options, and we try to make it very easy for the seller."

Short Sale:

Seller: "Short sales sound like way too much work. I'd rather not have to do that."

Investor: "Short sales are a lot of work, so I hear you there! Thankfully, my company has been doing short sales for ten years, and we have it down to a science. Yes, there is some effort on your part to get the paperwork the bank needs, such as financials, together. After that, we handle everything. We even have a team member whose sole job is to call the bank and make sure everything is going smoothly. After the paperwork from you, we handle the rest!"

List It:

Seller: "I think we will just list the property" or "I think we will try to list it again."

Investor: "I can see why you would go that route. You should decide if agents setting showings at all times of the day and evening, plus inspections, appraisals, and the buyer's financing are worth the headache. Agents can be great, but they will typically cost you 6 percent of the sales price, and the transaction can take a few months. Between the time on the market, your loan payoff, any repairs needed to sell to a buyer, and the agent costs, the costs required will be something you'll need to evaluate. If you sell as-is to us, there are no repairs, and we close quickly."

Rent It:

Seller: "I think I will just rent it out."

Investor: "Renting out the property can be a good idea if you know exactly what you are doing. Getting enough rent to cover the mortgage, taxes, insurance, and utilities is key, as is screening the renters with applications and credit checks so you aren't getting a deadbeat tenant. Renters also expect the owner to cover all repair costs and to have a move-in-ready place, which will require repairs up front. Even professional landlords I know complain about their renters; you have to have all of your ducks in a row for it to work."

Stay in My House:

Seller: "Can't you just buy it and let us rent it back from you?"

Investor: "I totally understand that moving isn't fun, and leaving your home is difficult. This sounds like a great option, but unfortunately, my company does not do this due to policy. It's simply too much liability. Most investors feel the same way, and some lenders who find you sold it and stayed in the property may have problems with the situation as well. Getting out from under this problem property will be a huge weight off your shoulders; believe me, I hear this all the time at closing."

Don't Trust You:

Seller: "How can I trust you?" or "How do I know this isn't a scam?" or "Aren't you just trying to steal my property?"

Investor: "I can see how having a stranger contact you about selling sets off red flags, but I can assure you that I do this for a living. We have helped over a hundred sellers in similar situations sell problem properties, and the testimonials on my website are 100 percent real. We want to find a win-win deal for you, and our number one goal is to help you through this process. I'll do everything I can to help you, just like I have with everyone I've worked with for the last ten years. Does that sound good?"

Attorney Review:

Seller: "It all looks fine, but I'll need my attorney to review this first."

Investor: "Absolutely! That is no problem whatsoever. I want you to feel very comfortable through this entire process and ensure you understand what is happening and what you are signing. I use a state-approved contract that goes through many reviews by the Department of Regulatory Agencies and the Real Estate Commission (as well as a bunch of lawyers), and I'm confident that your attorney will like what he/she sees."

Price (the most common objection):

Seller: "I was hoping to get more out of this property," or "Can't you pay more?" or "[Insert unrealistic price here] is my price to sell."

Investor: "I understand that you feel that your house is worth $200,000. I've looked up all the sales activity in your neighborhood and found these three comparable—apples to apples properties sold for $160,000, $155,000, and $165,000 in the last six months [show comps]. Factoring in the repair budget of $35,000 to sell at the top of the market [show repair budget], you'll see how we arrived at our offer price of $125,000. Our goal is to help you with the property, so you can get a fresh start and walk away from the house, and this is how we can make it a win-win sale."

If you are in this business long enough, you will hear all these examples and fifty more. The key is to address the concerns head on and let the seller know you hear them and are listening, then directly address their objection with a real-world explanation.

Techniques for Negotiating with Different Types of Sellers

Different sellers need different approaches to help them out of their unique situations. Here we will review some of the most common types of sellers, their motivation for selling, and how to negotiate with them so everyone comes away a winner.

Divorce

The obvious factors to a divorce sale are two adults who no longer want to live in the same house, where one party can't afford the house by themselves. Usually, one party calls you—let's just say the wife—and wants to sell. She still needs the signature of her soon-to-be-ex to sell, so you may feel less like an investor and more like a counselor going between the two parties to get everyone on board.

Sometimes a party will stall, stomp their feet, and throw tantrums to prolong the process. Negotiation here is simple—solve the problem, get the best price you can, and get both parties on board. One uncommon motivating factor here might be a court mandating the sale as part of the divorce decree. Basically, the judge says, "You have to sell for $200,000 so all parties can get paid and move on with their lives." If the court-mandated price is above your MAO, it is pretty much a dead deal. Negotiating with the court is like trying to knock down a brick wall with your skull.

Motivating Factors: Unwanted house that can't be afforded by one party alone, court order mandating sale, possible vacant property

Best Offer Terms: Quick or long close depending on the situation, rent-back if you are comfortable, seller can leave whatever they want

Bankruptcy

This opens a few cans of worms, and I don't want to get into legal advice territory here. Chapter 13 is a re-structuring of your debts, while Chapter 7 is a liquidation of the debts to pay the debtors. Either way, 7 or 13, it's going to add months to your timeline and your headache. Getting the sellers on board in talking to their attorney or trustee and going through the process of getting the court's permission to sell can be an uphill battle. The more you know about the bankruptcy process in your state, the better you will be able to negotiate and overcome objections. Knowledge is power, and having a good bankruptcy attorney on speed dial doesn't hurt either.

Motivating Factors: Need for a fresh start, can't afford the property anymore, court or trustee order mandating sale, possible vacant property

Best Offer Terms: Cash, quick close, helping with the bankruptcy process

Pre-foreclosure

I talked quite at length earlier in this book about folks in foreclosure. Negotiating with them is straight-forward. The more rapport and trust you've built, the better. Going from them not wanting to open your mail to their agreeing to a short sale can be a long process. Two big factors here include whether they have equity or not and the obvious time crunch before the foreclosure auction. A good investor who knows what she is doing can knock on the door of a pre-foreclosure on a Monday and buy the property on Thursday before the foreclosure auction on Friday. Knowing about your state's foreclosure timeline, laws, and redemption periods will go a long way in being able to help the seller. If there is equity, negotiate as normal. If there isn't equity, a short sale will be the best option for the seller.

Motivating Factors: Inability to afford the property, foreclosure sale scheduled zero to four months away, no longer making payments, possible vacant property

Best Offer Terms: Cash, quick close, help moving, short sale expertise, seller can leave whatever they want, knowledge of the foreclosure process

Bank Owned/REO

Ninety-nine percent of the time in the situation of an REO, you will be dealing with an agent who is listing the property. The good thing about negotiation here is that the party you are talking to has no emotional investment in the deal since the real decision maker is the asset manager at the bank. Sometimes you don't even talk to a person when submitting an offer; you just fill out a form online and upload your contracts. If you don't like people or emotions involved, this might be for you. Figure out your MAO, start under it, and let the bank come up to meet you at or well below your MAO. The asset manager simply runs the numbers, and if the deal works for the bank, congratulations. If not, expect a counteroffer. If you are in a hot market, you'll likely go up against multiple investors, so your highest and best offer from the start is expected. In my REO days, I've dealt with up to thirty-seven offers on one property, The asset manager said, "Pick the top five and upload those," and she picked one a few hours later.

Motivating Factors: Bank wants to get property out of their inventory, listing agent wants to get paid, property vacant

Best Offer Terms: Cash, quick close, waive your inspection, pay your own closing costs

Landlord

When a tired landlord calls you and doesn't want to deal with the property after their third tenant in a row trashed it, you can be the best solution to their problem. "I'm sick of this place. Just make it go away." These are most likely out-of-state landlords. They have to find local contractors to clean the property out and fix it, and they have to get it re-rented from across the country. Many landlords in this situation are so beaten down by problem tenants that they often don't care if they sell it for what they paid ten years ago. These super-motivated landlords are quite easy to negotiate with. Then there are, of course, the hard-nosed, super savvy landlords who want to get every dollar of equity out of the property. Convince them that you are the go-to problem solver for sellers in their situation, and back that up by keeping your word and maintaining professional demeanor.

Motivating Factors: Unwanted property, vacant property, can't afford the property, out-of-state owners

Best Offer Terms: Cash, quick close, waive your inspection, seller can leave whatever they want

Probate

This is when Uncle Herb dies and his property is left to an heir, multiple heirs, or nobody. Those parties want to sell the unwanted property, and this is where you come in. You'll need to understand the local probate process, where the deceased person's assets get transferred to a person or entity so they can then be sold. Not just any relative can sell Uncle Herb's house; they must go through the right channels and file paperwork with the probate courts or through a probate attorney. If you took ten calls from probate leads, all ten would probably be in a different stage of the probate process, so understanding the steps is key. Some might not know what to do, but know they want to sell. Going above and beyond and hooking them up with a good probate attorney or getting them county paperwork goes a long way in building rapport and trust. Many new inheritors see the property as a burden since they are saddled to paying maintenance, taxes, insurance, etc. and want to get the deceased's debts paid off as quickly as possible. Then again, others are attached to the property—and, of course, the equity in the property—and negotiating with them can be difficult. Trust, helping them through the process, and showing them the concrete numbers on comps and repairs usually goes most of the way to get them into your win-win deal.

There are times where the executor of the estate is an attorney, and negotiating with attorneys is always fun. Keep their client's best interests at the forefront and be professional. You might turn a tough negotiation into a win-win, and then that attorney could refer you more probate clients looking to offload a house quickly. That's a win-win-win!

Motivating Factors: Unwanted property, vacant property, can't afford the property, out-of-state owner

Best Offer Terms: Quick close, seller can leave whatever they want, helping with the probate process, having a good probate attorney on speed dial

Negotiating with Agents

Real estate agents have what's called a "fiduciary duty" to their client, where they're obligated to watch out for their clients' best interests and monetary stake in the property. They're also seeking to please their client, who often wants to "sell as quickly as possible" or "get an offer from a cash buyer." Since you aren't dealing directly with the seller and you can't be sure they are telling the seller the whole story, it can be a tough process. Some agents withhold information from their seller to try to get a higher price from another buyer; games like this give agents a bad reputation. I try to stay on the agent's good side and show them that I can be the solution to their client's problems. Of course, all the effort in the world won't help when you are dealing with an unreasonable agent, and sometimes communication breaks down. Most agents think they know more than everyone else, including seasoned investors. When things break down with an agent, it can sour the negotiation. If you think an agent is withholding your offer from the seller or doing something shady, don't hesitate to call the managing or employing broker at his company.

Motivating Factors: Wants to save the day, wants best deal for their client, wants to get paid

Best Offer Terms: Whatever will solve their client's problems, letting the agent double end the deal and earn both sides of the commission

Renegotiating the Deal

You made your offer, overcame objections, negotiated back and forth, and came to an agreement that works for both parties. Good work! Then something happens—a wrench thrown in the gears of your smooth deal. These wrenches usually appear in the form of an unexpected lien or unseen issue with the property. When a pricy issue comes up, you'll want to get the seller back to the negotiation table and renegotiate the price or terms. This isn't you going back on your word; this unforeseen issue has made the good deal a bad deal.

Let's say you uncover an issue with the property you didn't know about when you made the offer. It could be mold, radon, structural issues, oil tanks, bad septic, a broken sewer, twelve raccoons living in the attic, water damage, etc. There's often no way to see these things on your initial walkthrough, and they happen quite a bit. Thirty percent or so of my deals need to go back to the negotiation table after an issue is uncovered. Getting the seller to renegotiate price in these instances is fairly easy with concrete evidence of the problem and a bid in hand. Say you found some gnarly mold in the basement when you went back to do a more thorough inspection while under contract. You could get a bid and then show it to the seller: "Jim, unfortunately we found some gnarly black mold in your basement that we didn't know was there when we made the offer. That obviously would have affected our first offer because of the need to mitigate the mold and clean it up. This is clearly a health hazard and needs to be taken care of. We have a bid in hand from XYZ Mold Remediation for $5,500. Would you be willing to reduce the purchase price by that amount so we can tackle this problem, and then we can move forward to closing?" Highlighting the new issue with backup evidence will be the best way to break through to the seller, who has probably already mentally spent the money they were slated to get at closing.

Sometimes the issue isn't all about price or a price reduction. It might concern terms, the need for a longer closing than initially thought, or getting the seller to cover an item with their insurance policy. I'm currently in the middle of two deals where I got the seller to replace the roof prior to closing through their insurance company. It was an easy sell because instead of them taking the monetary hit at closing, their insurance covered it.

You might broach the subject as follows: "Jim, I had my roofer check out your roof a bit more closely than I could from the ground the other day. Your roof has bad hail damage [show report and bid]. He works with insurance companies daily for this kind of thing. Could we get the roof replaced under your insurance company with a claim instead of having to renegotiate the price to reflect his bid of $7,500? I've worked this with other sellers, and it involves a quick call to your insurance agent."

Since Colorado has had three major "hail events" in the last five years, if a roof is ten years old, it's pretty much guaranteed the insurance company will replace it at this point. I've never been told no by a seller when I approach it this way since insurance covering the issue is much easier to swallow than a $7,500 price reduction or the deal blowing up.

Negotiation is a fine art honed by real-world experience. I don't know many people naturally gifted in this skill or who learned it by reading a hundred books on negotiation. Get in front of people or on the phone and steel yourself to all the nos that will eventually lead to more consistent yesses as you get better. Becoming an expert negotiator will only benefit you throughout your life, from real estate to buying your next car to dealing with agents and lawyers. Build rapport, gain trust, and go forth and solve problems.

Case Study—Rapport Wins the Day

Type of Deal—Direct Mail
Investment Strategy—Fix-and-Flip

My letter reached the absentee owner of a property on the other side of town from where he lived. He called me after six or so mailings. His tenant had just moved out and left the property in bad shape. Dogs had their way with the carpet, the walls were badly banged up, and half of the kitchen cabinet doors were missing. I was one of three or four investors he called via direct mail letters. When I showed up, he was taking appointments back to back, trying to pit us against each other for the best price. I treated the appointment no different than any other, even though there were investors crawling all around the property. I built rapport, listening more than I spoke and asking questions about him and his family. We got along rather well at the end, considering he was pretty snarky when I got there. I submitted my offer to him, as did the other investors, and he decided to go with mine after reviewing everything. When I picked up the signed offer from him, he told me he could tell I was a professional. He then informed me that my offer wasn't the highest, but after meeting everyone, he was most confident that I could close the deal. Plus, he said he just plain liked me. Aw, shucks. This goes to show that genuine care can sometimes win out over price, even with stubborn old landlords.

CHAPTER 9:
Locking it Up

"Hot damn, we gotta find them boys and sign 'em to a fat contract."
−O Brother, Where Art Thou?, 2000

All the time, effort, and energy it took to get that lead is a complete waste if you cannot lock up the deal with contracts and get it to the closing table. You'll need to think through what to put in your contract to protect yourself and navigate the process that leads to signing on the dotted line at the closing table. That's what this chapter is all about—contracts and closing. First, let's explore the elements of a legally binding and valid contract:

- Offer

- Acceptance

- Consideration

- Mutuality of Obligation

- Competency and Capacity

- Written Instrument

Okay, let's see what each of these is all about.

- Offer. An offer from one party to another, this is the first step in a binding agreement. When you offer Jim $150,000 for his house

209

to close on May 30th and agree to throw away or donate anything left, those are the basic elements of an offer. One party is making the offer—it could be either the buyer or the seller.

- Acceptance. When both parties agree to the offer terms, there is, of course, acceptance. Both parties are in agreement when negotiation wraps up and everyone is amenable to the offer. This is when both parties' signatures bind the offer with the terms, dates, contingencies, and extras.

- Consideration. For a contract to be legally binding, both parties should offer something of value—the seller the property and the buyer earnest money. Earnest money shows the seller that you have funds tied to the contract and deal, whether that is $10 or $10,000. Consideration from the buyer does not always have to be money; it could be promise of services (disposing of Jim's stuff he leaves at the property) or a personal property exchange (giving Jim a cell phone as part of the negotiation). As you can see in these examples, it's usually earnest money of some type, but it doesn't have to be.

- Mutuality of Obligation. This means that both parties are obligated to perform by the standards of the contract. The dates in the contract, as well as the price, terms, and closing, all need both parties' action to accomplish. It comes down to performance. Are all parties involved mutually fulfilling the obligations to the contract? The buyer has a certain date he needs to get his earnest money in by, the seller must have the property cleaned out the day before closing, and both parties must do what is promised in the contract for it to be valid by closing. If one party doesn't perform, the other can legally cancel the contract. The idea is that everyone in the transaction needs to move forward in good faith to complete the terms of the contract. As soon as someone acts in bad faith contrary to the contract, the deal is in jeopardy of being canceled.

- Competency and Capacity. Competency is easy. Are both parties of sound legal mind entering the contract? I urge you to make sure everything is above board when dealing with possible mental illness or elderly sellers. You don't want to be that guy on the ten o'clock news found preying on people who had no business signing legal contracts. I've had to get family members involved, making sure that everyone was on board when a seller was in and out of a rehab treatment facility through the process. He was consistently drunk and not in his right mind when trying to sign contracts. Could he fully understand what he was signing? No. I certainly didn't want to be on the hook if he sobered up and accused me of taking advantage of him in a debilitated state. I asked the son to be granted power of attorney in one of the sober windows. Capacity has more to do with the seller having the legal right to sell the property. Is there more than one person on title? You will likely have to get everyone's signatures. Is it a probate property with ten heirs on the title? Ten signatures it is. I've dealt with a divorce situation where I was talking to the husband, and the ex-wife had moved back to Ukraine and hadn't been heard from for three years. He alone did not have the legal capacity to sell without her signature. This comes back to making sure you are dealing with the decision maker.

- Written Instrument. It's vital to get everything in writing, spelled out so it's understandable to all parties on a binding contract. There are hundreds of contracts out there, from guru one-page contracts to state-specific contracts to contracts you can buy at an office supply store like Office Depot. Most are fine to use. The more confusing and custom a contract is, the harder it might be for the seller to feel comfortable signing. If you are making MLS offers, a listing agent will likely make you use a state contract. If you are dealing with private sellers, you could easily get by with a one-page contract or something common like an Adams contract. This last one I mentioned is from a contract publisher, so a hundred lawyers have looked it over and deemed it safe to use in most situations. I use the state contract since I'm licensed and am required to do so. Lawyers, the Real Estate Commission, and the state have all okayed everything in there. I usually use the fact that that my contract can be found right on the Department of Real Estate's website as a trust factor. Some states allow verbal agreements or verbally binding contracts. I don't recommend it; I get all negotiation points in writing so there is zero confusion for all parties involved.

What Contracts Should I Use?

This is a common question. Usually, if you are licensed, you can only use the state contract, but non-licensed investors can use whichever contract they like.

- State Contract—available on your state website for the Department of Regulatory Agencies or the Real Estate Commission

- Adams Contract—available online or at an office supply store like Office Depot

- Lawyer Contract—available at your favorite real estate attorney's office; involves sitting down with them and crafting an offer template

- Guru Contract—available from many online real estate gurus; often a combo of the lawyer contract and the Adams contract; not a recommended option

Look over your local options, get advice from local real estate investors or your attorney, and decide what will work best for your business.

The basic elements of a contract include the price, the dates, the terms, and an explanation of what happens when those terms or dates are not met and what each party can do about it. Earnest money, as consideration from the buyer, is put up so that if the buyer defaults on the agreement, the seller's recourse is to keep the earnest money. The seller puts up the property; if he defaults, the buyer gets her earnest money back. This is a pretty typical scenario. Of course, there are many contingencies you could put in a contract, and we will go over which ones you can use to protect yourself and avoid losing your earnest money or getting involved with a lawsuit.

I like to think of the contract as one big timeline, where the contingencies are each attached to a date in the contract. This is probably my agent brain working. There might be fifteen dates and deadlines on a standard state contract, whereas an Adams contract or guru contract might have two dates, an escape clause, and closing. A typical closing timeline looks like this on a thirty-day closing. Not all contracts need all these things. What I offer below is a fairly exhaustive list:

Day 0—Sign or execute the offer/contract

Day 0-1—Get contract to title company/closing attorney

Day 2—Earnest money deadline

Day 7—Inspection deadline

Day 7—Escape clause deadline

Day 10—Title deadline

Day 10—Survey deadline

Day 14—Due diligence deadline

Day 20—Insurance deadline

Day 20—Appraisal deadline

Day 25—Financing deadline

Day 30—Closing deadline

- Earnest Money. This is the consideration the buyer has in the deal, some money down that shows the seller he is earnest about buying the property. Not all investors use earnest money for consideration, and like everything, the amount is negotiable. Do keep in mind that earnest money can be used as a negotiation tactic. Imagine a seller has two offers on the table that are similar, but one has $5,000 earnest money and the other has $10. Your average person will see the offer with substantial money down as more serious. I've used $10 down before. For me, $1,000 is typical, but I've paid up to $10,000 on a deal where I wanted to show the seller that I'm an investing professional who puts my money where my mouth is. I've talked to investors who have used the entire purchase price as earnest money; in those cases, $100,000 deposited at the title company shows that the investor is dead serious.

- Holding Earnest Money. Who should hold the earnest money? Easy answer—anybody but the seller. Let me repeat that: Never, ever make the check out to the seller then let the seller hold your earnest money deposit. The check should always be made out to and given to a neutral third party, like the title company, the escrow company, or the closing attorney. A seller has no incentive to give it back after depositing it, even if you wave the legally binding contract in front of them. In that case, your only recourse is to sue the seller for your money back if you cancel the contract for a valid reason. The closing attorney or title company will look at the contracts and release the money to the buyer based on the contract that was signed by all parties.

- Contingencies. These clauses, along with a deadline, are in the contract for specific reasons. The inspection deadline contingency means that if something is wrong with the property that was previously unknown, you can cancel based on that newfound information. If you notify the seller in writing on or before the specified deadline that you are withdrawing, your earnest money is safe, and the seller has no real recourse against you. These are built in to protect the buyer. In the below examples, I include a fairly typical timeline. Seven days would mean that the buyer has seven days after the contract is signed by all parties to cancel based on what you find via these contingencies.

  o Inspection—seven days. The buyer conducts a formal or informal inspection. If issues are found with the property that the buyer did not know about or could not find during initial walkthrough, the buyer can either renegotiate price or terms, keep going toward closing, or cancel the contract.

  o Title—ten days. The title performs title searches on the property and provides the buyer and seller a title commitment that shows what liens or judgments are against the property. A clouded title or other legitimate issue that affects moving forward with the transaction may arise.

  o Survey—seven days. A survey is when you pay some nice people to come out and measure the exact lot lines of the property and find out if any neighbors have built their driveway on your side of the line. A survey is usually used on properties sold to a developer, where the exact lot dimensions are measured and it is guaranteed that no neighbor is encroaching on the lot. If something is found during the survey process, you can cancel the contract based on this contingency.

  o Financing—twenty-five days. If you are getting any kind of loan, you may want to include a financing contingency in your contracts. If the lender denies you twenty days into the contract and you are past all your other dates, you will want this way out of the contract to get your earnest money back. If you lose your job while under contract and the lender can no longer approve your loan, you want a safety net, right? This also applies to hard money lenders who might decide ten days later that the deal isn't as good as they thought after pulling their own comps.

o Appraisal—twenty days. Often used for financed loans, this allows you to withdraw from the deal if the appraisal comes in low and your financing will not cover the purchase price any longer.

o Insurance—twenty days. If your insurance company goes out to the property and decides that the property cannot be insured for some reason or claims the property's history would cause the price to insure to be astronomical, you would be allowed to back out with an insurance clause.

o Due Diligence—fourteen days. Due diligence is your homework on the property. Verify the rents from the landlord, double-check with the city on whether the lot can be split before you sell the property to a developer, and check zoning laws to figure out exactly what can be built or done with the property.

o Escape Clause—seven to fourteen days. This is a catchall clause that grants the buyer the right to cancel the contract and receive back their earnest money with no reason given. A "get out of jail free" card, it looks something like this: "Buyer reserves the right to terminate this contract for any reason, given in writing to the seller, within seven days following execution of purchase contract. If cancellation is made within the seven-day window in writing to seller, buyer will have earnest money released to him."

Some sellers will object to an all-out escape clause or maybe one of the other contingency clauses you try to use. Still, these clauses protect both you and the seller, keeping everyone moving in good faith to the closing table. There are such things as non-contingent offers, where you waive everything and have no protection. These offers are for when you are comfortable with the condition of the property, sure that title will come back fine, confident that your insurance company will insure the house, and having completed all your due diligence. The fewer contingencies—or as the seller sees them, obstacles—the stronger your offer looks.

You could even include in your offer that your earnest money is non-refundable, no matter what contingencies are in the contract. That puts forth bold terms that the seller cannot ignore. The money is on the table and his, whether you close or not. Crafting an offer that is strong—but also protects you with some contingencies—is an art. You don't want to give away the farm up front, but if you knew the seller would jump at an offer that waived inspection and you are comfortable with it, it makes your offer more likely to be accepted. A cash offer at a slightly lower price with no financing or appraisal contingencies will likely beat out a more highly financed offer.

When I sell a completed flip project, I vet offers based on their contingencies and timelines. If a cash offer comes in $3,000 lower than an FHA offer, I'll take it over the $3,000 higher offer. Earning $3,000 less is worth the removed contingencies and headaches that the financed offer can bring. I've beat out other investor offers when my offer was lower but had the strength of a cash offer with fewer contingencies. I've also beat out offers on a property because I built the most rapport. The other buyer was difficult, and that buyer's personality was a negative contingency to the seller. He knew the next month he'd have to deal with that guy's personality and liked the thought of working with me better.

There is a hierarchy of cash or financing terms. Let's say you have four offers on the table, with everything else being mostly equal:

Cash > Conventional Financing > VA Financing > FHA Financing

Cash is obviously the best since it contains fewer contingencies. There are no financing or appraisal obstacles to overcome. Conventional beats VA and FHA since the conventional appraisal process is much more friendly than VA or FHA. I like VA over FHA most days of the week, but they are pretty equal otherwise. At the bottom of the pile is FHA. With strict guidelines for lenders, FHA may raise eligibility and appraisal concerns that factor in condition of the property.

Case Study—Nine-Offer REO

Type of Deal—REO
Investment Strategy—Wholesale

Ever hear that awesome old saying, "Fall down eight times, get up nine"? That sums this deal up for me. The deal was an MLS-listed REO. I didn't have an inside track with the agent, and all offers had to be submitted online. I knew and loved this area and was sure it was a deal, but a quick call to the listing agent told me there were ten offers on it already. I decided to throw my hat in the ring anyway. A week or so later, I heard back that another buyer got the property. Then a week after that, I got an email saying it was back on the market and to "resubmit your offer if you are still interested," so I did just that. Again I was told I lost out, and again I was notified a week later that the property was back on the market. This happened eight times!

Each time, I submitted my offer and waited. I found out that the deal kept falling through due to a structural problem that caused the buyers to run away screaming. My last offer waived my inspection contingency, so the bank jumped on it since the last eight buyers backed out due to inspection. For the ninth time, I submitted my offer—and it was accepted! I easily found a buyer for it and double-closed. The lesson here is that it pays to be persistent and to craft your offer to be the strongest possible. My buyer told me at the closing table that he had been putting offers on it too, right up until the eighth time, and then he quit when it came back on the market that last time. He then ended up buying it from me. Persistence pays off.

CHAPTER 10:
Closing the Deal

"A-B-C. A-Always, B-Be, C-Closing. Always be closing, always be closing."
                                                    –*Glengarry Glen Ross*, 1992

You didn't think I could fill a real estate book with semi-relevant movie quotes without something from this movie, did you? Like Blake says in *Glengarry Glen Ross*, "Always be closing." You got the lead, you built rapport with the lead, you negotiated with the lead, and you locked the deal up with a contract. Now it's time to close the sale. Need more money? Close on more houses. ABC. But remember: A deal under contract can be blown up a hundred different ways; I never count my money until after closing.

You may have a hundred properties under contract, but until they close, you shouldn't count on a dime of that money. I've seen sellers back out the day after we have signed a contract and walk away from the closing table before signing anything. A deal can fall apart at any time, for almost any reason.

So, you have a signed contract between you and the seller Jim. Now what? Your first task is to get it submitted to your chosen title company, XYZ Title, along with any earnest money per your agreement. Your purchase price is $150,000 cash, and the earnest money is $500. XYZ Title runs a comprehensive title search on the property. They pull any ownership and encumbrance reports (O&E) to see if there are disputes about ownership and mortgages, liens, or judgments associated with the property. Turns out

Jim has one mortgage for $99,000 and a lien he didn't know about for $1,000 from a contractor he had a payment dispute with. The contractor filed a mechanic's lien against Jim's house, and now it's attached and must be paid at closing.

The title company's job is to pull the title reports, provide title insurance, and act as an escrow company—basically, handle the money for everyone. Before closing, XYZ Title will provide you with all the math of the deal, including what all the fees will be and, of course, how much you need to bring to closing and how much Jim will walk away with. On the day of closing, you bring in your $150,000 plus any fees. Title takes all the money and distributes it to the mortgage company to pay off Jim's loan, to the county to pay off his mechanic's lien, and to themselves—and then cuts a check to Jim for his equity. Title also settles the taxes owed for property tax, and if Jim pre-paid some of those, he gets his money back. Title also deals with utilities in many states, notifying the water company that change of ownership has occurred. They provide you, the buyer, with a deed to the property that conveys ownership from Jim to you.

$150,000 Purchase Price	$150,000 Purchase Price
$500 Closing Costs	-$1,200 Closing Costs, Title Insurance
$750 Tax Payment for 2016	-$99,000 Mortgage
-$500 Earnest Money	-$1,000 Mechanic's Lien
	$500 Tax Credit for 2016
$150,750 Check from you to title at closing	$48,300 Check to Jim at closing

Title takes your $150,750 check (a bank wire transfer most of the time)—and then you get the property, and Jim gets a $48,300 check after everything as far as taxes, insurance etc. is settled.

They don't just hand Jim a check for the purchase price of $150,000 and trust that he'll pay off his mortgage and lien. As part of the process, the escrow company makes sure everything is paid off so that the new owner is handed a property free and clear of any issues. What would happen if the title company did hand Jim a check and he didn't pay off his mortgage? It would be a nightmare to deal with, which is why it's handled at closing.

Let's dive deeper into some of these terms, starting with the most obvious: What is the difference between a title company, an escrow, and a closing attorney? You might be surprised that there's a lot of overlap. A title company also handles escrow; a closing attorney may be the one to order title insurance and act as the escrow agency.

So, why would you use one over the other? It's not quite that simple. Twenty-two states have a law in place that says an attorney must be used, and separate title/escrow companies do not exist in those states. If you are on the East coast and have real estate experience, you might be wondering what the heck a title company is since closing attorneys are the norm there. On the West coast, I've never used a closing attorney in any of the thousand transactions I've been a part of. Make sure you know which your state uses before diving in to this process.

Which are those twenty-two states that use attorneys? At the time of this writing in 2017, they include Alabama, Connecticut, Delaware, District of Columbia, Florida, Georgia, Kansas, Kentucky, Maine, Maryland, Massachusetts, Mississippi, New Hampshire, New Jersey, New York, North Dakota, Pennsylvania, Rhode Island, South Carolina, Vermont, Virginia, and West Virginia. This list informs whom you should look for in each area. If you live in New York, you have to use an attorney, so get to know some good ones. Here in Colorado, title companies handle all title and escrow.

The closing process can be confusing. I've thrown a ton of terms at you without backing up each one, so let's dive a little deeper. Title is evidence that the owner lawfully possesses that property, while a deed is the legal instrument executed by the seller, then acknowledged by the buyer and recorded with the local county government. This notifies the county who the new owner is, who to send the tax bill to, etc. There are dozens of types of deeds, and many vary by state. The difference is where they come from and how much protection they offer:

1. Warranty Deed/General Warranty Deed. This deed is most typical in residential real estate transactions, acts as a guarantee to the buyer that the seller has the right to sell the property, and ensures that the property will be conveyed free of liens, debts, and judgments. It covers the entire history of the property.

2. Special Warranty Deed. The buyer is only protected for the time that the previous owner owned the property and not for any time

before that. REO/bank owned properties convey with this type of deed.

3. Quit Claim Deed. The quit claim deed is most commonly used by family members and in divorce situations. This achieves a simple swap of ownership and can involve no payment at all, such as when an uncle gives a property away that he owns free and clear. There is not any warranty that protects the buyer against past transfers of claims. This type of deed does not require a sale and allows the property to be transferred by filing the deed with the county.

4. Bargain and Sale Deed/Sheriff's Sale Deed. This is usually used in court-seized situations, where the property is sold after being taken from an owner. Some states on the East coast use the bargain and sale deed regularly for typical real estate transactions. It involves limited or no warranties, just like a quit claim deed.

5. Personal Representative's Deed/Executor's Deed. This deed is for when a personal representative or executor of an estate in a probate situation gains control of the property. The court transfers title from the deceased individual to the personal representative so the personal representative can then sell or deal with the property. In some states, this just means that if you bought the property from an estate or personal representative, you also get the personal representative's deed for some reason. It possibly carries no warranties from before the deceased owned the property.

6. Tax Deed. This deed is given after a tax sale, where the county took the property for non-payment of taxes. It's very similar to the sheriff's deed above.

7. Deed in Lieu of Foreclosure. When a homeowner has missed payments and is in pre-foreclosure, often the bank will offer for the owner to "give the property back" before foreclosure. The seller then signs the property back to the bank instead of going through the whole foreclosure process.

I just want you to be aware of the different types of deeds that are out there and in which situations these deeds are used. Nine times out of ten, you will be given a general warranty deed, the kind of deed that gives you the most protection, but if you buy an REO property or a property from a tax sale, know what you are getting into. Improperly recorded documents, another person claiming ownership, fraud, liens, encroachments, easements, and other items that are spelled out in the title insurance can all pop as title defects. This includes anything that can keep an owner from transferring ownership to the next person. An issue like a title defect can take an hour to clear up, while other problems can last for months.

So, Mr. Buyer, what happens after you have owned the house for six months and one of these two happens?

1. Jim's cousin knocks on your door claiming to be the rightful owner and that Jim had no right to sell the property.

2. The title missed a lien against Jim for $50,000, and now they try to come after you, threatening to foreclose or put another lien on the property.

This is exactly why title insurance exists; it insures the buyer and the buyer's lender against any financial harm that might come from circumstances like these.

How to Find an Investor-friendly Title Company or Attorney

Not all title companies or attorneys are created equal; some are friendlier toward investors and know how to handle investor transactions. Most can get the job done if you are just buying houses from homeowners because these look a lot like normal purchase transactions. It gets a little more complicated when you're wholesaling or if you need "outside the box" services. My advice is to find several referrals from other investors, from real estate investor club members, or from those on BiggerPockets. Calling each one and asking questions goes a long way to make sure that you are both comfortable with each other. A good title company or attorney will take the time to answer questions and walk you through their process. If, for some reason, you can't get any referrals in your area, call ten or so companies and ask the following to weed out the non-friendly ones:

- "Do you do hold open title policies?" When purchasing a property for fix-and-flip, many title companies will issue a "hold-open" policy, so when you sell, you don't have to pay the title insurance twice.

- "I often buy properties, come to closing as the buyer, and then turn around and close on it as the seller the same day or with a double closing. Does your company do these types of transactions?" When wholesaling and performing double closings, it's imperative to get a company who actually does these transactions on board.

Double closes, hold-opens, assignment fees, pass through closings, and wet and dry closings are terms savvy closers know. Getting a referral takes the hard work out of calling title companies who mostly don't know what you are talking about for that one that gets it.

What does closing cost? What does the closing company (title or attorney) charge? Each state, county, and city likely has a different closing cost structure. I know some counties that charge a certain tax or extra closing fees, while others don't—and that's in the same state. Some common fees include recording fees, notary fees, transfer taxes, settlement fees, state stamp taxes, and more.

Building good closing relationships will serve your real estate career for a long time. Get to know the closers, the reps, and the attorneys, as well as their fees, inside and out. That way, when you sit down with a seller, you can better explain the closing process and what to expect for closing costs. Know what you are doing and get good closers on board with your business strategy.

Case Study—Short Sale Time Machine

Type of Deal—Networking Referral, Short Sale
Investment Strategy—Fix-and-Flip

This deal still gives me recurring nightmares. Because of this experience, I no longer handle my own short sales (I now hire a negotiator) and avoid working with divorced sellers who cannot communicate directly with each other. In this case, all communication between the two parties had to be through attorneys. This short sale ended up a two-year process.

After putting in a contract for $125,000 in January of 2012, the bank proceeded to lose our paperwork ten times, we had seven different negotiators, I escalated it to upper management twenty-two times, and I got referred to "the special office of the president of _____ [insert big bank name here]" three times. I begged and pleaded to push this short sale through.

In the meantime, the title company uncovered four judgments that had to be dealt with before we could close. For each one, I had to call and negotiate a lower payoff so that the sellers could walk with a little money and we could get the deal done. The title company was a lifesaver in this process, helping me find out who each lien belonged to, as well as the contact information for each. My closer at the title company knew more about this file than I did, and we broke open some champagne together when it finally closed.

Two years later, we finally arrived at the closing table (though, in two different locations due to the sellers' restraining orders on each other). The bank used an old 2012 appraisal when we closed in 2014. The price was locked in from two years prior, and in a rising market, that was a very good thing.

CHAPTER 11:
How to Build a Business Around Finding Deals

Dr. Peter Venkman: For whatever reasons, Ray, call it … fate, call it luck, call it karma, I believe everything happens for a reason. I believe that we were destined to get thrown outta this dump.

Dr. Raymond Stantz: For what purpose?

Dr. Peter Venkman: To go into business for ourselves.

—*Ghostbusters*, 1984

Here we are at the end. We learned how to find, market for, contact, fund, negotiate, and close real estate deals. As some famous president said, "Mission accomplished."

Wait, you wanted to become a bona fide professional deal-getter guy? Not just a hobbyist who works on deals every third weekend? You closed a deal or two, so now what? Or should I say, so what? Anyone can luck into a deal or two. It takes setup and work to make a legitimate business out of finding deals. Figuring out that these methods work is amazing, isn't it? But now what do you do? How can you build a successful career out of finding deals?

Consistency is the key here. Of course, this book isn't about building or structuring your business, but I will hit on some important pieces here to give you a good start, and you can take the information past your first, second, or tenth deal and build something more out of it. There are four key elements to scaling up the techniques discussed in the previous chapters: the big picture, systems, image, and re-investment.

Big Picture

When you first start out, it can be daunting to learn the entire acquisitions part of this business, from where you want to start in real estate (flipping, wholesale, or buy-and-hold) to whether you want to get licensed, your web presence, branding, business cards, phone systems, office, and more. It can be hard to think about what you want your business to do or look like. Your business needs to begin with the end goal in mind—whether that is to close one deal or a hundred deals or to use deal money to take your husband to Hawaii. The best part is that you can take that goal and then reverse-engineer it to see how much action you will have to take to hit it. It keeps the goal within sight and shows exactly how your daily actions snowball into a much bigger goal.

Back when I talked about marketing, I mentioned the "let's make a crap-ton money this year" equation. It's a great way for a flipper or wholesaler to figure out how many deals they need to close to meet their goal, as well as the marketing costs involved.

Wholesaler Who Wants to Make $100,000 a Year

1. Set a goal for how many deals you'll need to wholesale to reach $100,000/year, assuming each deal nets you $5,000:

   Average Profit/Deal: $5,000

   Target Profit/Year: $100,000

   Deals/Year: $100,000/$5,000 = 20 deals/year

2. Work backwards to figure out how many letters you'll need to send to reach your goal, assuming a 5 percent response rate and a 2.5 percent close rate of those who call:

   Direct Mail Response Rate: 5%

   Close Rate from Responses: 2.5%

Conversion Rate: 5% x 2.5% = 0.125%

Letters Needed: 20 (target number of deals)/0.00125 (conversion rate) = 16,000 letters/year

3. Calculate marketing cost based on letters to be sent, assuming your expenses are 80 cents per letter:

Cost: 16,000 (letters/year) x $0.80 (cost/letter) = $12,800

Fix-and-Flipper Who Wants to Make $100,000 a Year

1. Set a goal for how many deals you'll need to flip to reach $100,000/year, assuming each deal nets you $25,000:

Average Profit/Deal: $25,000

Target Profit/Year: $100,000

Deals/Year: $100,000/$25,000 = 4 deals/year

2. Work backwards to figure out how many letters you'll need to send to reach your goal, assuming a 5 percent response rate and a 2.5 percent close rate of those who call:

Direct Mail Response Rate: 5%

Close Rate from Responses: 2.5%

Conversion Rate: 5% x 2.5% = 0.125%

Letters Needed: 4 (target number of deals)/0.00125 (conversion rate) = 3,200 letters/year

3. Calculate marketing cost based on letters to be sent, assuming your expenses are 80 cents per letter:

Cost: 3,200 (letters/year) x $0.80 (cost/letter) = $2,560

Start out by figuring out what is realistic and then breaking down how much marketing will cost you to get there. You may not know your response or conversion rates for your marketing, but try the numbers above and find out what it will take to make the amount of money you want this year.

This system of taking the end goal and breaking it down into daily steps has helped me as both an agent and an investor. It can apply to many acquisition strategies, networking, Internet marketing, bandit signs, cold calling, door knocking, and more. Knowing what daily steps I need to get done to dominate my big picture goal gets me leaping out of bed each morning to tackle those actions.

Systems

Systematizing and automating pieces of your business is key when you work alone (as many of you will start out doing). Remember that pesky "consistency" word I keep using? I mentioned this at the end of my first BiggerPockets Podcast episode as advice to new investors. I probably say it ten times a day: Systems ensure that your marketing is consistently sent out so that deals come in the door, whether you feel like going through the actions or not. Most businesses, especially lone-wolf businesses, have huge pains when it comes to growth.

You might be asking, "Um, I'm just starting. Do I need to do all of this?" The answer is *yes*. By breaking down and documenting things like "how to pull comps" or "how to follow up with leads," you can always go back in a pinch if you forget an important step. Or you might wing it for a few deals, then start documenting as you grow. Still, the earlier you start, the earlier the habit becomes a solid rock of your business. When you start hiring others to take over tasks for your business, you will have the systems documented ahead of time to hand your new team members.

I personally break down my entire business into boxes or tasks—what happens first, what happens second, and so on—using a flow chart. It's a big picture view of my business as a whole. This shows how I can insert any new person into a box or procedure. Doing this work early in my business ensures I can plug the right person in at any time.

Imagine looking at an online map of your city. Trying to pinpoint your house, you know where it is but can't see it on this big map. As you zoom in, small details appear as you go from the entire city view down to your neighborhood. Zoom in more, and you can see your house, the trees in your yard, your car in the driveway, and your kid's lost Frisbee on the roof.

- These are big picture, general tasks, like "run comps"—the city view of your business.

- Each of those boxes breaks down into more specifics for that task—the neighborhood view of your business.

- Then the task is documented in detail, including step-by-steps and how-tos—the "my house" view.

System Tools

Systems by themselves are amazing; brilliant people have been implementing systems in business since the beginning of business. When you pair systems with technology tools, you can achieve a high level of efficiency and automation. Here are some real estate investor tools to help every deal-finder out there:

1. CRM. CRM is short for "customer relationship manager," but good ones do so much more. Whether in the form of a client database, computer software, or an Internet-based system, these tools allow you to enter in and keep your information centralized. A CRM helps with rapport and can keep a record of your last conversation with the seller. Some CRMs are not geared toward real estate, but can be customized and tweaked to do almost anything. There are literally hundreds of CRM software programs; some are free, but most aren't.

2. Deal/Repair Analysis. Using online tools to help you evaluate deals can help you and your team standardize the way you look at prospects. A few different calculators can be found on the BiggerPockets website at BiggerPockets.com/analysis. As a new investor, playing with these calculators can help you learn how more experienced investors evaluate deals.

   a. House Flipping Calculator. Using this calculator, you can input the purchase price and the ARV price—and there is even a place to break down your repair costs, financing, holding costs, and other expenses like utilities and insurance. After inputting all the data, you'll receive a clean one-page report on the property that you can show to potential investors or lenders!

   b. Rental Property Calculator. This offers many of the same features of the House Flipping Calculator, but has more detailed sections for financing, potential rent for the property, and any repairs needed. You get a complete investment snapshot of the property, including a one to thirty-year look at the investment, factoring in value and equity.

   c. Wholesaling Calculator. Much like the House Flipping Calculator, the Wholesaling Calculator has a place for all the important data like your purchase price, ARV, and repair costs. You can input desired profit, and it will give you an MAO, the price for which you would sell it to another investor, and a few report output options to keep or show to potential buyers.

3. Mailing Services. People usually love or hate direct mail. The idea of putting together a hundred or a thousand mailers sounds terrible to some people. Others love the hands-on process and don't mind the work it takes to write or print a bunch of letters, stuff them into envelopes, put a stamp on them, and take them to the post office. Thankfully, we don't live in the Stone Age any longer. There is a half dozen or more companies willing to do this work for you. This type of system keeps many investors consistent because of how easy this makes setting up and scheduling mailings with a few clicks online.

4. File Storage/Sharing. Everybody in business needs a place to put their files, preferably in a central place that can be accessed at home, at the office, in your car, or thirty thousand feet in the air. Keeping your important files organized and in an accessible place is invaluable. You never know when you'll need tour spreadsheets, your Word docs, your PowerPoint presentations, your PDF files, your property photos, and your contracts. When you grow and need an assistant to access business files, you'll want to have these services set up beforehand.

5. Electronic Signatures. Gone are the days of meeting a seller with contracts to sign or mailing contracts back and forth. Of course, the seller must have an Internet connection, and you will run into many sellers who will only provide signatures the old-school way: in-person or mailed out. With online e-signature software, you can upload your contract and sign with your mouse, then email it to your seller so they can review the contracts and sign with their mouse. If you or your seller is on a phone or tablet, you can sign with your finger and call it a day. Some are free and some are not, so do your research.

6. Online Phone System. The Internet can do pretty much anything these days. It would only make sense that you can now set up a new phone number to make and receive calls from your computer, right? You used to have to install a new phone line in your home

or office or carry around three cell phones. No longer, my friends! How about voicemails that are automatically emailed to you or the ability to pick up your new online business number calls from your cell phone?

Tools and systems are indispensable in today's age of technology. The upfront work to set up business systems and tools is sizeable, but the end payoff will save you time, effort, and energy. It's better to be proactive and scale up your systems and tools before you need them than to try to play catch-up after growing too big, too fast.

Image

Whether you have done a hundred deals or are just starting out, you should be working on your personal and company image. I've become known as the guy with his own name on his hat. Well, it's my company name, and it serves a purpose: branding! It's cohesive with my business card, my website, my YouTube channel, and my email signature.

Branding entails having a consistent look on all the media you use. It goes a long way in giving your business credibility. Many, if not most, sellers will look you or your business up online before calling or deciding to do a deal with you. The more trust you can build with a professionally-branded website and social media, the better. Even if you just send yellow letters, having a brand presence online and in follow-up emails is still a good idea. Here are places where your company logo and brand should be used:

- Business Cards

- Social Media

- Yard Signs

- Email Signature

- Website

- BBB (Better Business Bureau)

I spent the first six years of my business having no brand—no consistent image that I could present—and I now know that was not a smart decision. If you stay in your market for any length of time, you will eventually become known. Your reputation, for better or worse, gets tied closely with your image, either your name or your company. Ten years later, you could have agents excited to show your fix-and-flip project based on your brand name alone.

233

Reinvestment

So, I hear you want to grow your business? Go from four deals this year to twenty the next? It's an amazing feeling to get your first check and think to yourself, "This actually works!" Then you repeat what brought you success, getting more leads in the door. Now that you're bringing in deals, what should you do with your money? How can you get to the next level in your business and grow organically? You should strategically reinvest your profits into the thing that brings more deals in the door—marketing!

That's right, you sent letters out or put bandit signs up to get those deals, so now you should reinvest some of that fat, juicy profit right back into the machine. Every single month, as deals close, reinvest 10 percent of that right back into marketing. Each month, enlist more mail, more bandit signs, or more online advertising. This is one way to set that snowball flying down the hill. Your $1,000 marketing budget last month grew to $1,500 based on the last deal you closed. If you keep re-investing a percentage of your profit, you will reach amazing numbers relatively quickly. You can't always expect to grow your results by keeping your input the same. Reinvestment allows you to grow exponentially over a short time. Still, remember to do what's appropriate for you and the business; only you can decide if this is right for you. Set a marketing budget and stick with it for the first six months to allow yourself to tweak the lists, the medium, and the message.

You start out with a marketing budget of $1000 per month, and reinvest 10% of any deals profits back into marketing.

	Jan	Feb	Mar	Apr	May	Jun	Jul
Initial Budget	$1000	$1000	$1000	$1000	$1000	$1000	$1000
Feb Deal 10%		$500					
Mar Deal 10%			$250				
Apr Deal 10%				$500			
May Deal 10%					$500		
Jun Deal 10%						$1000	
Jul Deal 10%							$1500
Total Marketing Budget for Month	$1000	$1500	$1250	$1500	$1500	$2000	$2500

The more you invest back into marketing, the more potential leads will come in the next month, growing your potential profits exponentially

Parting Advice

I still love real estate, even after detailing every bit I know into this book. During the writing of this book, I've moved my family into a new house, I've bought a dozen houses, and I've sold a dozen more. Each day of writing, I was in the middle of all kinds of deals. My hope is that you took action while reading this book—or that you'll launch your plans after finishing these final words.

- Don't get stuck in analysis paralysis.

- Don't take an investor to coffee and tell them you want to "wholesale or flip houses," then disappear.

- Remember that no matter the area of real estate you decide to work in, finding deals is always an amazing skill to have. The ability to find better deals than the next guy will set you apart from the competition.

- Act with integrity, professionalism, and a spirit of truly wanting to help others to set yourself up for win-win situations in any deal.

Case Study—Ten Cats Live(d) Here, Two Are Missing

Type of Deal—Door-knocking, Pre-foreclosure
Investment Strategy—Fix-and-Flip

After all we have gone over in these past eleven chapters, I bet you're still wondering if some of these techniques really work. I regularly get asked the question, "Does door-knocking still work?" Here's a little story of exactly how effective it can be.

My partner was door-knocking pre-foreclosure properties when he ran into an owner outside. After talking with her and building rapport, I realized she was interested in accepting our help to buy her out of her problem house. To come to a price, we needed to see inside. She was reluctant to let us in, stating it "was a bit of a mess." After several attempts to set up a time to see it, her sister called and gave us the scoop.

She was a hoarder, and no, she wasn't hoarding glitter and Christmas presents. Trash and cats were the vices of choice, and it is, to this day, the worst house I've ever been in. Due to the condition, we could only offer her what she owed, plus a few thousand dollars to move; otherwise, she would go through foreclosure and get nothing. She moved out prior to closing, leaving almost everything behind. While our crews emptied the house, her sister grabbed important things from the piles. We caught eight cats, found two dead, and made sure not to open the plastic containers left downstairs next to the out-of-order bathroom.

After $65,000 in work (and lots of oil-based Kilz primer), you could walk through the property without your eyes stinging, your lungs burning, and an intense feeling of claustrophobia. The fix-and-flip profit we made—not to mention helping someone out of a tough situation—made that door knock well worth it.

Now it's your turn. So, get out there!

ACKNOWLEDGEMENTS

"I say never be complete. I say stop being perfect. I say let—let's evolve, let the chips fall where they may."

—*Fight Club*, 1997

"Write a book," they said. "It will be easy," they said. Something about "it will only take a hundred days." Well, this is my first attempt at writing a book, and sometimes I was afraid it would break me. Not one to quit, I continued forward through a start-stop eighteen-month process. I wrote, edited, tweaked, and beat the words into submission—all while running a full-time real estate investment business and making time for family. I wrote at my home office, plenty of coffee shops, and multiple breweries—anywhere I could step away from distractions and get words down.

I'm grateful to Stacy, my wife, who is an amazing rock star. Thank you for loving me and hanging with me through this real estate journey, and more importantly, through this crazy life! Your support is immense and invaluable. I love you! And, of course, thank you to our son Wesley for showing me how much fun it is to be a dad and reminding me daily why I work so hard. I've never met a funnier person who I enjoy being around more.

To my family—my brother Adam, his wife Debby Young, and my awesome niece Noelle—thank you for more than I could ever put into words, including letting me live with you twice. Thank you to my in-laws, Sharon and Dave Marston, whose support every step of the way since I was seventeen has been incredible. Robert and Lauren Marston, I'm lucky to call you my brother and sister-in-law. Let's go hike a mountain! Elizabeth and Keith Matthews, thank you! Andy and Stacey Schuler, best friends since I was fifteen, and your unwavering support. To my dad, Karl, and his wife, Lori, and my Grandpa Charlie, thanks for raising me to find the deal in everything and for supporting me.

To my mother Kathleen, who passed away in 1989, I love you, Mom. This is also for my insightful and protective brother Aaron, who passed away in 2014. I hope I can make you both proud.

Thank you to my network of friends, colleagues, real estate buddies, mastermind groups, clients, and people whom I admire, especially Chris and Christine Sanders, Micah and Betsy Joseph, Joshua and Julie Dorkin, Paul Selck, Brian Davis, Matt Nockles, Tucker Merrihew, the DFA, Ryan Dossey, Nathan Adams, and Brandon Turner. To my mentors who didn't even know their huge impact on my life: Mike Litman, Tony Robbins, Tim Ferriss, Ryan Holiday, Gary Vaynerchuck and Grant Cardone.

ABOUT THE AUTHOR

Anson Young is a full time real estate investor and licensed agent, living and working in Denver, Colorado. Specializing in the types of distressed properties the average person runs away screaming from, his mission is to help homeowners out of bad situations and change neighborhoods for the better. Having completed hundreds of deals in his eleven year career, he currently focuses on fix and flip investments, watching crappy houses get turned into nice ones. Well versed in short sales, REO, asset management, foreclosures and probates, he has built real estate experience through real world hard work. A longtime contributor to the BiggerPockets community, Anson also started the first BiggerPockets local meetup group which has grown since 2012.

Born and raised in Colorado, when not working you can find him and his family adventuring outdoors in and around the beautiful Rocky Mountains.

MORE FROM BIGGERPOCKETS

If you enjoyed this book, we hope you'll take a moment to check out some of the other great material BiggerPockets offers. BiggerPockets is the real estate investing social network, marketplace, and information hub, designed to help make you a smarter real estate investor through podcasts, blog posts, videos, forums, files, and more./ Sign up today—it's free! www.BiggerPockets.com

Be sure to also read:

The Book on Rental Property Investing

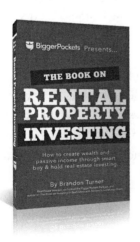

The Book on Rental Property Investing, written by real estate investor and co-host of the BiggerPockets Podcast Brandon Turner, contains nearly 400 pages of in-depth advice and strategies for building wealth through rental properties. You'll learn how to build an achievable plan, find incredible deals, pay for your rentals, and much, more more!

If you've ever thought of using rental properties to build wealth or obtain financial freedom, this book is a "must read."

The Book on Investing in Real Estate with No (and Low) Money Down

Is a lack of money holding you back from real estate success? It doesn't have to! In this groundbreaking book from Brandon Turner, author of *The Book on Rental Property Investing*, you'll discover numerous strategies a real estate investor can use to buy real estate using other people's money.

Less "hype" and more "practical strategies," you'll learn the top strategies that savvy investors are using to buy, rent, flip, wholesale properties at scale!

The Book on Tax Strategies for the Savvy Real Estate Investor

Taxes! Boring and irritating, right?

Perhaps. But if you want to succeed in real estate, your tax strategy will play a HUGE role in how fast you grow. A great tax strategy can save you thousands of dollars a year - and a bad strategy could land you in legal trouble.

That's why BiggerPockets is excited to introduce its newest book, The Book on Tax Strategies for the Savvy Real Estate Investor! To help you deduct more, invest smarter, and pay far less to the IRS!

The Book on Flipping Houses

The Book on Flipping Houses, written by active real estate fix-and-flipper J Scott, contains more than 300 pages of detailed, step-by-step training perfect for both the complete newbie and the seasoned pro looking to build a killer house-flipping business.

Whatever your skill level, *The Book on Flipping Houses* will teach you everything you need to know to build a profitable, efficient house-flipping business and start living the life of your dreams.

The Book on Estimating Rehab Costs

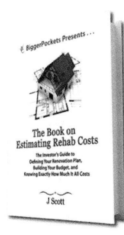

One of the most difficult tasks for a real estate investor is estimating repairs. To help you overcome this obstacle, J Scott and BiggerPockets pull back the curtain on the rehab process and show you not only the cost ranges and details associated with each and every aspect of a rehab, but also the framework and methodology for estimating rehab costs. You'll discover how to accurately estimate the variety of costs you will likely face while rehabbing a home as well as which upgrade options offer the biggest bang for your buck.

Whether you are an experienced home renovation specialist or still learning how to screw in a light bulb, this valuable resource will be your guide to staying on budget, managing contractor pricing, and ensuring a timely profit.

FREE: *The Ultimate Beginner's Guide to Real Estate Investing*

The Ultimate Beginner's Guide to Real Estate Investing is a free guide designed to help you build a solid foundation for your venture into real estate. In the eight chapters of this book, you'll learn how to best gain an education (for free), how to pick a real estate niche, and how to find, fund, and manage your latest real estate investment.